Health and Social Care
for Advanced GNVQ

3rd edition

Health and Social Care

for Advanced GNVQ

Liam Clarke, Bruce Sachs & Sue Ford-Sumner

stanley thornes *GNVQ*

First published in 1994 by:
Stanley Thornes (Publishers) Ltd
Ellenborough House
Wellington Street
CHELTENHAM
GL50 1YW
United Kingdom

Second edition published 1995
Third edition published 2000

00 01 02 03 04 / 10 9 8 7 6 5 4 3 2 1

A catalogue record for this book is available from the British Library

ISBN 0 7487 3510 0

Line illustrations by Angela Lumley; Barking Dog Art

Typeset by Florence Production Ltd, Stoodleigh, Devon
Printed and bound in Spain by Graficas Estella S.A.

Contents

Acknowledgements   vi

Introduction   vii

Assessment for GNVQ   ix

Unit One   Equal opportunities and clients' rights   1

Unit Two   Communicating in health and social care   41

Unit Three   Physical aspects of health   79

Unit Four   Factors affecting human growth and
                development   121

Unit Five   Health, social care and early years
                services   187

Unit Six   Research perspectives in health
                and social care   253

Bibliography   308

Glossary   311

Index   319

Acknowledgements

The authors and publishers would like to acknowledge the advice of Graham Ford Williams, who provided extremely useful comments on the manuscript throughout the writing process.

The authors and publishers are grateful to the following for permission to reproduce previously published material:

- Alzheimer's Disease Society – p. 249 (right).
- Her Majesty's Stationery Office – p. 3. Crown copyright material is reproduced with the permission of the Controller of Her Majesty's Stationery Office.
- National Meningitis Trust – 249 (left).
- The Guardian – p. 212.
- Women's Royal Voluntary Service – pp. 242, 243, 244.

Every attempt has been made to contact copyright holders, and we apologise if any have been overlooked. Should copyright have been unwittingly infringed in this book, the owners should contact the publishers who will make corrections at reprint.

Photo credits

Age Concern – p. 236 (top).
John Birdsall (www.JohnBirdsall.co.uk) – pp. 10, 104 and 236 (middle left and bottom).
Angela Hampton - Family Life Picture Library – pp. 12, 95, 101, 156 and 201.
National Osteoporosis Society – p. 132.
Photofusion – pp. 50 (Sam Tanner), 55, 61, 62 (Paul Baldesare), 64, 72, and 229 (Paul Doyle).

Introduction

Since publication of the highly successful first two editions of this text, we have learned much about what health and social care students value in a book of this sort.

First, this book is written from a perspective of health and social care practitioners. The authors have had extensive first-hand experience working in the caring professions, and bring that perspective to each chapter. The GNVQ requirements are explored in relevant and realistic ways. Although much of our time is now spent externally verifying GNVQ courses, we are still care professionals first, and wouldn't want it any other way.

Second, we have provided a depth and detail of knowledge which the serious student requires. This is not a revision aid, but rather a useful reference source. It has been written to provide the student with more than just basic GNVQ knowledge. We would expect that this text will serve the student well in further, more advanced courses, such as HND level. In fact, HND students will find this text to be an invaluable resource. In addition, this text will meet many of the requirements of the new BTEC Nationals in Caring, Health Studies and Early Years.

Third, in providing depth, we have not departed from the basic GNVQ knowledge requirements, which are set out clearly and plainly. Depth of knowledge does not mean complex, difficult texts. An Advanced GNVQ must be at A-level standard, and we have tried hard to maintain that standard. The ways in which we have explored complex issues is precisely what the advanced GNVQ student will require to get better grades. We have presented here a straightforward presentation of the Advanced GNVQ in Health and Social Care – a course which we were responsible for writing, and we view this book as the companion for the course.

This book covers all of the mandatory units of the Advanced GNVQ in Health and Social Care, and as such will support students registered with any of the awarding bodies: Edexcel, OCR or AQA. It will also provide background reading and vital underpinning knowledge for candidates for NVQs in care at both levels two and three.

Whilst this book comprehensively supports the structure and content of the mandatory units, we have developed the material beyond minimum requirements in order to put it clearly into a proper vocational context. Many of the Case Studies and perspectives expressed in this book come from the real experiences of the authors.

We have placed an emphasis on active learning with Activities and Case Studies used to illustrate and expand upon the contents of each unit. How the book is used will to some extent be determined by the way in which the GNVQ is tackled. We suggest that the student makes extensive use of work placement opportunities in relation to all of the subjects covered in this book. Students should also be acquainted with the methods of assessment used for GNVQs, so that work may be planned with assessment in mind. A brief section on this topic follows.

Each chapter concludes with Revision Questions and example Assignments. The Revision Questions are based on the knowledge and understanding for the units. The Assignment at the end of each chapter has been designed to address all of the requirements for each unit.

The Advanced GNVQ in Health and Social Care is a challenging and worthwhile achievement. It will provide the student with a thorough knowledge of Health and Social Care, and an opportunity to experience working in care settings. As a qualification, it may provide the means directly into employment for some. For most, it will provide access to higher education, including courses toward social work and nursing qualifications. The vocations and professions included within Health and Social Care are some of the most personally rewarding jobs there are. They require special people, willing to devote themselves to the well-being of others. The authors of this book have considerable direct professional experience in the Health and Social Care industry. We know how important this work is, and the devotion that one needs to possess in order to succeed. We dedicate this book to all those who use it, for the purpose of making a better, more caring world for all people. Good luck, and work hard!

Liam Clarke
Bruce Sachs
Sue Ford-Sumner
April 2000

Assessment for GNVQ

What is a General National Vocational Qualification (GNVQ)?

GNVQs are alternative qualifications to A levels or GCSEs and can be taken at three levels:

Foundation
- **Part One GNVQ (Foundation)** – equivalent to two GCSEs at grades D–G
- **Foundation GNVQ** – equivalent to four GCSEs at grades D–G; these normally take one year of full-time study

Intermediate
- **Part One GNVQ (Intermediate)** – equivalent to two GCSEs at grades A–C
- **Intermediate GNVQ** – equivalent to four GCSEs at grades A–C; these normally take one year of full-time study

Advanced
- **Advanced GNVQ (called 'vocational A levels')**
  - **Full award (12 units)** – equivalent to two A levels; these are normally taken over a two-year period of full-time study
  - **Single award (6 units)** – equivalent to one A level; these are normally taken over a one-year period of full-time study
  - **Three-unit awards** – these have been designed to encourage students to study GNVQs alongside other qualifications such as A levels, AS levels or GCSEs

How is a GNVQ structured?

All GNVQ courses are made up of units:

- **Mandatory units** – these are units you must study
- **Optional units** – these are units you choose to study.

What is a GNVQ unit?

All Advanced GNVQ units are of equal size and value and are organised in the same way.

You will be provided with a set of specifications from your awarding body. **Section 1** tells you about the unit and gives you brief headings of what you will learn about. For example:

Unit 4: Factors affecting human growth and development

About this unit

This unit will give you the basic understanding of human growth and development needed to develop a knowledge base for working with people in every stage of life.

You will learn about

- development from infancy to later adulthood
- skills developed through the lifespan
- the range of factors that can influence growth and development, including genetic, environmental and socio-economic factors
- theories of development

It will also tell you how the unit will be assessed, for example:

Unit 2, Communicating in health and social care; Unit 3, Physical aspects of health; Unit 5, Health, social care and early years services; and Unit 6, Research perspectives in health and social care are assessed through your portfolio work and the grade that you get for that work is the grade for the unit. Unit 1, Equal opportunities and clients' rights and Unit 4, Factors affecting human growth and development will be assessed through external assessment (a test or examination set by the awarding body) and marked by that body. The grade for the external test will be the grade for the unit.

Section 2 tells you in more detail what you will need to learn. For example:

Factors affecting development

Human development is affected by both genetic and environmental influences. You will need to examine the positive and negative effects of the following factors on growth and development:

- inherited, genetic factors, and how genetic factors interact with environmental influences

---

- socio-economic factors, including the effect of income, housing, nutrition, education, and access to health services
- local and global environmental influences, for example the impact of pollution on health.

You need to investigate how genetic, socio-economic and environmental factors are interrelated.

Section 3 is called Assessment Evidence. This section will tell you what you have to do to gain a pass, merit or distinction. For example:

Assessment evidence

The external assessment will be based on your understanding of human development based on a study of the human development of two individuals at different life stages (the youngest must at least eight years old and the other at least 19 years old). You need to show you understand the way the individuals have developed and why this has been the case.

Your study must include:

- the growth and development of the two individuals at different stages of their development
- how two major skill areas developed in each individual
- factors that affect human growth and development
- theories of development and learning

To achieve a pass you must show you can:

- clearly describe the growth and development of two individuals at different life stages
- trace the development of two major skill areas in each individual
- describe the range of factors that may have affected the development of the two individuals
- describe four main theories of development, relating them to the individuals.

To achieve a merit you must also show you can:

- compare and contrast the differences in the development of the two individuals
- explain accurately the influence of the skill areas on the development of the two individuals
- use appropriate theories to analyse the influence of the range of factors on development and present well-considered conclusions.

To achieve a distinction you must also show you can:

- present coherent arguments based on a comprehensive analysis of the relative importance of the factors that affected the development of the individuals

---

1.2 The legal framework and policies for promoting equality

Throughout this unit, we have been referring to both legislation and policies relating to equal opportunities and clients' rights. While we have emphasised that the development of good practice in care work, on the part of both individuals and organisations, is paramount to protecting people's rights, a knowledge of relevant legislation and policies is important for two reasons:

*   Much practice in health, social and early years care is circumscribed by legislation and policies. In fact, the reason many services exist in the first place is that they fulfil statutory responsibilities.
*   When practice and organisational policies fail, the legislation provides an important safety net in protecting individuals.

Legislation supporting non-discriminatory practice

Some legislation makes it illegal to treat individuals unfairly because of prejudice or stereotyping, or seeks to promote the interests of groups who are vulnerable to discrimination. The following legislation is all relevant.

*   The Local Government Act 1966 provided money to local government to work with immigrants from the Commonwealth. Only recently has this money been more accountably targeted to help the groups for whom it was intended.
*   The Sexual Offences Act 1967 legalised consensual activity between men in private, provided that both parties were over 21 years of age (in England and Wales). Recently, this has been controversially lowered to 18 years of age, but still does not provide equality for homosexuals with heterosexuals, for whom the age of consent is 16 years.
*   The Chronically Sick and Disabled Persons Act 1970 suggested a range of services to be made available to disabled and ill people, including the provision of telephones and functional adaptations to their homes. This Act only set out guidelines.
*   The Equal Pay Act 1975 made it unlawful to discriminate between men and women doing the same jobs, in terms of their pay and conditions. Despite this landmark piece of legislation, statistical evidence shows that women still face discrimination in employment and pay. In addition, occupations such as nursing, which are perceived (wrongly!) as being largely women's work, remain extremely low-paid.
*   The Sex Discrimination Act 1975 and 1986 set out the rights of all individuals in issues regarding gender. It makes it illegal to discriminate on the grounds of gender or marital status in education and employment. The Act also allows for positive action in some cases, where being of a particular sex may be regarded as a genuine occupational requirement for a job. This Act set up the Equal Opportunities Commission to monitor and provide advice on promoting sexual equality.
*   The Race Relations Act 1976 made it illegal to discriminate on the grounds of race, colour, ethnic origin and nationality. This Act is monitored by the Commission for Racial Equality (CRE), which the Act established and to which complaints may be brought. The CRE carries out research, provides information and advice, and has the power to investigate complaints. The law

allows positive action to ensure the involvement of all racial groups in society. Specific responsibilities are placed on local authorities, which have a duty to eliminate racial discrimination and to promote equality. Nevertheless, racial discrimination still pervades British society.

- The Education (Handicapped Children) Act 1980 intended to integrate children with special educational needs into mainstream provision where possible. This responsibility was placed on local authorities. Children with disabilities are to be assessed and 'statemented'. The 'statement' would define the specific educational needs of the child, which the local authority was to meet through mainstream provision. The massive resource implications of the Act meant that it could not be effectively implemented.

- The Mental Health Act 1983 was implemented to safeguard the rights of patients compulsorily admitted under the Act to hospital. The Act ensured that patients were made aware of their rights, and increased the role of the 'approved' social worker, in recognition of the importance of balancing medical and social factors in psychiatric illness. The Act is monitored by the Mental Health Act Commission. The Act fails, however, to safeguard the rights of patients being treated 'informally'.

- The Disabled Persons Act 1981 and 1986 increased the rights of disabled people by establishing the necessity for them to be informed about provision and consulted about their requirements. There are four main rights:
  - Assessment of need is required by the local authority.
  - Resources must be provided, appropriate to the individual, that help the person to live as independently as possible.
  - Representation is a right of all disabled people. (Where the ability to express one's own needs is limited, representation may be made by another person or an advocate.)
  - Monitoring and review are necessary to reflect the changing needs of individuals with disabilities.

The Act intended to involve disabled people and their carers fully. However, the effectiveness of the Act nationally has been limited, as it only set out guidelines and suggestions. No responsibilities were imposed on either the NHS or local authorities. Recent attempts to improve the rights of people with disabilities have been systematically defeated and discouraged by the government.

- The National Health Service and Community Care Act 1990 ensured that individuals in need of care are appropriately assessed and have rights of complaint. The Act allows for service-purchasing by authorities and sets out responsibilities for all care agencies, both statutory and independent, to work collaboratively. It had been anticipated that an individual's needs and preferences could be better met through these provisions. However, inadequate funding and competition among agencies for money have rendered the Act far less effective than it might have been. In addition, the Act restricted real choice for those individuals who could not wholly finance their care independently.

- The Criminal Justice Act 1992 places a duty on those administering the criminal justice system to avoid discrimination on the grounds of race or gender. In addition, its new sentencing structure was meant to provide more alternatives to prison. Since the introduction of the Act, prisons have been pushed beyond their capacity.

Activity 7

Choose either the Sex Discrimination Act or the Race Relations Act and identify what behaviours are described as discriminatory.

The charters

In addition to legislation, there are a variety of government charters that indicate the rights and legitimate expectations of service users. These include:

- *The Citizen's Charter*, which outlines what all users of public services have a right to expect. If services do not meet the required standards, the procedures for complaints are made clear.
- *The Patient's Charter*, which sets out the rights of all users of the NHS. It establishes minimum waiting times and other quality criteria, and how to complain if standards are not met. The Patient's Charter only covers administrative standards. Concerns about GPs, opticians, pharmacists and dentists are expressed to the local health authority. Community health matters, including hospital closures and service cutbacks, are dealt with by the Community Health Council. Complaints about hospital doctors are made through the Regional Health Authority. In addition, the service user always has recourse to his or her Member of Parliament (MP) or legal action. Difficulties with local authority services should be expressed to local councillors, and those concerning independent organisations to the local social services department or health authority's inspection units.

The above legislation and charters will be relevant in many different care settings, and you will need to know which is applicable in the settings you are familiar with.

It is also important to be aware of the ways in which service users can be become aware of their rights. Many care organisations will make the effort to inform clients of their rights and to provide them with appropriate leaflets and booklets. Some legislation, such as the Mental Health Act 1983, requires a hospital manager to see every detained patient personally in order to explain their rights to them. National charters such as the Patient's Charter and the Citizen's Charter should be readily available. In addition, all service users in all services should be formally advised of how to proceed in making a complaint, as this is a vitally important way for an organisation to monitor its compliance with laws and policies. Independent sources of advice and help are also important in ensuring that those who use care services are fully informed of their rights. Some organisations, such as MIND in the field of mental health, view this as a major part of their work.

Activity 8

a Individually, or in groups, visit or contact some of the organisations referred to above, and collect leaflets describing their functions and services. Discuss in class the roles and responsibilities of the various organisations.

b Identify conflicts that may arise in some of the legislation described above between individuals, or between individuals and organisations.

Monitoring quality

Quality in health, social care and early years services is the ordered and systematic approach to meeting the needs of service users, care workers, managers and other stakeholders. It is about continuous improvement and excellence.

Quality assurance procedures of many care organisations refer to legislation applicable in their services as well as their own policies, and set out ways in which compliance can be monitored. By incorporating equal opportunities and client rights into the standards set for the care service, monitoring is possible as well as inspection, which many services require.

In order to monitor a service for good practice in relation to equality, it is necessary to establish observable and measurable standards. For example, have clients had their rights regarding confidentiality explained to them, or how many complaints have clients made about unfair treatment? Does the library in a nursery have books that promote positive images of different races? Such monitoring can be undertaken regularly by the organisation itself through the collection of data. The data can be used to inform the service if its internal standards are being met, and to identify areas in which improvements may be made.

Some services, such as residential and nursing homes and nurseries, are required by law to be inspected externally. The inspecting organisation (currently the local authority, but this may change) often establishes criteria relating to equality and clients' rights. The inspectors are empowered by law to enforce the criteria they set. In some circumstances, inspectors can remove the registration of a service if its standards (including those relating to equality and rights) are not being met.

Why does the concept of quality in care services incorporate the promotion of equality and rights?

1.3 Understanding the effects of discriminatory practices on individuals

The bases of discrimination

In this section we shall investigate and discuss some of the more prevalent forms of **discrimination** in our society, and how individuals may be affected. In addition to discrimination in relation to health status and disability, the requirements of the UK's 2.5 million non-white population pose considerable problems for health and social care services. While 40% of this group are British-born, the others are not and they may experience considerable communication difficulties when insufficient regard is paid to language and cultural differences by care professionals. The easy response is to create specialist services and workers to deal with minority groups. However, while expedient, this response still leaves ethnic minorities outside the mainstream and does little to lessen the discrimination that exists. The needs of all minority groups should be met by generally more responsive and educated health and social care services. Some forms of discrimination, such as racism and sexism, have received much public attention, but the types of discrimination go well beyond these and particularly affect those vulnerable groups who are likely to use health and social care services. Discrimination results in inequality in access to services, and this in turn is reflected in statistics of the nation's health and social problems.

Activity 9

On page 18 are three examples of discrimination in job advertisements. Identify who is being discriminated against and discuss your findings.

WAREHOUSE PERSON

Due to recent company expansion a further person is required to assist in our fabric warehouse.
Working within a team, the person we require should be flexible, aged 23–35, and be able to work on their own initiative. A knowledge of goods in/despatch procedures would be advantageous as well as the ability to work well under pressure.
In return we offer an excellent salary, bonus and pleasant working conditions in the heart of the Peak District.

Production Manager c£30,000
Shift Manager c£25,000

A major brand leader in East Anglia requires two ambitious career minded managers for a high volume 3 shift food packing operation.

You will have a degree of appropriate qualification and will be:

Production Manager
With 3 shifts reporting to you, you will be in your late 20's to early 30's and able to demonstrate a track record of change management in a modern production environment.

Shift Manager
Aged early to late 20's, you are probably looking for your first major career move.

Both positions command an attractive salary and a relocation package.

CONSIDERED WORKING IN AMERICA?

NOW YOU CAN ...
WITHOUT LEAVING HOME

CHICAGO *Diner*

Stunning opportunities for stunning people

All American concept Licensed Bar and Diner opening soon

Attractive and fun to be with Staff required daytime and evening, full and part-time

VACANCIES

Chefs	Commi-Chefs
Bar Staff	Receptionists
Glass Collectors	(Night-time)
Kitchen Porters	Waiters/resses
Cellar Man	D.J./V.J.
Meeter/Greeters	Door Supervisors

Interviews being arranged now

Phone RACHEL or DAVE on

or send details with a photograph to

CHICAGO *Diner*

What is discrimination?

Making use of generalisations and stereotypes is part of human nature. It is how we make sense of the world. We put things into categories about which we may make general assumptions based on our previous experiences and education. Sometimes, however, generalisations and stereotypes may be based on ignorance and fear, resulting in prejudice, intolerance and discrimination (unfair treatment), and hence oppression for other people.

Where such discrimination is widespread in a society, it systematically undermines groups of people materially and psychologically. Their experiences become invalidated. Such discrimination results in exploitation and abuse. It disenfranchises groups of people from mainstream society. The dominant value system in a society often perceives the only worthwhile culture and attributes to be those positively valued by the majority of citizens. In the UK, this tends to be white, middle-class, Anglo-Saxon, Protestant, intelligent, young and healthy. Discrimination is not restricted to particular groups in society. It is aimed at anyone who, for whatever reason, possesses attributes that are not culturally valued. On the basis of having such 'negative' attributes, assumptions are made about the individual. Such ignorance and intolerance is widespread throughout society. All of us are likely to be both victims and perpetrators of discrimination.

Activity 10

In small groups, discuss ways in which each of you has been discriminated against. Consider not just your race, but your age, sex, disability, etc.

The problem of discrimination is extensive. The list below identifies some of the common types of discrimination we may encounter in our society. What links all forms of discrimination is the concept of intolerance. It is not unusual to be suspicious of those not like us in appearance, beliefs, background and much more. The real challenge in developing antidiscriminatory practice in the caring services is to develop a more tolerant attitude to differences between people. If the underlying cause of intolerance is fear, then the objective of antidiscriminatory practice must be to remove the fear.

Elderly people are largely written off as being of little use, and prone to disease and deterioration

Activity 11

a In groups of three or four, discuss the ways in which individuals may be different from each other.
b When your group has agreed, write these differences down in a list. Decide what positive points and what negative points are associated with each difference.

In the activity above, you may have listed some of the more common bases of discrimination, which appear below.

Common types of discrimination

- *Age* – The culturally valued age to be in UK society appears to be between 18 and 35. The views of children tend to be disregarded. Much of the interaction between parents and children is corrective in nature. People over 35 will begin to experience the effects of discrimination in the job market. Elderly people are largely written off as being of little use and prone to disease and deterioration.

- *Class* – There is considerable evidence that discrimination on the basis of social class is widespread. Significant differences exist in educational opportunities, work and health care. Many people will assume a person's class from their accent, but class is far more complex than this.
- *Culture* – There are many subcultures in the UK based on race, religion, place of origin, lifestyle and more. In fact, much discrimination is cultural discrimination. There is much intolerance of lifestyles that are not considered to be 'the norm'.
- *Gender* – We are all aware of discrimination on the basis of gender. Women are still generally paid less than men and appear to be excluded from certain positions (sometimes called the 'glass ceiling'). Both men and women are victims of sexual stereotyping, are expected to behave in certain ways and fulfil particular roles.
- *Health status* – Those in our society suffering from chronic, recurring or terminal health problems are often excluded from social and employment opportunities. They may also be perceived as 'problems' by health and social services agencies and considered to be a burden on social security budgets.
- *HIV status* – In recent years, we have seen much fear and ignorance about HIV and AIDS. Those who are HIV-positive have been assumed to be homosexuals or drug addicts, and there is much irrational fear about having contact with them.
- *Marital status* – Assumptions are still made about individuals on the basis of whether they are married or not. Married men are seen as more conventional and trustworthy. Married women, on the other hand, may be perceived as an employment risk because they are likely to want or have children.
- *Cognitive ability* – This means the ability to learn and process information effectively. Those of low cognitive ability are often perceived as being unable to participate in society. If employable at all, they are often exploited on ridiculously low wages. Children of limited cognitive ability are frequently abandoned by the educational system and are often removed from mainstream education into 'special' units. The 'performance' requirements imposed on schools has made this problem even more acute, as schools compete for the 'more-able' students.
- *Mental health* – Those people experiencing mental health problems are frequently treated with suspicion. They are often perceived wrongly as being violent or dangerous. Attempts to house some individuals with mental health problems in the community sometimes result in protests and anger. Similarly, people with mental health problems are often denied decent employment opportunities.
- *Offending background* – It is not uncommon to find that someone who has broken the law and has been in prison is denied employment, and sometimes housing.
- *Physical ability* – Those of limited physical ability are frequently denied access to public places and suitable housing. Physically disabled children are sometimes denied mainstream education.
- *Place of origin* – Those whose place of origin is other than the UK often have different customs, beliefs and diet. Their experiences are often invalidated, and they are put under considerable pressure to appear to be British. Sometimes, they must disguise their accents and abandon their native dress in order to 'integrate'.
- *Political beliefs* – Although the UK may be more tolerant of diverse political beliefs than some other nations, political allegiances are still frequently the basis on which many assumptions about individuals are made. Extremism of any kind is frowned upon.

- *Race* – The colour of one's skin is still an overwhelming source of discrimination. The human species is racially diverse, but this is not always reflected in communities, education or employment. Racism remains one of the major sources of discrimination in the world.
- *Religion* – Many different religious beliefs and practices can be witnessed throughout the UK. Rather than being a source of interest and education, religious differences are regarded with suspicion and hatred. Religious differences have been the cause of many wars throughout the world.
- *Responsibility for dependants* – Discrimination exists, primarily in the employment market, against those who have children to care for, as they are perceived to be less reliable. There is also some discrimination against men by the legal system in custody disputes.
- *Sensory ability* – We live in a world that assumes that everyone can see and hear. The needs of those who cannot are sometimes not considered in the provision of services.
- *Sexuality* – We live in a society that is largely intolerant of anything other than heterosexual relationships. Homosexuals are treated with suspicion and sometimes violence. They were legally considered to be mentally ill until the 1960s. In addition, certain behaviours are perceived as promiscuous, or out of the ordinary, and are not tolerated by society in general. Those perceived to be sexually different from 'the norm' are denied both employment and social opportunities.

What are your assumptions?

The above list is not exhaustive, but it is easy to see that there is a risk of discrimination wherever individuals or groups are perceived to be different from 'the norm', or what is commonly encountered and valued in mainstream society.

The effect of discrimination on the individual is serious. Victims feel dejected and powerless. They lose their self-esteem, motivation and confidence.

Activity 12

Divide the class into working groups. Each working group will concentrate on a particular part of society that is discriminated against. Identify the rights available to that group through legislation. When this is completed, each working group should present a summary of its findings and the class will make notes of inconsistencies in rights, where they exist.

Case study

In September 1993 the press reported a case in which Mr Green, a black insurance salesman, and his pregnant white girlfriend, Miss Jones, were awarded £24 233 by an industrial tribunal after they had been simultaneously dismissed from the sales department of the company for which they both worked.

The tribunal was told that, when Miss Jones informed her employer that she was pregnant, he swore at her and refused to allow her to attend antenatal classes (her right in law) saying, 'I ain't running a charity, I'm running a business.' He gave her additional work to do at home, saying that if she had worked 'instead of playing with that black', she would not have become pregnant. He referred to her as a 'slag' and 'stupid cow', among other abusive terms. His business partner was equally abusive towards her.

When Miss Jones was 5 months pregnant, she was sacked, along with Mr Green. She said, 'They did everything . . . to make me walk out of my own accord.'

The company claimed that the couple were made redundant after a fall in orders, but later admitted to the tribunal that staff numbers had actually increased from 20 to 40 after the redundancies!

The award of £24 233 covered injury to feeling and loss of earnings. The case was the first since the European Court of Justice had removed the limit of £11 000 on award for injury to feelings. The tribunal chairman described the treatment received by Mr Green and Miss Jones from their former employers as 'grotesquely offensive' and said it had made them both feel disadvantaged.

ⓠ *In small groups, discuss and summarise the issues raised by the case study.*

In what ways might discrimination be a problem in care services?

Because discrimination is such a problem, groups discriminated against may still find attitudes and access to services less than even-handed in spite of legislation.

The vicious circle

Although discrimination begins with the attitudes of other people, negative social expectations cause individuals to devalue themselves and to act accordingly. Victims begin to behave in the negative ways expected of them. This reinforces initial prejudices and makes them even stronger. This process is called a vicious circle and is illustrated opposite.

Most vicious circles begin with statements that start with 'Everybody knows . . .'. What 'everybody knows' is likely to be an unquestioned, limiting assumption about an individual's or group's potential and their right to enjoy opportunities. If we can understand the vicious circle and how it works, we can work systematically to reverse its effects. Intervention into the vicious circle means changing our attitudes and the policies in the places in which we work. We have here many targets for change. We can work to change expectations. We can expand opportunities for individuals and groups, and, by doing these things, increase the status, power, self-esteem and confidence of those discriminated against. Turning vicious circles into virtuous circles is one of the essential tasks of health and social care. It is why the value base of care is so important.

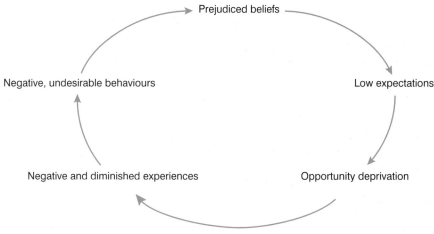

The vicious circle

Let's look at an example of how the vicious circle can be used to understand discrimination.

1 *'Everybody knows . . .' statement* – Everybody knows that Afro-Caribbean boys don't work hard in school.
2 *Prejudiced belief* – Afro-Caribbean boys aren't worth educating.
3 *Low expectations* – Joe is an Afro-Caribbean boy attending a mixed-race school. Because Afro-Caribbean boys don't work hard, Joe won't work hard.
4 *Opportunity deprivation* – Joe doesn't get the attention from the teacher that the other children get, because it is perceived that it would be a waste of time.
5 *Negative and diminished experiences* – Joe is neglected and not receiving support with his work from the teacher. He is not learning as much as he should.
6 *Negative, undesirable behaviours* – Joe is losing interest and falling behind the other children. As a consequence of falling behind, he fulfils the prophecy – this is the 'I told you so!' statement. The teacher believes that Joe's falling behind is proof that Afro-Caribbean boys don't work hard in school, and this further strengthens the original prejudiced belief.

The vicious circle model of discrimination is important, because not only does it explain the process of discrimination but it also gives us methods of introducing non-discriminatory and antioppressive practice. In the example above, we can work on changing the prejudiced beliefs by doing the following:

- Properly training the teacher, with a view to changing the teacher's attitudes and behaviour. Perhaps the Education Department has an ongoing programme in order to achieve this with staff.
- Challenging the teacher's behaviour using an Education Department policy or code of practice. Alternatively, the teacher may be accused of a breach of the Race Relations Act, and charged.
- Providing opportunities for Afro-Caribbean boys such as Joe. By showing that Joe can do well, we would be providing a strong positive image, which would challenge the prejudiced belief.

Which of the above methods of intervening in the vicious circle do you think would be most effective?

Activity 13

a Divide the class into pairs. Each pair should choose a group subject to discrimination in society. The list of types of discrimination on pages 19–21 might prove useful. Using the model of the vicious circle, explain how changing one or more of the elements of the circle can result in a virtuous circle. Express the 'prejudiced belief' as an 'Everybody knows . . .' statement.

b When each pair has satisfactorily completed the exercise, present it to the rest of the class for discussion and evaluation.

1.4 How care organisations promote equality

This section of the unit will examine the many ways in which care organisations may promote equality and rights. Generally, this will be achieved through both policies and procedures.

- *Policies* explain in broad terms what the organisation is trying to achieve.
- *Procedures* set out in detail how work within the organisation must be conducted. A procedure will state the ways in which decisions will be made, by whom and within what time-scale.

There are many things to consider when developing policies and procedures relating to equality and rights in care services. There often has to be a balance between bureaucratic mechanisms and professional judgements. Firm but sensitive handling is often required, and this is a very skilled area of work. As we have seen, it is made even more complex by the fact that sometimes the service itself must make decisions that involve clients' rights. We will examine some of the complexities found in this area of work, before drawing some general conclusions.

The contexts in which discrimination may occur

As we have seen, discrimination may take the form of individual behaviour, which is the most obvious. This occurs when an individual or group members are treated differently because they look different, speak differently or have different beliefs from us. This often results from stereotyping another individual, resulting in unfavourable and distorted perceptions. We might unthinkingly avoid someone who is gay, or assume that older people are irritable and boring.

Societal discrimination occurs when the stereotyping is so widespread that it is largely unquestioned. Discrimination may be reinforced unintentionally through the normal working of the system. The Swann Report (1985) described it as 'a range of long established systems, practices and procedures which have the effect, if not the intention, of depriving marginalised groups of equality of opportunity and access to society's resources'. Examples may be the design of buildings without access for people with disabilities, or unequal pay for equal work.

All organisations and systems provide evidence of structural or institutional discrimination. These inequalities often persist in spite of efforts to change them. Racism may represent the attitudes and actions of individuals, which may be addressed by training and development or, in more serious cases, by disciplinary action against the individuals concerned. However, even more serious is the concept of institutional racism. This is where the policies or practices of an organisation systematically discriminate against one or more minority groups. The concept of institutional racism is controversial, as it suggests that racism is not simply the actions of a few individuals but rather is deeply rooted in both the policy and practice of the organisation. It is likely that health, social care and early years services are no more immune to institutional racism than any other type of organisation, in spite of the high profile that these issues are given. Recent criticisms of British police are evidence of how far such problems may extend.

What is institutional racism?

Power and empowerment

Empowerment is the act of providing information and skills to less powerful groups or individuals so that they may take more control over their own lives and make a more active contribution to society in general.

An intention of care values is to create equality for all individuals. This idea challenges the historical notion of power that has previously existed in professional caring relationships. Most professional care workers are employed by agencies that have considerable power. Social services departments, health services and independent providers all have responsibilities in law to others besides service users. While we emphasise the therapeutic, supportive and counselling roles of care workers, these workers are also responsible to their agency of employment, and often to the general public, whose interests they also serve. The allocation of resources, and the soft 'policing' duty involved with many care jobs, backed up by legislation, require care workers to combine their caring roles with that of bureaucrat and controller. The compatibility of these roles is very difficult to manage. The care worker may be economically advantaged compared to the client. The worker may be better educated and, by definition, possesses more power through position than the client.

The social or health problems of some service users may create real dependency. To be perceived as anything other than fit, able and making a valuable contribution to society is to be stripped of power. Some care services inadvertently reinforce this problem in the way they provide their services. Those who provide care services are not immune from the attitudes of the society into which they themselves have been socialised. They may have attitudes that reinforce many of the prejudices society has about people who are different, for whatever reason. Care settings may mirror the effects of power on vulnerable individuals in both public and private settings.

The power of assessment

There is often compliance in making the exercise of power legitimate. Those who are perceived to be in power must make very conscious efforts to encourage (i.e. enable or empower) the user of care services to take an interest and to participate. The provision of care for those who need it is now perceived to be based on partnership. This means that the client is no longer regarded as a passive recipient of services but has an integral part to play in decisions regarding the client's own welfare.

> ## Activity 14
>
> In a care setting (which may be a work placement), observe the behaviour of other care workers. Make a list of some of these behaviours, which may include things like assisting with bathing, eating or bedtimes. Decide for each of the behaviours that you listed whether the client is being empowered or whether the care worker is exercising power over the client, and why.

In order to attempt to correct institutionalised inequalities in care services, care organisations need to pay attention to two key areas:

* recruitment and selection of staff
* assessment of the values and attitudes of those who wish to work in their organisation, as many applicants for jobs will share the prejudices that may be found in society generally. Not everyone is suitable for care work.

Ongoing staff training and development

By having a continuous programme of staff development, which addresses issues of equality and rights, care organisations will give out clear messages about their commitment to positive practice, and at the same time help to develop and reinforce desirable responses in staff.

You will read more about this below under Organisational responsibilities (pages 32–33).

Ways of handling ethical issues and dilemmas

Real power results from knowledge and choice. Historically, care organisations met the requirements of groups in society other than clients themselves. The needs of those perceived to be more able, including families, neighbours, professionals and politicians, dictated policies in respect of those perceived to be less able. Care professionals often made decisions with reference to significant others first and the client second. The problem was compounded by the lack of choice in service provision, with particular services being offered by only one local provider, almost exclusively in the public sector. Clients had to accept what was offered or have no service at all. Financial constraints on available provision have also been a major factor in limiting the choice of clients. All these factors, over many years, have developed into an institutionalised belief that care providers know better than clients what is needed, or wanted.

It is now apparent that such attitudes significantly contribute to the problems of those disadvantaged through health or social difficulties. The very process of health or social disadvantage results in a loss of power in society.

A prime aim of health and social care is empowerment in respect of a client's rights and choice. Not only is such an aim morally correct but it is also highly effective in terms of meeting the needs of those who require care services. By promoting and supporting individual rights and choice within service delivery, we may ultimately reduce a major source of difficulties that care workers themselves impose on clients.

Maintenance of individual rights and choice

Essentially, clients should have the same choices and rights as are afforded to all of us in everyday life. This means that clients' perception of their problems and preferred responses to them should be encouraged, listened to, acknowledged and recorded. This is very dependent on the effective communication skills of the care worker, which will be discussed in Unit Three. Options, rather than solutions, should be presented to the client, and the differences among the options should be fully explained. Options should always be considered in respect of risk, but only in exceptional circumstances should the right to take risks be removed from the client. Most commonly, such a situation may arise when it is deemed that the client cannot make a reasonable assessment of the risk, such as in a case of mental illness or severe learning disability. In such a case, the client's rights are legally protected by the Mental Health Act 1983.

We often talk of independence, but perhaps interdependence better describes the relationship that most clients would wish from a care service. For many, the care service becomes an important part of their lives and the support offered should be emotional as well as practical. Care workers are often not allowed sufficient time to meet other than urgent practical needs. Therefore, it is important that clients are encouraged to develop relationships with their carers and that these relationships are based on mutual respect. Such relationships will be dependent on the carer's ability to promote and acknowledge the individual's rights and choices. This may entail sensitive areas, such as the right to have sexual feelings and to express these in activities and relationships. Particular attention is drawn to this area because, in the past, many clients of care services have been denied such rights.

In what ways might care services empower service users?

Activity 15

a In groups, discuss the ways in which you would support a client in making choices in an institutional setting, such as a hospital or a residential home.
b How might your activities create conflict within the work setting?

A client may not choose to be as independent as the professionals involved believe the client is capable of being. Moving individuals towards independence can only be done by encouragement: the right of individuals to choose their preferred level of independence is what is important. For example, elderly people may wish more to be done for them because they choose not to push themselves. This process of disengagement is not unusual. Coercive pressure in this situation may be a consequence of the care worker's own feelings about the process of ageing.

Carers must not only develop tolerance towards different types of individual but must also actively promote and support individual rights and choice. This requires good interpersonal skills.

Effective interpersonal skills are particularly important in dealing with challenging behaviour. Service users may be angry or aggressive, and the care worker will need good rapport and listening skills to calm the situation down. However, care workers need to be careful not to expose themselves to dangerous situations, and may need to call on the support of others, including the police, where necessary.

will be reflected throughout your GNVQ education and should be continued in higher education and employment. The emphasis put on care values in the Care NVQs, and a profound understanding of them, is an important recognition of the importance and complexity of ethical issues.

Professional supervision is also of great importance, as it supports and enables the ethical development of the care worker. In recognition of the ethical complexity of most care decisions, case conferences are an effective means of exploring the values of different interested parties. Even where decisions may go against a certain individual's values, the case conference provides an opportunity for people to be listened to and their views to be recorded.

Organisational responsibilities

We discussed in 1.1 Promoting equality in care practice, the many ways in which care service workers can promote equality through their own practice, and this will be further reinforced in Unit Two, which looks at interpersonal skills. It is important to focus on the individual care worker, because the service user's experience of the service will be largely based on direct contact with individuals. It should be clearly understood, however, that the organisation has very clear responsibilities in ensuring that the client's contacts with care workers reflect the best possible practice. This can be achieved in a number of ways, as discussed below.

Training and professional updating

As we have explained, ethical issues are difficult and the development of good practice in care workers requires that they are afforded appropriate training opportunities. Many services run programmes within their organisation but this may not be feasible for smaller services. However, many of the organisations that represent service user interests provide programmes of training for care workers, and service users themselves often make a significant contribution to developing appropriate awareness and skills among workers. In fact, much of the initiative for raising awareness of cultural diversity has been taken by ethnic minority communities themselves.

Through appropriate training and development, staff can not only develop their awareness and understanding but also become informed about agency policies and procedures. Such training should form part of an induction programme for new employees. Continuing training in these areas will enable staff to remain alert to issues and to continue to foster positive attitudes. Training sessions is also a safe arena within which to challenge inappropriate attitudes and behaviours. This might be achieved through role-plays and case studies in group settings. Such training is an effective way to foster positive attitudes in staff.

Staff selection

It is very difficult to determine people's attitudes and values using the sorts of selection procedure that most care services use. It should be obvious that the success of any service in promoting good practice depends on the care workers themselves and there is always a risk of employing individuals with strong opinions that would be contrary to the policies and practice of the organisation. Selection procedures should focus as far as possible on determining the values and ethics of applicants. The recruitment process itself should encourage applications from disadvantaged and under-represented groups, as this will provide effective positive images for others within the community.

Management structures

In view of the fact that the area of equal opportunities and clients' rights is so complex, it is important that clear systems of accountability are established within care organisations. We have already mentioned how quality procedures need to account for practice in this area, and it is advisable to have a named person within the organisation who is responsible for overseeing practice relating to rights and equality. Such a person would ring-fence this as an area of priority for the organisation and be able to develop expertise that might otherwise be lacking within the service. A specialist in equality and opportunity would be able to provide support for both workers and service users, develop and monitor policies, ensure compliance with legislation, ensure that care values are being applied in practice and contribute to staff development and training.

It is also vital that managers also demonstrate their own personal competency in promoting equality. This is called 'modelling'. Modelling appropriate behaviour to promote equality and rights creates a culture within the organisation where such behaviour is copied and valued.

Notification procedures

Care organisations need to be aware that gender, age, race and poverty all play a role in abusive relationships. Central to understanding abuse is the concept of inequality – the belief that one sex or one race is superior, for example. Within care services, child and adult protection has achieved a very high profile in recent years, and such abuse occurs within care services, just as it occurs in the wider community. Most services now have both policies and procedures for dealing with abuse when it is found, but it should be appreciated that it can be very difficult for an individual worker to challenge bad practice within their own organisation. There should be support for workers who wish to report abusive practice and information available about what they can do both inside and outside their employing agency. Sometimes it may be service users who report abuse, and they too should be supported within the service, so the procedures need to be clear. The reporting of abuse within a service is sometimes referred to as 'whistle-blowing'.

Issues for health, social care and early years services

- Staffing should reflect the diversity of the local population
- Strong links should be developed with groups from local minority communities
- Publicity and information materials should ensure that they include positive images of members of minority communities
- A fully detailed policy on equality should be developed and monitored
- It is important to keep ethical considerations at the top of the agenda in care practice. It is only through such open recognition, discussion and resolution of competing values that the care industry can reflect in practice the real complexity of the issues it faces. There are no rules.

Identify the ways in which care service organisations can promote equality and rights.

1.5 Sources of support and guidance

There are numerous sources of support and guidance about issues relating to equality and rights available for care workers, clients and organisations. Much support is available on a national basis, but help is sometimes even easier to obtain

Key terms

After reading this unit you should be able to understand the following words and phrases. If you do not, go back through the unit and find out, or look them up in the Glossary.

Attitude   Social exclusion
Discrimination   Stakeholder
Empowerment   Values
Quality

Review questions

1 Define discrimination and explain the effects on individuals.
2 Explain how, in certain circumstances, using legislation to prevent discrimination may be effective. When may it not be effective?
3 Identify sources of information and support in matters relating to discrimination and equal opportunities.
4 What forms of discrimination are prohibited by legislation? What forms are not?
5 Explain how the use of language is important in antidiscriminatory practice.
6 a Do you believe that antidiscriminatory practice should be an issue for discipline and legislation or education and training?
   b What are the positive and negative aspects of each approach?
7 Describe the relationship between ethical issues, and attitudes and values.
8 Define the concept of empowerment and what role it has in care services.
9 What are the threats to individual rights and choice in care services?
10 In law, what rights with regard to confidentiality exist for clients?

Assignment

You will be asked to prepare a study investigating a code of practice or a charter of rights that promotes equality, as well as one piece of legislation. You will also need to investigate how one health, social care or early years service supports clients and workers in promoting equal rights.

This chapter has discussed codes of practice and charters of rights, as well as identifying relevant legislation. We have also identified a variety of ways in which services support clients and workers in promoting equal rights. It is suggested that you review these sections now.

Get the grade

To get an **E** grade you must complete tasks 1–4

To get a **C** grade you must complete tasks 1–7

To get an **A** grade you must complete tasks 1–9

Tasks

1 Select one care setting with which you are familiar. Find out what codes of practice or charters of rights are used in or are relevant to the service you have selected. Also find out about what legislation and policies are used in the service to promote clients' rights and confidentiality. Make notes about how the policies, codes of practice and legislation are used in the service you have chosen. You will need to discuss this with staff in the service you have chosen, as

▶▶

they will be a valuable source of information. Explain how these policies, codes of practice and legislation are actually used in day-to-day practice, giving examples.

2   On pages 22–23, we explained the vicious circle of discrimination. Use this model to explain how clients in the service you have chosen are affected by discrimination. You will need to explore a variety of 'Everybody knows . . .' statements in order to get a full picture. Be sure that you address the long-term consequences, such as disempowerment and lowered self-esteem.

3   Show that you understand why non-discriminatory practice is an important part of the care service you have chosen, and how non-discriminatory practice helps to 'empower' service users.

4   Show the ways in which the service you have chosen actively promotes clients' rights. It would be useful to provide examples, which you can discuss.

5   Analyse how the organisation supports workers in promoting clients' rights. Analysing means looking at the *range* of methods used by the organisation and discussing the pros and cons of each method. You will need to draw a conclusion at the end, which means expressing your own opinion, clearly supported by the evidence you have presented.

6   We have explained in the text a number of reasons why users of care services are particularly vulnerable to infringement of their rights. You will need to explain this yourself very clearly and fully, using examples.

7   Show the ways in which the service promotes clients' rights, as well as how codes of practice and charters are used. Now, analyse how use of a code of practice or a charter influences day-to-day practice. This may mean how it affects worker behaviour, or how procedures are in place to protect clients. How do clients benefit from this? Remember that 'to analyse' means to cover a variety of evidence and discuss pros and cons.

8   In the text we have reviewed a range of equal opportunities legislation. Can a law itself change people's attitudes, or is more required? Care workers need to have the right attitudes and demonstrate the correct behaviours in order to promote equality of opportunity. How effective is the equal opportunities legislation in affecting values and behaviour? Evaluate its effectiveness, which means supporting your opinions with facts that you present clearly, and determining how reliable your information is. Be sure to use several examples of legislation and suggest for each how it might be improved.

9   In order to improve the quality of their practice in promoting equal opportunities and clients' rights, care workers may use a variety of sources of information and support. This may involve accessing information from organisations such as those listed on pages 35–37, going on training courses or reading books and professional journals. In addition, staff are often supervised in the work they do. Explain how care workers can make the most of these opportunities, and give examples, perhaps from the care service you have chosen to study.

Key Skills

	You can use this Assignment to provide evidence for the following Key Skills
Communication C3.2, C3.3	When you are describing a code of practice, a charter of rights or a piece of legislation, or explaining the effects of discrimination. The vicious circle would be evidence of communicating using an image.
Application of Number N3.1	In assessing the effectiveness of equal opportunities practice, you may want to consult and interpret different sources of information, including data.

Communicating in health and social care

What is covered in this unit

2.1 *Types of interaction*
2.2 *Effective communication*
2.3 *Communication skills in groups*
2.4 *Evaluating communication skills*
2.5 *Maintaining client confidentiality*

At the end of this unit, you will be asked to produce a report on how effective communication skills are used in a health, social care or early years setting of your choosing. You will also need to produce records which you have made on your own interactions in a one-to-one interaction and a group interaction, using different client groups for each. If you would like to see further details of the tasks you are likely to need to carry out for assessment please refer to the end of the unit where an assignment has been set (see pages 75–78).

This unit is assessed through your portfolio work. You will receive a grade for your report and for your records of your communication skills. This grade will be your grade for the unit.

Materials you will need to complete this unit:

- Books on communication skills (there are many available)
- Access to care settings and their clients
- A video camera
- A communication expert to talk with, such as a social worker, psychologist or counsellor.

2.1 Types of interaction

Introduction

There is no aspect of care work more essential than effective communication. Successful outcomes in care work are often reliant upon the care workers having appropriate communication skills and the barriers to good communication being removed or minimised.

Communication skills are the ways in which we transmit information and include oral (using words), non-verbal (using body language) and written types of communication. Information includes facts, feelings and opinions.

The ways in which we communicate with others can have either positive or negative effects. By making individuals feel as if they are part of a community, the care worker can increase the client's sense of wellbeing. Emphasising the worth of others and giving others the time that they need is important. In order to optimise the sense of wellbeing in others, care workers need to systematically develop their skills. In order to achieve this, they must be committed to becoming more effective and the care organisation must be committed to providing the appropriate support and training. Failure to do so may result in the negative consequences of clients becoming disempowered, feeling oppressed and losing their sense of self-worth. Care workers must be vigilant and attentive in their interactions with others, recognising that interactions may have both positive and negative effects.

The importance of interpersonal interaction in health and social care

Care is a service industry, where workers have an unusually high degree of contact with service users. Cowell, writing in 1984, said 'People are as much a part of the product in the consumer's mind as any other attribute of the service'. He explains that in service industries, such as health and social care, the 'product' of the service is created by the interpersonal interaction of its workers. Bateson (1977) argues that, because the behaviour of the people who deliver the service is so important, the determinant of that behaviour should always be 'What benefits the service user?'. He calls this the consumer benefit concept. The consumer's view should always be central to the service being offered. This is critical to the success of the service in meeting needs.

Activity 1

Select a care setting and describe a number of physical aspects of that setting (eating arrangements, sleeping arrangements, visiting, decor, etc.). List these aspects and for each one describe how the client benefits. If you cannot find any benefit for the client, you may need to ask some questions as to why the setting has been organised in that particular way.

Draw conclusions from this activity as to whether the setting is person-orientated or institutionally based.

Gronross (1982) states that quality in a service is determined by:

- the attitudes of employees
- the behaviour of employees (interpersonal interaction)
- the general service-mindedness of personnel
- the elevated status of employees within the organisation who have direct contact with service users.

Activity 2

In small groups, decide what attitudes care workers should have in order to provide a quality service. Make a list of these and discuss why each is important. Consider both social care and health care settings.

The client's preferred method of communication should always be used

The values and attitudes of care workers can only be expressed through interpersonal interaction. The values and the behaviours appropriate to care have been established in the value base unit for the NVQs in Care (Unit O2).

The value base and interpersonal skills

Health and social care is a service that requires not only a great deal of technical skill in physical care but also considerable skill in emotional and psychological care. The style of help is of equal importance to any physical support offered. Indeed, some care services, such as mental health, are wholly dependent on proficiency in emotional care. All users of care services have emotional needs, so the ways in which care workers respond to them are crucial.

Surveys carried out in the USA on user satisfaction in care show that satisfaction with a care service is always measured in relation to the interpersonal skills of the staff. Recent publications from the Royal College of Nursing also recognise this, drawing attention to the differences between technical quality (purely practical skills like taking blood pressure or applying dressings) and functional quality (how the carer interacts with the patient in meeting the patient's emotional needs). In some businesses, functional quality is taught through 'customer care training'. However, this can be 'parrot-fashion' and can sound false if the attitudes of the staff are not also fundamentally changed. Attitudes result from values, and these are very difficult to learn or change.

Activity 3

Why do you think that attitudes are difficult to change? Give examples from your own experience.

Interaction in health and social care

There are several types of interaction important in health and social care. These include the following:

- *Language* – the use of words in making statements and asking questions, also known as verbal behaviour. The use of language includes how we emphasise words, and our tone of voice.
- *Sensory contact* – This includes non-verbal behaviour such as body language, facial expression, distance from the other person and touching.
- *Activity interaction* – This may consist of activities such as music, arts and crafts, drama and movement. Sometimes it is more effective to allow individuals to communicate through activity, and opportunities for this may be provided by, among others, occupational therapists. All forms of effective interpersonal interaction require skill and training.

Within health and social care, there are very specific reasons why interaction is so important:

- *Exchange of information* – Much of the work within health, social care and early years services requires information to be exchanged between workers and service users, between workers and workers, between workers and their organisation, and between organisations. For example, in order for an assessment to be made of the needs of an individual, some form of interview must occur. The skills of the care worker will need to be good in order to extract and record reliable information. Although the bulk of such an interview will be orally conducted, the facts will also need to be recorded in written form, and what is written will often form the basis of a resource allocation. Information is wholly dependent upon good communication skills, and accurate information forms the basis of all decisions made about services and clients. Workers need to effectively communicate not just with service users but also with managers, colleagues, other professionals and clients' relatives. Clear, unambiguous communication is essential for effective service delivery.
- *Explaining procedures* – The world of health and care services is often confusing and bewildering for those who use services, and it is the care worker who is often their guide and interpreter for the services they are using. Clarity in communication is essential when explaining procedures, so that mistakes will not be made and also so that the client has all the information necessary in order to make informed decisions. Procedures may include health treatments or investigations, how an assessment works, or even how complaints and appeals procedures work.
- *Promoting relationships and offering support* – Effective communication is also the core of the caring relationship – it communicates warmth, support, concern and approval. It is through effective communication that we can value people as individuals and make them not feel as if they are being processed by the systems that regulate care services.
- *Getting to know clients and assess their needs* – If we can communicate effectively with clients, we will achieve a much better understanding of how they perceive their situation, and as a result make better assessments. Although there is a formal aspect to assessment, much assessment is informal and achieved on a day-to-day basis through interaction between care workers and service users.
- *Negotiation and liaison with clients, family members, colleagues and other professionals* – Care work requires effective communication with many different individuals who have an interest in the service being offered. These individuals are called

stakeholders. Stakeholders need to remain involved and informed, and this is most effectively achieved when the care worker has the necessary skills.

- *Promotion of interaction between group members* – Much care work (but not all!) requires working with a group or as part of a team. Care workers need to be able to make useful contributions to the group as well as be able to promote and support the contribution of others.

These are only some of the purposes of interaction in care work. It is important to remember that effective communication always requires a clear purpose, and care workers should be aware of the purpose of any interaction they are involved with and be able to explain that purpose to others. It is also important to note that the professional care worker will always assume full responsibility for the effectiveness of an interaction and never place the blame for misunderstanding on others. For this reason, care workers will possess a range of skills that they can adapt effectively to fit most situations. There is a doctrine among professional communicators that states: 'The meaning of a communication is the result that you get. If you are not getting the result you require, *change* what you are doing!'

Much interaction in care services may be informal, e.g. getting to know clients and chatting with colleagues. While such interactions may seem natural and undemanding, the care worker will understand that the quality of service the client receives and the environment within which the care worker works are highly dependent upon the quality of those interactions. Cowell (1984) emphasises that, in service industries such as health and care, the concept of quality as defined by service users is almost wholly associated with the interpersonal skills of staff. The attitudes, behaviour and service-mindedness of staff are *the* key features of successful service delivery. Where clients express dissatisfaction with services, it is almost always a dissatisfaction with the interactions experienced with staff. Researching health care, Cleary and McNeil (1988) observed that 'the most consistent finding is that such health care provider characteristics as communication skills, **empathy** and caring are strong predictors of patient satisfaction'. Patients often emphasise in quality assessments that caregivers were or were not friendly and polite.

Other interactions will be more formal, and these may include explaining decisions or procedures to clients and their families, assessing needs and confirming information, case conferences and staff meetings. In these situations, while clarity and accurate information are critical, the skills of the worker in being sensitive and caring are still paramount.

Explain why effective communication is of particular importance in health, social care and early years services.

This chapter identifies the basic skills required and how they may be used to enhance interaction. In addition, for interpersonal interaction to be effective, it must consider issues such as gender, age and culture.

2.2 Effective communication

We have implied that some communication may be less effective than other communication. It is very important that you understand the differences between effective and non-effective communication. In this section, we shall explore the factors that enhance interaction and those that inhibit effective interaction.

It is important that care workers are able to identify barriers to effective communication. Some of the barriers may be due to poor skills development in the care worker. Other barriers may be due to the physical environment – poor building design, noise or lack of privacy. Some clients may have special communication needs, such as deafness, a speech impediment or memory problems. Some attitudes can create barriers, such as stereotyping, maintaining class differences or lacking respect for cultural and ethnic differences. Of course, not everyone speaks English, and interpretation may be necessary. Another major barrier can be anger or distress, which effectively prevents open and honest communication. Identifying such barriers is the first step to overcoming them. This section will explore some of these issues.

Using effective communication to empower

Interaction between care workers and clients should be **empowering** for the client. Class, age, disability, gender and race may all contribute to individuals feeling that they lack power – that they are somehow 'unequal' to others. One of the goals of effective interaction is to equalise relationships: to establish a sense of partnership with clients. Skilful listening and questioning, as explained below, can help to empower clients. Awareness of people's rights and preferences, helping people to talk about the past and listening attentively to clients' experiences can all help to empower. Of course, gaining consent from clients to explore issues with them is central to any interview or formal interaction.

Effective communication in health and care services can only ever be empowering because:

- it respects people's preferences and beliefs
- it promotes **confidentiality** and respects people's privacy
- it enables clients to express their views and be heard
- it promotes clients' rights
- it helps to develop individual identities in clients and supports personal development.

An important aspect of interpersonal skills is to understand outcomes. An outcome is a specific, desired result of an interaction. The care worker should be clear what outcomes are desired in interacting with a client, and gain client agreement. Outcomes should incorporate care values – the client should experience the worker's positive regard for choice, confidentiality, personal beliefs and identity. There are three distinct phases of acquiring effective interpersonal skills.

- *Thinking* – Intellectual awareness is developed. An understanding of the reasons behind the skills is acquired.
- *Doing* – New behavioural skills are learned through practical exercises and analysis. The nuts and bolts of interpersonal skills are practised.
- *Feeling* – To develop feeling, the skills are used in real-life situations, with real feedback. Workers gain an emotional insight into their effect on others and how others affect them. In this stage, the values associated with the new behaviours are internalised and the new behaviours become more natural.

When the learning of interpersonal skills is limited to just thinking and doing, the values of the worker may not change. For example, care workers may learn how to express themselves in a politically correct, antidiscriminatory way but may still possess discriminatory beliefs. In such a situation, the workers will display incongruence – the subtle, non-verbal cues betraying their discomfort with their own behaviour. Workers' posture, eye movements and other body language will communicate a message different from their words. To develop feeling requires considerable determination. The value base of care cannot be communicated to clients simply because one has read it, or practised a few exercises. However, reading about the values of care and practising exercises are the essential first steps.

Effective interpersonal interaction is:

- gaining an understanding of the value base on the feeling level
- being able to communicate that to service users, both verbally and non-verbally.

A desirable outcome of interpersonal interaction in health and social care is the development of understanding. Care workers will need to be understood on both emotional and intellectual levels. They will also need to understand others and be able to communicate their understanding to clients on both the emotional and intellectual levels. Successful communication is about the results we achieve from being understood and expressing understanding. In health and social care it is always the client who determines whether the worker's communication is effective. If a client does not understand, the worker must find a different way of achieving the outcome of understanding. The responsibility for achieving understanding in health and social care always lies with the care worker. This is the nature of the professional relationship. Therefore, the care worker needs to have a repertoire of varied interpersonal skills to call upon. Each of us is unique and different. Good communication skills:

- acknowledge the uniqueness of individuals and bridge the differences
- increase understanding by focusing on outcomes and not problems. Ideally, the care worker and the client can share outcomes, such as a sense of belonging, increased independence, more support where needed or accessing appropriate resources. All goals should be set with clients, in line with the value base.

What factors makes communication effective?

Usually, words just come and talk just happens – the process is automatic. However, the demands on care workers to communicate competently and effectively make them suspect that they could do better. There are numerous factors that can enhance or inhibit interaction. We shall start by looking in some detail at interactive skills.

The skills required to enhance communication

To promote antidiscriminatory practice, support individual rights and choice, acknowledge personal beliefs and identity, and maintain confidentiality, the most important skill is to communicate effectively. Effective communication is essentially mutual understanding between the client and the care worker. The responsibility for mutual understanding clearly lies with the care worker. If care workers are not being understood, they must find another way of expressing themselves. If the client is not being understood, the care worker must use a different technique of communication.

Effective communication begins with the recognition that each of us is different and unique. Good interpersonal skills bridge these differences.

The first steps toward effective interpersonal interaction

- Observe what is going on around you, and make conscious decisions about how to respond.
- Acquaint yourself with the values of care.
- Avoid generalisations about people. Regard all people as unique individuals, with their own views and feelings. Show an interest in the ways in which people are different.
- Work only with goals, not problems. It is easy to see what individuals cannot do. It takes skill and vision to see what they may aspire to.

The skills of interpersonal interaction

There are five basic skills in enhancing an interaction with a service user:

* questioning
* self-disclosure and prompting
* active listening
* giving information
* rapport.

Each of these involves both verbal and non-verbal skills.

Questioning

Questioning is the seeking of information, clarification, views, feelings and thoughts. There are two basic types of questions: closed and open.

Closed questions
Closed questions are questions that can be answered in one or two words, often 'Yes' or 'No'. 'What is your name?', 'How old are you?', 'Do you eat chips?' and 'What is your nationality?'. are examples of closed questions. They are essential for ascertaining facts. They should, however, be minimised in a conversation, as long strings of them make people feel interrogated and uncomfortable. Closed questions may inhibit conversation.

Open questions
Open questions are questions that require a more extended answer. For example, instead of asking a client, 'Do you eat pork?', the care worker might ask, 'What sorts of foods do you like or dislike?'. Such an open question feels more comfortable, and allows clients to answer in their own way. The use of open questions communicates to the client that the care worker is interested in the whole range of responses that the client might make. Open questions typically begin:

* How . . . ?
* Why . . . ?
* In what ways . . . ?
* What sort of . . . ?

By using open questions, the care worker will find that much of the information that needs to be ascertained is freely given, without the need for interrogating the client endlessly with lists of closed questions.

It appears that the use of closed questions comes more naturally in our culture. In order to develop skill in open questioning, practice is required.

Activity 4

In pairs, ask each other questions about anything of your choice.

a If you are asked a closed question, give a one-word response. Do not give any more information than you are asked for.
b If you are asked an open question, give as full an answer as you believe appropriate.

This activity will make you pay attention both to the sorts of questions you ask and the sorts of questions asked of you. It is important to do this activity by the rules, as, if you just have a chat with your partner, you will learn very little about open and closed questions.

Self-disclosure and prompting

Self-disclosure is another means of enhancing a conversation when seeking information. It is often used in conjunction with questioning. The purpose of self-disclosure is to make clients more comfortable and forthcoming, by telling them something about yourself. This helps to establish areas of common interest. Self-disclosure is necessary for making clients feel that the are not under scrutiny. It turns an interview into a conversation. Some examples of self-disclosure, used with an open question, may be:

* 'I don't like hot desserts. What sorts of dessert do you like?'
* 'I broke my leg once and found using crutches very difficult. How are you managing with them?'

Activity 5

a In pairs, repeat the exercise on open and closed questions, but this time add self-disclosure to the conversation. Keep to the same rules.
b At the conclusion of your conversation, spend a few moments discussing how different this exercise made you feel compared to the one where you asked only questions.

Self-disclosure is a type of prompting. Prompting is a means of getting clients to talk when they are finding it difficult. Most of us prompt quite naturally, by nodding our heads or by saying 'Yeah' or 'I see'. These sorts of phrase, combined with an attentive gaze and raising of the eyebrows, are effective prompts. They tell the client that we are expecting a response. In seeking information, a care worker may need to focus the client's responses. An information-seeking interview can easily evolve into a social conversation, with little being disclosed. The care worker may need to bring the conversation back to the topic being discussed. This can also be done by using prompts. A simple reminder will often work, such as 'Does any of that affect your relationship with your son, Mrs Jones? I'd like to discuss that, if it's OK?'.

Active listening

Questioning, prompting and self-disclosure are the ways in which we obtain information and enhance interaction. However, it is important that the care worker shows that the client has been listened to and understood. This is called active listening. Active listening is a powerful way of optimising interactions. There are two types of active listening:

* paraphrasing
* reflective listening.

Some of the ground rules are as follows:

* Avoid saying that you understand when you don't.
* Avoid jumping in with your own points of view.
* Use open questions.
* Pay attention to body language.

Paraphrasing

Paraphrasing is a simple and effective way to test understanding. A paraphrase is a repetition or a summary of what the client has said. It might begin with a phrase

49

Good communication skills acknowledge the uniqueness of individuals

such as 'What you have been saying, if I've got it right, is . . .', and then repeating or summing up what the client has said. Paraphrasing checks for accuracy of understanding and provides the client with an opportunity to correct any misunderstanding. Importantly, it communicates to the client that the care worker has been listening and trying to understand.

Activity 6

Work in groups of three. Two of the three will initially take an active part in the activity, while the third is an observer.

a   Choose a subject for discussion (preferably one that can produce some heated debate or disagreement).

b   One participant starts off with an opening statement.

c   When the first participant concludes, the second has to respond. However, before doing so, he or she must summarise what the first person has said.

d   The third person assesses whether the summary was correct.

e   The second can then continue.

This process continues for as long as has been agreed. The third person then takes the place of one of the first two, and the process repeats with a different subject, and then again, until each pair in the trio has had a discussion and has practised paraphrasing. A variation of this activity can be played with a larger group. The individual who initiates the discussion passes a stick on to a person of his or her choice. This second person must then paraphrase the first person's contribution before proceeding with their own. On concluding, the second contributor passes the stick on to another and so on until the agreed time for the activity has elapsed.

Reflective listening

Reflective listening is less concerned with the summarising of facts, and more involved with understanding the emotions and feelings that are being communicated. All interactions between people communicate only three basic things:

- emotions and feelings
- needs and wants
- facts or opinions.

In reflective listening, the listener sorts out the information received from the other person into these categories, and responds only in the order above. Emotions and feelings are the first and most important to respond to, using emotion and feeling words. Some examples of feeling words are:

- happy
- worried
- sad
- excited
- concerned
- angry
- frustrated
- frightened
- depressed
- disappointed.

How many more can you think of? Feeling words are important for identifying the emotions of those with whom we converse.

Example 1

Mrs Robertson: Mike usually helps me with my bath. He will be here in an hour. Can you help me now instead?

Care worker: You seem worried about Mike giving you your bath.

Mrs Robertson might feel inclined to discuss what is worrying her because the care worker was able to label her emotion for her. If the care worker was mistaken, and Mrs Robertson was not worried, she had an opportunity to correct the care worker's mistaken perception.

Example 2

Bob (aged 8): The teacher caught me messing around and kept me in during playtime.

Care worker: You must have felt embarrassed in front of your friends.

The care worker invites Bob to talk about what happened at school by suggesting that he might have felt embarrassed. To have been condemnatory of Bob would have shut him up.

Essentially, in reflective listening we are saying that how people feel is often more important than the facts or details of the situation. Care workers will use both verbal and non-verbal cues to determine how they believe the client is feeling. This is then checked with the client. It does not matter if the care worker is mistaken. A feeling misread can give rise to many more incorrect responses. Reflective listening is one of the major skills of childcare. Children need to have their feelings acknowledged. Much of our interaction with children is directive, prescriptive and factually based. Many of the problems we have with children are due to these forms of interaction. Telling a child that you can see when he or she is upset, happy or worried works wonders. Because you have acknowledged the child's feelings, the child is likely to talk more. Perhaps it is because we often do not use reflective listening with children that children grow up without learning this important skill themselves. All forms of interaction are learned by modelling. Those care workers who work with children need to demonstrate desirable forms of behaviour.

Activity 7

Working in threes, start off with two participants and one observer. The two have a discussion about a topic of their choice, while the third scores them both for reflective listening. The observer will be watching each participant for the use of feeling words in checking out the other's emotions. This is repeated until all three have been observers.

Note: All the activities in this section are for you to experience the interaction techniques being described. Considerably more work would be required to master these techniques. At this stage it is important that you develop an understanding of what the techniques are.

Giving information

Information has to be provided to clients in ways of their own choosing and subject to their capabilities. Barriers might include language, hearing, visual impairment or mental state. It is important that clients always have as much information as possible in order to exercise their right to choice.

Rapport

All the interpersonal skills described above will be ineffective unless **rapport** (sometimes called 'meshing') is established. When rapport is not present, it will become the top priority in communicating. Rapport is a powerful way of optimising the effectiveness of interactions. It has already been stated that care workers are most effective when they can match their outcomes with those of their clients. Your outcomes, or goals, will not be achieved unless the other person also achieves theirs. The purpose of information seeking is to determine what outcomes the client desires. The care worker will then dovetail, or mesh, the worker's own outcomes with the client's, so that both achieve satisfaction. When a client's outcomes are not realised, the care worker's outcomes are not either, and the care worker experiences dissatisfaction at work. An aim of all care workers is to finish the day's work knowing that something has been achieved, and feeling good about the part they have played in it.

So much of the care worker's effectiveness depends on the skill of rapport. Rapport is composed of a number of basic skills, which take much knowledge and practice to master. For example, the following skills can be used.

- *Mirroring and matching* – Both the verbal and non-verbal behaviour of the client can be mirrored by the care worker, including body movements and tone of voice. To mirror effectively, the care worker just hints at the client's movements or tone, but is careful not to mimic them. This skill is only used very subtly. For example, if the client is moving his or her head from side to side when talking, the care worker may only very slightly use the same movement. The care worker may adopt the same body posture as the client, such as crossing legs or leaning forwards.

• *Pacing* – The pace of speech or the breathing pattern of the client can also be mirrored, and then changed if necessary by the care worker. For example, if clients are anxious, they are likely to be breathing quickly. The care worker can pace his or her own breathing to match the client's and can then begin a process of slowing down, taking the client with him or her. The care worker can establish rapport with the client by matching the pace of speech. If the client speaks slowly, the care worker should change tempo accordingly. Pacing can be particularly effective when faced with challenging behaviour.

Rapport is the process of developing a shared understanding with the client and is therefore one of the core essential skills of health and social care. It is a process that we all engage in naturally up to a point. When brought into conscious control as a caring skill, its effect is powerful.

Explain the five basic skills of effective interaction.

Activity 8

a Work in groups of three. One person will be the observer. One of the other two engages in ordinary conversation about a topic of his or her choice. The other practises mirroring body movement. The observer's job is to ensure that the other two do not get carried away by the conversation. The observer will describe how effective the mirroring has been. The first student will also describe how it felt to be mirrored. The exercise is repeated until all three students have been the observer. Remember not to mimic. Mirroring is a minimised reflection of the other person's behaviour. This exercise can be repeated with pacing.

b Repeat the exercise, but this time mismatch as many verbal and non-verbal cues as possible. For example, if one person is speaking slowly and quietly, the other speaks quickly and loudly.

Neuro-linguistic programming

The understanding of how we both give out and interpret even the minutest of physical cues has been enhanced through the ongoing development of neuro-linguistic programming (NLP). In spite of its unfortunate full name, NLP is highly practical in its models, skills and techniques, which are very basic and easy to learn. NLP has studied what makes outstanding individuals so successful and presents the patterns and skills of success in a way that is learnable. The process is called modelling. For an excellent introduction to this developing and influential area of psychology, the book *Introducing Neuro-Linguistic Programming* by J. O'Connor and J. Seymour is recommended.

NLP was developed by Richard Bandler and John Grinder in the USA in the 1970s. The 'neuro' part of NLP refers to the fact that all behaviour results from the neurological processes of sight, hearing, smell, touch, taste and feeling. Our neurology is also responsible for the visible, physiological reactions we make to feelings and events. The 'linguistic' part of NLP emphasise the importance of language in ordering our thoughts and behaviour, and in communicating with others.

NLP is based on three essential ideas:

- Know what you want – have a clear idea of your desired outcome.
- Rely on alert and sharp senses to notice what you are getting.
- Be flexible in changing your own behaviour until you get what you want.

Heightened sensory activity needs to be developed to be successful. You need to see, hear and feel all that is happening around you and have a sufficient number of responses to what you are experiencing. The more choices open to you, the more chances of success. Communication is so much more than the words we say. It has been estimated that body language makes up 55% of communication, tone of voice 38% and words only 7%. NLP develops the ability to respond effectively to others, and to understand and respect their model of the world. There are many techniques for doing this, some even based on intricate observation of eye movements.

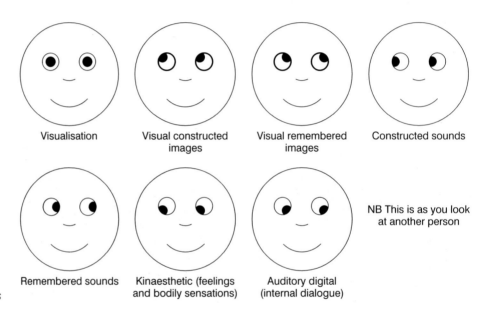

Visualisation   Visual constructed images   Visual remembered images   Constructed sounds

Remembered sounds   Kinaesthetic (feelings and bodily sensations)   Auditory digital (internal dialogue)

NB This is as you look at another person

Eye movements

Eye movements can indicate the 'representational system' used by a person. Some individuals rely mostly on visual, auditory or kinaesthetic (feelings) senses in processing information. It is important to know which, so that we can present information to them that will be compatible with their information-processing system. For example, we might refer to 'seeing what you mean' (visual), 'hearing what you are saying' (auditory), or 'being moved or touched by what you have said' (kinaesthetic). Achieving rapport is helped by matching an individual's representational system.

Non-verbal behaviour and body language

Interpersonal skills depend not only on verbal skills but also on non-verbal skills and body language. We converse with our whole body, including facial expressions, eyes, gestures, physical distance and skin tone. Although we read body signals all the time, it takes considerable practice and skill to do this consciously. The non-verbal aspects of communication provide valuable clues about how an interaction is progressing and about the feelings of the other person.

It is the patterns of body language that are important, rather than single incidents.

Body language is easy to misread, and making false assumptions can create strong barriers to understanding.

Facial expressions

Our faces communicate complex and subtle messages. A smiling and alert face strongly attracts. A forlorn and helpless face arouses sympathy and concern. A tense and grumpy face sends out messages to stay away. While it is possible to smile and feel sad, the eyes and eyebrows are less amenable to control and are therefore valuable indicators of feeling. A long, silent gaze with raised eyebrows evokes speech in the other person. We use our eyes to continue speech and to obtain feedback. We end conversations by looking away. People look more at the person they talk to when they like them, and also look more at the other person when listening than when talking.

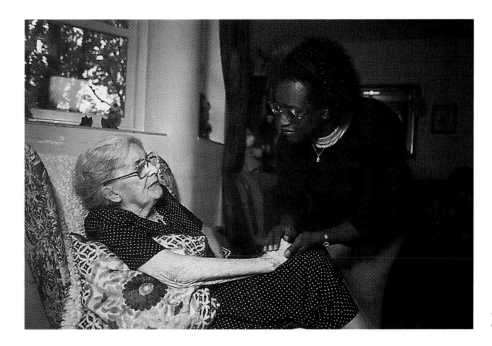

Holding hands can give comfort and reassurance

Personal space

All of us require personal space. The amount that we require is partly determined by culture as well as by personal preference. The amount of personal space used in an interaction is important in relation to intimacy and dominance. The closer the person gets, the more intimate or dominant they wish to be. We all like to be in control of our personal space and the situations in which we wish to be close (intimate) with someone. For example, in a doctor's waiting room, people maintain distance from each other, unless numbers force them next to one another. To sit down right next to another person in an otherwise empty waiting room would make that person extremely uncomfortable.

Body contact

Body contact is another area of intimacy. Here also the British use less physical contact than many other cultures. Touching is an area of great importance in care; some clients will welcome physical contact while others will not. It is a good idea to be guided by the way the client uses touch. If clients are physically expressive, they may not mind you mirroring their use of touch. However, if a client appears not to use touch, it is better to interact with them in the same way.

Gestures and body postures

These are popular topics of study. Here again, cultural differences need to be taken into account. Gestures can reveal a great deal about an individual's emotional state. For example, fiddling with things and tapping can indicate stress, and so can embracing oneself or placing the hands on the back of one's neck. In social situations, grooming, nibbling and tidying can indicate social anxiety. Preparatory movements provide strong messages about the desires of individuals. Packing one's case to end a meeting, opening a door or rising from a chair to say goodbye to someone, or looking at one's watch to communicate an end to a conversation, are all powerful non-verbal signals. Holding one's chin up communicates a desire to dominate. Nodding when listening communicates interest and support, and prompts the other person to continue to speak. The skill of reading body language is important for an effective care worker, and the student is well advised to develop such skills.

Activity 9

On your own, watch individuals and groups – on the bus, in restaurants, in family groups, etc. Watch for:

a facial expressions
b eye contact
c physical proximity
d gestures and postures.

Consider what you believe is being communicated. Repeat the exercise, watching your own body language in different situations.

The first step in acquiring skills in non-verbal behaviour is to observe.

Activity 10

Try making observations of interactions between individuals whom you cannot hear. You can watch people in restaurants, buses or other public social contexts. Or, you can watch a TV play or film with the sound down. Look for the factors discussed above and try to guess what is being communicated.

Assertive behaviour

Assertive behaviour is a way of behaving with other people, when a situation demands it, with a view to expressing honestly how we feel and encouraging others to express their needs effectively. This way of behaving was popularised in the 1970s, as an off-shoot of behavioural therapy. Today, it is sometimes called 'personal effectiveness' and training in these skills is widely available, particularly for women.

The theory behind assertiveness assumes that there are three ways in which individuals may interact:

- *Aggressive behaviour* – The overall goal is to win and demolish the other person's resistance. The rights of the other person are often violated and the interaction is characterised by raised voices and angry personal attacks. It is virtually impossible, when being aggressive, for an individual to perceive another person's point of view. Aggressive individuals will often attempt to dominate the conversation.

* *Passive behaviour* – The overall goal is to placate everyone and avoid conflict at all costs. To achieve this, the individual may refuse to respond appropriately, thus blocking further communication. Passive behaviour may be used to arouse guilt in another person. Passive individuals attempt to manipulate others.

* *Assertive behaviour* – This is a way of behaving that fulfils six major requirements:
  – assertive behaviour is direct
  – assertive behaviour is honest
  – assertive behaviour is appropriate
  – assertive behaviour is informational
  – assertive behaviour is open to further discussion
  – assertive behaviour is responsible.

If you have expressed what was important to you and allowed the other person to respond in his or her own way, you have been assertive, regardless of the outcome. Assertive behaviour is not about winning battles. It is about offering a choice in how to respond in a given situation where, perhaps, none existed before. Assertion is an effective way to convey warmth and sincerity, through responding emotionally with reflective listening. Although assertive behaviour is primarily a verbal technique, it is supported by non-verbal techniques such as touching and posture. Putting an arm around someone in distress, or mimicking posture and movement, make assertive behaviour more effective. We learn very early in life not to express our own needs in certain situations, where we allow ourselves to be dominated by other people. This is particularly true when dealing with people we perceive to be more powerful than ourselves. Assertive behaviour, however, assumes equal rights of expression for all people. For example, we all have the right:

* to change our minds and break commitments
* to make mistakes
* to make decisions or statements without justification
* not to know something or not to understand
* to feel and express emotions, both positive and negative, without feeling that it is weak or undesirable to do so
* not to get involved in someone else's problems
* to refuse demands made on us
* to be the judge of ourselves and our own actions and to cope with the consequences
* to do all of these things without giving any reasons for our actions.

The important thing about understanding interpersonal rights is they are just that – rights! You need not behave in these ways if you choose not to. However, it is your right to do so if you choose. Assertive behaviour is about alternatives and choices. There are times when it may be best not to be assertive, perhaps because you would not be pleased with the consequences. It is, however, important that you can be assertive where you feel you need to be, and where you feel that, by doing so, you will achieve outcomes and goals that you set. Assertive behaviour is ineffective unless rapport is established at the same time.

Assertive behaviour is an important skill in negotiating, or working out differences between people. In reaching agreement or compromise, you begin by forgoing those demands that are relatively unimportant to you but may produce difficulty for

What is the difference between assertive and aggressive behaviour?

the other person. The other person should do the same for you. An effective compromise should take into account just a few items that really mean a lot to both of you and can be dealt with without much resentment. It is very difficult to work out an effective compromise if assertive skills are not being used. Some of these skills, such as reflective listening and self-disclosure, have already been discussed.

The support needed for effective interaction

In order for interaction to be effective, the situation within which the interaction takes place must be as supportive as possible. This essentially means removing as many sources of stress from the situation as possible. This may be achieved by doing the following:

- Clearly introduce yourself.
- Clearly introduce any others present.
- Provide information about the background to the interaction.
- Ensure that the physical environment is suitable, in that it is confidential and private, not noisy and uncomfortable.
- The arrangement of seating should not reflect perceptions of power (e.g. one chair higher than another, or one participant behind a desk).
- All participants should have a clear view of each other.
- Establish rapport, making full use of non-verbal behaviour.
- Use open questions and self-disclosure where appropriate.
- Use reflective listening.
- Ensure that all the participants' uncertainties are resolved before concluding. All the skills explained in this unit, whether in relation to individuals or groups, share the common objective of optimising the support of the interaction and reducing the anxieties of participants.

In addition, care values should always be applied. This means that the individuality of the participants is to be respected and responded to positively. Examples include arranging for translation where appropriate, respecting opinions that differ from your own and exhibiting patience with those who have communication difficulties.

Factors that can enhance or inhibit effective communication

So far, we have reviewed the skills required for effective communication. We will now identify the other factors that can enhance or inhibit effective communication.

Physical factors – non-verbal communication

Non-verbal communication may be classed as a physical factor because it concerns the ways in which we use our bodies to communicate. We have already discussed effective non-verbal communication and how the care worker must be a good observer. Changes in the body language of others will provide reliable information as to whether the person is angry, distressed, threatened, relaxed, happy, etc.

The physical environment

The physical environment is also a major factor in effective communication. Interaction needs to occur in an appropriate environment. If confidentiality is a concern, privacy will be important, so that the interaction will not be overheard. Too much noise or too many distractions can seriously inhibit the effectiveness of an interaction. Comfortable seating can also help.

Porras (1987) describes four aspects of the physical setting that have been shown to significantly affect behaviour. These are space configuration, physical ambience, interior design and overall architectural design.

Space configuration

How the space in the care setting is actually laid out affects clients' and care workers' behaviour in two ways. Physical restrictions may limit or direct the behaviour of people in the care setting as well as having psychological effects. Issues such as noisiness and privacy are important. Walls are good in that they may provide some privacy, but they may also create isolation. Both privacy and the opportunity for interaction are necessary, and creating the right balance in the physical environment is not easy. In all care services, space configuration is an important consideration where interviews or interaction will occur. In residential and day services, the location of lounges, eating areas, administrative facilities, bedrooms, activity areas and so on determine what relationships are formed, who people approach for help and advice, and who they trust.

Physical ambience

This aspect of the physical setting includes lighting, heating, levels and types of noise, odours and general cleanliness. These rather subtle variables can have a significant influence on the degree of comfort the client experiences. Making service users comfortable is important. The physical ambience in the office, for example, should communicate that visitors are welcome.

An often debated issue in health and social care is the wearing of staff uniforms in residential and day care settings. This issue involves many complex variables and it should not be assumed that there is one simple answer. One variable is the requirement of protective clothing where needed. Some jobs in health and social care require the worker to wear suitable protective clothing. This will certainly be evident in hospitals, nursing homes and some residential homes.

Another variable is the specific role of the care worker. For example, in working with young people or some individuals with learning disabilities, particularly in the community, the care worker may need to dress casually and inconspicuously.

In important meetings or case conferences, the care worker may need to be dressed more smartly and formally. Psychiatric nurses are an important example where uniforms have been largely abandoned in the last decade. This resulted from a

There are advantages and disadvantages associated with uniformed staff

shifting view of the mentally ill as sick to a view of the mentally ill as individuals with problems who need to be befriended, supported and helped.

Many clients in hospitals and residential homes for elderly persons consistently express a desire for the staff to be uniformed. In fact, research from other service industries generally supports the view that where service personnel are in uniform, the 'feel-good' factor in using the service is enhanced. Hence, we now are seeing the staff in many service industries in uniform: in banks, shops, hotels, etc. The use of uniform in the personal service industries is said to create a stronger corporate image and to reinforce the image of trustworthiness and professionalism of the staff. There remains, however, a deep unease in the care industry about uniforms. It has long been felt that uniforms put barriers in the way of truly caring relationships. However, it is possible that uniforms may, in some instances, enhance the caring relationship. Our concerns about a home help in uniform may reflect our own prejudices and discomfort about our clients. There may be an argument to create strong corporate identity in caring services, to reflect pride in the work that care workers do and to develop a higher profile in the community. Should care workers be embarrassed about their vocation?

Activity 11

a Divide the class into a number of small working teams. Each team will be assigned one client group. The team will then explore the range of care workers involved in providing services to that group and discuss the pros and cons of staff uniforms.

b Each team should then present its arguments to the whole class, with whom further discussion will take place. It may be interesting to put some of the suggestions about when uniforms might be appropriate to a vote.

Interior design

Many individuals use both social and physical cues from their environment to figure out what others think about them. Their perceptions of this often affect how they perceive themselves. Where clients are allowed an influence on the design of their immediate surroundings, they typically feel more a part of the care system and more valued. Personalising the care setting results in more positive attitudes in clients. Many care services aim to provide soft, home-type settings even in offices. In residential settings, this may be achieved by using more personal effects – from plants and pictures to items of furniture. While this may be obvious in the client's personal space, much may also be achieved by allowing clients to personalise communal areas as well.

Generally, people feel more comfortable in 'warm' environments where there are soft seats, subdued lighting, carpets, curtains and pot plants. By involving clients, and avoiding harsh furnishings and lighting, the care setting can be optimised for supporting interpersonal interaction.

Architectural design

This refers to the overall structural design of the building in which the care service is provided. Many of the same comments about the architectural design can be made as with the interior design. The overall design of the building has a massive influence on how both clients and care workers perceive how others feel about them, and how individuals function in the care setting.

Activity 12

Choose a care setting with which you are familiar and, using the headings above, describe its physical aspects. For each physical aspect you described, explain the effect on clients. Make recommendations for improvement.

It is true to say that a day centre is not a service; an elderly persons' home is not a service; a hospital is not a service; and nor are clinics. These are all physical settings within which services are provided. The nature of care services is interpersonal – from person to person. However, it should be understood that the physical setting itself has a great effect on how and when clients and care workers interact.

Physical setting has a significant impact on care service delivery

Explain how physical settings can be improved in order to optimise effective interactions.

There are, however, constraints on optimising interactions in the care setting. Foremost is probably the cost. Cost should be borne in mind in relation to all possible improvements. Low staffing levels and old and dingy buildings are real problems in care services. Optimising the care setting for effective communication would require these factors to be addressed and improved upon. The effects of the physical environment can both enhance or inhibit interactions. Care services need to consider such issues when designing settings for care service delivery.

Activity 13

Describe any problems as you see them occurring over the course of a working day in a care setting. Explain how these problems might relate to:

a the physical aspects of the care setting
b the 'culture' of the care organisation
c poor management of the service.

Emotional factors

Communication can be greatly enhanced by having a relaxed manner and communicating understanding, sincerity and warmth. We have already reviewed some of the skills required in order to achieve this. However, care workers need to understand that, regardless of their own training, the most demanding situations will still arise. The professional caring relationship can be highly charged emotionally and it is important that care workers maintain absolute focus upon the client.

The care worker needs to understand and communicate understanding on both the emotional and the intellectual level

While it is important that the relationship be focused on agreed issues of care, it should not be clinical in nature. The relationship will be as human as the care worker is capable of. Rigid responses should be avoided, and flexibility is an important attribute of the relationship. In order to make the caring relationship comfortable and more natural, it should reflect all that is involved in life. It should not just be task-based, but include subjects such as poetry, music, books, fun, politics and hobbies. Almost all caring relationships are temporary in nature and you should never lose sight of this fact. Clients should not be led to believe that you personally will always be there for them. However, the relationship can still be something quite special, and this may be best achieved by thoughtfulness in attending to detail.

Controlled involvement

The professional caring relationship is made up of a controlled involvement. Biestek (1957) provided a useful model of how the involvement may be controlled:

- *Sensitivity* – The care worker must demonstrate sensitivity to the client's feelings at all times. This is not just understanding on the part of the care worker, but effective demonstration, using the skills previously described.
- *Understanding* – The special kind of understanding that is typical of the caring relationship is understanding that is wholly in relation to the client – who they are and what difficulties they may be facing.
- *Response* – While there may be many practical tasks involved in caring for the client, response must always incorporate feelings. These feelings may be communicated either verbally or non-verbally. The response the care worker makes to the client should communicate an acceptance of that client. Acceptance is communicated through warmth, courtesy, respect, concern and interest. Clients may possess beliefs that we do not share and behave in ways of which we do not approve. Clients usually both fear and expect disapproval, because they sometimes lack **self-esteem**. It is important to note that acceptance does not mean approval.

Activity 14

Using the three headings above (sensitivity, understanding and response) discuss each one with reference to the skills described earlier in this unit. It is important that the concepts underpinning the nature of the caring relationship are clearly linked to the skills required.

Activity 15

Using observations made in a care service of your choice, discuss the relationships you observe with reference to the concepts developed in this unit.

A conceptual understanding of the nature of the caring relationship does not provide the skills required for either establishing or maintaining it. These skills are developed through repeated intelligent practice, enhanced by skilled supervision on the job. The concept of coaching or supervision in care services is built around developing skills in professional caring relationships. This is why care work is one of the very few vocational areas where the ongoing supervision of workers is

expedient – taking the easiest course This results in inappropriate ruthlessness, where clients' feelings are not considered. The recognition of stress in care work is important. Methods of stress reduction at work should be used and care workers should be taught the techniques of stress management. Caring and concerned employers also establish staff counselling services. The care organisation must address this most problematic and inevitable outcome of ruthlessness and expediency caused by understaffed resources, overworked care workers and unskilled managers.

The six problems for caring relationships described above are serious and commonplace. They are issues that must be focused on by every care organisation. If they are not addressed and resolved, it will be the professional caring relationship that will be damaged, and along with it the individuals who use care services.

What is the relationship between effective interaction and the concept of the 'caring' relationship?

/ **Activity 16** /

Analyse a care setting of your choice for problems in care relationships. Interview staff about their feelings with regard to the six problem areas listed above. Draw conclusions and make realistic, valid and constructive recommendations for improvements.

Social factors and special needs

Some aspects of the social factors affecting communication have already been discussed, such as attentiveness to the client, respecting the client and the consequences of losing respect. However, other social factors can enhance or inhibit interactions in health and care services.

As we discussed in Unit One, the care worker may possess prejudices that may find their way into interactions. Stereotyping particular individuals, negative attitudes towards particular ethnic groups or gender inequalities could inhibit effective interaction. There are also situations when the client may not easily understand the care worker.

Why might the client not understand?
The problem may simply be one of language. The client may not speak English very well. In such a situation, the care worker would need to find an interpreter. The client may be hearing-impaired, in which case the worker may have to use an alternative method, such as signing or writing. The client's preferred method of communication should always be used. A common problem is the use of technical jargon, particularly in medical settings. This should always be avoided, and the worker should attempt to communicate with the client in ways that are consistent with the client's level of understanding and perceived abilities. Commonly, the client may not understand what the care worker is trying to communicate because the care worker lacks good interpersonal skills, both verbal and non-verbal.

/ **Activity 17** /

Find out how care agencies in your area assist individuals for whom English is a second language.

Another use of effective communication in care work is working with life histories. Working with people's life histories enables them to establish and maintain a sense of identity. Life histories are useful because:

- they highlight the different experiences that individuals have and enable them to share those experiences more effectively
- they identify and increase awareness of stigmatised or hidden experiences
- when encouraged to talk about the past, clients can take a more active role in managing change within themselves
- they help individuals to establish a clearer identity.

The skills used in working with life histories include many of the conversation management skills discussed above, particularly open questions, paraphrasing and reflective listening. Clients are entitled to use life histories to gain knowledge about themselves, their families and the circumstances they may find themselves in. The care worker needs to handle life history work with patience and sensitivity (life histories can take some time to work with). Confidentiality here is also of paramount importance, as the client must perceive the care worker as entirely trustworthy. Life histories are usually very private stories. Examples of using life history work by care workers are working with children in care in order to establish a sense of identity, and also with older people in order to maintain identity, particular where memory is poor. This is also sometimes called reminiscence.

The major point about communicating effectively as a care worker is that the responsibility for being understood *always* lies with the professional care worker.

2.3 Communication skills in groups

Much work in health and social care involves working in groups. Workers may be organised into groups, as may service users. Some of these groups will be natural and informal, while others may be structured and organised formally for specific purposes. A formally organised group may be a residential setting, for example. Informally, groups may arise because of shared interests or problems.

Groups require an atmosphere of security, and all members of the group should have some sense of ownership over group processes and activities. Groups have a life of their own and the processes that occur within groups can have powerful effects upon us. They are likely to have both formal and informal structures. Managed effectively, groups can help individuals who would otherwise feel isolated and disempowered and have negative perceptions of themselves.

Sometimes care work is organised into a group model not because of the benefits to clients but because of financial efficiency. Managing people in groups can be less expensive than individualised approaches. Communal living, for example, can be problematic, as it can tend toward repetitive regimes, with individuals regularly coming and going within the group. Such situations need very skilful management.

Some basic understanding of group processes is helpful in effectively managing a group. Groups always grow and mature, and it is possible to identify distinct stages of group development.

The stages of group development

- **Forming** – At this stage, members of the group have not yet developed a group identity. They are still very much individuals seeking to establish their own personal identities within the group and to make personal impressions upon others.
- **Storming** – This uncomfortable period in the group's life is often marked by conflict. Members begin to reveal their own personal goals within the group, and clear differences usually emerge. Members begin bargaining with each other about what each wants, both individually and collectively, from the group.
- **Norming** – During this stage, the group creates a framework for the relationships within it. Who will do what and how it will be done are addressed. These working rules set the norms of behaviour within the group.
- **Performing** – This is the fully mature group, which should now be able to get on with whatever its purpose is. Not all groups reach this stage, however, as some get stuck in the earlier, less productive stages.

Groups are composed of individuals, so much of what we have already discussed in relation to individual interaction is also highly relevant for groups. Listening skills are very important, as are assertive skills. Individuals in groups possess the same rights, choices and freedom from discrimination that we have already discussed in relation to individuals. Groups are natural and wherever people have contact with each other, groups will form. Individual members of a group will have their own personal expectations of what the group needs to give them. For many, this will be a sense of belonging, safety and identity. On the other hand, the group itself will develop its own expectations. A group may exist to deal with specific tasks, share experiences or provide support. Once group goals are defined, there will be certain expectations, which members may need to fulfil. Groups develop their own 'rules', and adaptation to these rules is part of the process of socialisation. Groups can be very useful and productive in a number of areas:

- problem-solving and decision-making
- processing and sharing both information and feelings
- gathering ideas and suggestions

- gaining feedback on previous decisions
- increasing commitment and involvement
- negotiation and resolving conflicts.

Compatibility among group members helps the group to stabilise and survive.

Developing cohesion is a primary objective of all groups. Cohesion is helped when:

- goals are clear
- all members listen
- all members contribute
- disagreements are comfortably dealt with
- hidden agendas are dealt with through assertive behaviour.

Hidden agendas are individual goals that oppose the outcomes desired by the group and threaten group cohesion. Just as in interpersonal communication, groups should possess the ability to turn goals into outcomes. Goals, or desired outcomes, should be clearly determined by the group early on, and rapport should be established among the members. Individuals in groups should be aware of the interactive processes going on. Behaviour that demonstrates warmth, understanding and sincerity is a vital element in a successful group. Sensitivity is important. Tension must be detected early, and dealt with, as well as any bad feelings that are created. Negative acts produce negative responses in other people, so individual group members should remain positive and not personally critical of others. Negative escalation will destroy group cohesion. Where there is potential for disagreement and negativity, the secret is not to challenge the person, only his or her information. This is where assertive behaviour can be really valuable. Just as negotiation was discussed with reference to assertive behaviour, it is also an essential group skill.

Tips on negotiating in a group

- Establish rapport.
- Validate any proposal the other side makes as legitimate and worthwhile for discussion.
- Summarise what you understand to be the other side's point of view or position.
- Do not become defensive.
- Do not attack.
- Do not personally insult.
- Remain flexible.
- Do not blame or accuse.
- Provide reasons before making proposals – only a few important ones, or the point might be lost.
- Express feelings as well as facts.
- Emphasise areas of agreement.
- Recognise and respect the value system of others.
- Question positions but do not ignore them.

Groups are opportunities for close interpersonal contact, and work best when the goals of the group and the expectations of individual members are simultaneously met.

Behaviours helpful in group work

- **Questioning** – seeking information, opinion and ideas.
- **Listening** – showing verbally and non-verbally that you are paying attention and understand what others are saying.
- **Informing** – giving helpful information, opinions and ideas.
- **Clarifying** – clearing up confusion, defining terms and pointing out alternatives.
- **Sharing** – inviting comments using listening skills, keeping the communication channels open and making people feel involved.
- **Supporting** – recognising the individual rights, choices and identity of group members.
- **Encouraging** – helping those who are shy, nervous or reluctant to contribute; this involves being friendly, warm and responsive, both verbally and non-verbally.
- **Harmonising** – recalling disagreements, reducing tension and getting people to explore their differences constructively.
- **Assertion** – using the rules of assertion, particularly in negotiation, to promote clarity and accuracy.
- **Constructive disagreement** – not upsetting people when there are disagreements. Other people's viewpoints may be incorporated into your own, so that the discussion becomes constructive. Focus first on what is agreed before disagreements are dealt with.
- **Humour** – reduces tension.
- **Relaxation** – creating an atmosphere of calmness and confidence.
- **Cohesion** – referring to the group as a team rather than as a collection of individuals.

Activity 18

Observe a group in action. This may be a meeting in a care service, or even an activity in class. Using the headings above, make notes on the extent to which each behaviour is in evidence. Is there room for improvement?

It is important to remember that the communication needs of particular individuals within the group may need to be supported, so the group facilitator should actively achieve this. The group facilitator must:

- identify the communication skills of each group member
- support each member of the group and promote effective communication
- observe and interpret interactions within the group.

Effectively managing a group activity helps individuals to develop skills in co-operative behaviour, promotes individual potential and develops an awareness of others. Some service users may be intimidated by working in a group. This will manifest itself as:

- non-attendance
- not participating or contributing
- attempts to dominate the group, or disrupt the group by inappropriate talking or changing the subject
- being aggressive or unsupportive of other group members.

By paying careful attention to the suggestions above, and by gaining as much experience and training as you can, it will be possible to avoid these difficulties.

2.4 Evaluating communication skills

In what ways is effective communication in a group the same as in a one-to-one interaction? In what ways is it different?

It is important that we have some measure by which we can evaluate how effective interpersonal interactions are. Listening is an important way of finding out how effective you are. Developing a style of interaction that effectively but unobtrusively checks out whether your understanding of the other person is correct and whether what you have said has been understood is of vital importance. We shall be examining in this section some techniques that you may wish to consider. Specific training in interpersonal skills is essential for work in care. This will provide the opportunity, in relatively safe situations, of experimenting and practising. Your own improvement may be thereby systematically monitored for:

- the quality of your contribution
- improvement from previous occasions
- knowledge and understanding.

This monitoring should be done using a variety of methods:

- *Verbal feedback* may be obtained from the individual with whom you are interacting, or an observer, or both.
- *Written feedback* is best obtained from an independent observer, who may rate you against specific criteria (e.g. how many open questions were used).
- *Video observation* is useful, because you can observe your own behaviour and may observe things that you missed when in the process of interacting. An advantage of video observation is that you can watch it again and again.
- *Self-reflection* is useful in addition to the above three observational techniques. It is worth recording your own experience of the interview in some detail. The process of writing it down often makes things clearer. A traditional training method in social work is called 'process recording', which is a very detailed self-reflection on client interviews.

Observation of interaction is vital to understanding. Not just observing and reflecting on your own skills but observing others is also extremely valuable, and using video will allow you to evaluate your own interpersonal effectiveness and that of other care workers. Taking a step back to evaluate enhances care workers' sensitivity to the interpersonal world around them. Ultimately, the care worker assumes a primary professional responsibility for the success of the interaction. Any misunderstanding on the part of the client must be addressed by the care worker.

Activity 19

You will need to develop good observational skills before you can meaningfully evaluate your own interpersonal skills. Watching others and evaluating their skills is good practice. You can then apply the same criteria to yourself, perhaps using videotapes. Such exercises can be done as roleplays in class.

▶▶

Score interpersonal skills using the following frameworks:

1. Frequency of skill use

Skill used   **Frequency**

Open questions
Closed questions
Self-disclosure
Other prompts
Paraphrasing
Reflective listening

2. Non-verbal skills and rapport

Skills used   **Notes on use**

Facial expressions
Eye contact
Physical proximity
Posture and orientation
Gestures
Rapport

Effective interaction requires **reflective practice**, and even the most advanced practitioners are continually striving to improve their skills.

Written feedback is best obtained from an independent observer

2.5 Maintaining client confidentiality

We have already covered some aspects of confidentiality in Unit One, particularly the legislative and policy aspects. We have stressed that one of the most important aspects of effective communication in health and care services is maintaining the confidentiality of information. If care workers are careless with information about clients, the trust upon which the care relationship is built will be lost.

Clients and patients have many rights in respect of confidential information. Some of these rights are enshrined in law. The Data Protection Act 1984, the Access to Health Records Act 1990 and the Access to Personal Files Act 1987 all set out the legal rights of health and social care service users. Both the legislation and local procedures establish the requirement of care workers to breach confidentiality where risk to the client or others exists.

It should be apparent that the essence of the care values is the importance of the client as a person in every conceivable situation. The choices, wishes and needs of clients are the main determinants of service provision. However, in ascertaining the client's views and needs, much information needs to be obtained, and much of that information must be recorded and shared with others. The privileged position of care workers in determining and maintaining information about the individuals who use services has often been taken for granted. At its worst, breaches of confidentiality involve careless talk about the client with others, sometimes where it can be overheard. Chat on buses, in the staff lounge or even with the care worker's own family about information disclosed in confidence is not uncommon. One of the most important of all clients' rights is the right to have control over the disclosure of information pertaining to them.

The Patient's Charter guarantees confidentiality of health records and access for patients. Relatives and friends may only be given information about the patient if the patient so wishes. The Access to Health Records Act 1990 allows patients to see all National Health Service (NHS) notes made after November 1991. However, access to your notes can be refused if a doctor considers that such access could be damaging to your physical or mental health. It is also permitted for a doctor to withhold certain information without your knowledge. Although the intention of the Act is good, it is not an entirely satisfactory piece of legislation and is open to professional abuse. The European Convention on Human Rights also guarantees privacy and confidentiality, as does the 1995 European Directive on Data Protection.

Aside from legislation, there are other formal means of protecting client confidentiality. These include the following:

- *Agency confidentiality policies* – All health and care organisations will have written policies on confidentiality. The purpose of such policies is to lay down strict criteria on when information about a client may be disclosed and when it may not. The policy will also specify internal procedures for ensuring confidentiality.

- *Contracts of employment* – Contracts of employment in health and care services usually stipulate that failure to follow the agency's confidentiality policy can be a dismissable offence.

- *Professional codes of conduct* – Some health professionals are members of professional associations and will be bound by codes of conduct pertaining to confidentiality. Such professionals include doctors, nurses, occupational therapists, chiropodists and clinical psychologists. Breaching a professional code of practice can lead to disciplinary action, resulting in the member being 'struck off', which means that they will not be allowed to continue to practise.

- *Civil law* – If an individual believes that his or her confidentiality has been breached, and can show that there has been some consequential and tangible harm as a result, the individual can sue for damages.

- *Complaints procedures* – Health and care organisations will have complaints procedures that allow a client to complain formally about a member of staff the client believes has breached his or her confidentiality.

The values of health and social care go even further. They require that access to personal information be limited and agreed by the service user. The service user must understand any limits placed on the confidential information. Care workers should always explain to the client what information will be collected about them, what the information will be used for, where it will be stored and with whom it will be shared. Sometimes, where there is a perceived risk to the service user or others, information may need to be passed to others without permission. In such circumstances, the service user must be told what is being done with the information and why. Examples of this might be in relation to a child at risk or a suicide threat. A care worker can never be certain what it is that is going to be told to him or her. If asked by a client, 'If I tell you something, will you keep it to yourself?', the only acceptable response is 'That depends on what you are going to tell me'. Care workers are never fully at liberty to keep secrets between themselves and clients, as the workers represent their organisation and may need to let specific individuals know any critical information, particularly where the client or others might be at risk.

Sometimes, information may be transmitted by telephone. The identity of interested parties must be made clear beforehand. In fact, proof of identity should be obtained where there is any doubt. Proof may consist of personal knowledge of the person to whom the information is being communicated. In addition, identity cards may need to be used in face-to-face situations. Obviously, the use of fax machines is not recommended, as no control exists over who will receive the information.

Entries into case files should contain only factual information and not personal opinions or hearsay. Entries should be checked by the service user for accuracy, and amended accordingly. It should always be explained to the service user exactly who has access to files.

What a care worker learns about an individual should always remain confidential. The temptation to discuss such things in a social context is often great, but must be resisted. It has been said that, despite their best efforts, health and care organisations are often 'leaky' through the gossiping of staff. The maintenance of confidentiality is not only an important interpersonal skill, but is also intrinsic to organisational procedures. The good practices specified by care organisations in respect of confidentiality will help care workers to develop their skills in this important area.

Key terms

After reading this unit you should be able to understand the following words and phrases. If you do not, go back through the unit and find out, or look them up in the Glossary.

Assertive behaviour
Closed questions
Confidentiality
Empathy
Empowerment
Non-verbal communication

Open questions
Rapport
Reflective practice
Self-disclosure
Self-esteem
Verbal communication

Review questions

1 Give examples of how interpersonal skills can help to:
   a encourage personal preference
   b encourage choice
   c convey respect for others
   d convey warmth and sincerity.
2 What is the relationship between the client's understanding of a quality service and the interpersonal skills of the care worker?
3 Define both verbal and non-verbal communication and give examples of each.
4 Explain how effective listening can help understanding.
5 Define group cohesion and give examples of obstacles to it.
6 Explain the differences between aggressive, passive and assertive behaviour.
7 Identify and describe the different types of effective listening.
8 Discuss how our interpersonal skills can convey warmth, sincerity and understanding, with particular reference to:
   a choice of words
   b tone of voice
   c body language.
9 What sources of data are used to evaluate effective interaction?
10 What are the four aspects of the physical setting that can be analysed in relation to effective interactions?
11 What support do care workers need in monitoring their caring relationships?

Assignment

For your assessment in this unit, you will need to collect information both about your own communication skills and about how good skills are used in a care setting. For the purposes of evaluating your own skills, you will need to interact with two different client groups. If possible, you should collect your evidence for this from a work placement. However, the use of role-play is also acceptable, particularly if you do not have easy access to two different groups.

To get an **E** grade you must complete tasks 1–3

To get a **C** grade you must complete tasks 1–5

To get an **A** grade you must complete tasks 1–7

Tasks

1   For this task, you must collect information on how effective your own skills are in a one-to-one interaction. By doing this, you will begin to develop the skills of reflective practice.

   a Select a client with whom you can have a useful interaction. The interaction can be a formal interview, although a more informal interaction would be just as acceptable. Interact with the client for a period of time (a minimum of 10 minutes is suggested).

   b Make notes during the interaction. These notes will be about the interaction, not about the client. If making notes during the interview is uncomfortable, ask someone to do it for you, or use a video camera to record the interview so that you can make notes afterwards. The notes you make should correspond with the headings in **c**.

   c Organise your observations under five headings:

   i *Factors in the environment* – Describe the immediate environment within which the interaction occurred. You will want to describe the room, the seating arrangement, the time of day and whether anyone else was present.

   ii *Body language* – Describe your body language. For example, you should discuss your posture, gestures, facial expressions, body contact, personal space and eye contact.

   iii *Interpersonal skills* – Describe in as much detail as possible what skills you have used (for example open questions), and provide specific examples for each skill identified. Your examples could include your spoken words, as well as a description of your tone of voice. Try not to just give examples, but explain *why* specific skills were chosen. Identify as many skills as you can.

   iv *Enhancing factors* – Describe the physical, emotional and social factors that helped to make the interaction effective. Refer to the relevant sections of this unit for examples of what sorts of factor you can describe. Be sure to explain *why* any factor you have identified as enhancing made the interaction more effective.

   ii *Inhibiting factors* – Describe the physical, emotional and social factors that made the interaction less effective than it might have been, and why.

2   For this task, you must collect information on how effective your own skills are in a group interaction. The group must involve a different client group from the one you have used in the one-to-one interaction, or it can be role-played. Once again, you will have to make notes of the group interaction under the following headings.

   a *Factors in the environment* – Describe the immediate environment within which the interaction occurred. You will want to describe the room, the seating arrangement, the time of day and who the members of the group are.

b *Interpersonal skills* – Describe in as much detail as possible what skills you have used in the group setting and provide specific examples for each skill identified. Some of these skills may be the same as those you used in the one-to-one interaction, but others will be different, and specific to working with a group (for example, encouraging, harmonising and informing). Try not to just give examples, but explain *why* specific skills were chosen. Identify as many skills as you can.

c *Enhancing factors* – Describe the physical, emotional and social factors that helped the group interaction to be effective. You will be covering the same sorts of factors that you discussed for the one-to-one interaction, but within the context of the group. Be sure to explain *why* any factor you have identified as enhancing made the group more effective.

d *Inhibiting factors* – Describe the physical, emotional and social factors that made the group less effective than it might have been, and why.

3 Choose a care setting in order to make notes on how effective communication is used by the service as a means of valuing people as individuals. You will need to make these notes over a period of time, and may also wish to ask questions of members of staff. You will also have to find out about how the service promotes confidentiality. There should be written policies on this.

a Using specific examples from your notes, explain how the care service uses effective communication. For example, you may wish to describe how service users are given choices, encouraged to express themselves, and are effectively listened to. You must describe specific interactions, and explain how the interaction respected and promoted the individual's dignity and self-esteem. Make sure you provide sufficient examples.

b Describe how the organisation stores records and information about clients, and explain what rights clients or others may have to client information. You should refer to both legal requirements and organisational policies in order to discuss this. In what ways are service users made aware of their rights regarding confidentiality by the organisation?

4 You have reviewed your skills in both a one-to-one and a group setting. Using the same headings as in **1** and **2**, suggest ways in which you might have used interpersonal and group skills more effectively. In order to make the suggestions useful, relate your performances to the qualities of effective caring relationships earlier in this unit (for example sensitivity, understanding, empowerment, self-awareness, respect and sincerity). Make sure you show that you can use some of the key terms of this unit effectively.

5 Identify some examples of poor or inappropriate communication that you have observed in your chosen care setting. Fully discuss why you believe your examples are poor or inappropriate interactions, and what the effects might be on the clients involved.

6 You have already evaluated your skills and made suggestions about how they might be improved. Now you must develop an action plan that you can use to help develop your skills. In order to develop the action plan, you need to do several things:

a For each of the skills you have identified as needing improvement, clearly state what best practice would consist of. It is best practice that you will be aiming for.

b Your action plan should then clearly explain how you might develop your skills from where they are currently to best practice. You will want to explain how opportunities for supervised practice, as well as training, can be used to develop your skills. You may also want to consider the use of keeping reflective journals, as well as reading books on interpersonal skills. You may want to consider more advanced approaches such as NLP, or learning counselling skills.

7 You have already identified examples of poor or inappropriate communication in your chosen care setting. Now, write a report that could be of use to the managers of the care setting, which:

a explains why appropriate communication skills are important in the chosen setting

b discusses some of the skills being used appropriately in the setting

c identifies which skills may need to be improved

d suggests ways for the service to improve the skills identified.

Remember to refer to concepts of best practice and justify your observations and suggestions.

Key Skills

Opportunity

	You can use this Assignment to provide evidence for the following Key Skills
Communication C3.1a	By presenting evidence of your involvement in a group situation, along with a record from someone who has observed you or a videotape of your work.
Communication C3.3	When you compile a written report evaluating your own skills in both a one-to-one and group interaction, and also when you evaluate how skills are used within a care service.
Information Technology IT3.1	If you use the Internet to find out about legislation, or charters of rights, as well as finding out about sources of help and support by collecting information from organisation websites.

Physical aspects of health

What is covered in this unit

3.1 **Physiology and anatomy**
3.2 **Homeostasis**
3.3 **Physiological measurements of individuals in care settings**
3.4 **Safe practice**
3.5 **Accuracy of results**
3.6 **Accurate analysis of results**

At the end of this unit you will be asked to carry out an investigation into the interaction of human body systems and how physiological status is measured. If you would like to see further details of the tasks you are likely to need to carry out for assessment please refer to the end of the unit where an assignment has been set (see page 119). This unit will guide you through what you need to know in order to complete this work. You will be assessed on this work and awarded a grade and the grade you receive will be the grade for Unit Three.

Materials you will need to complete this unit:

- A peak flow meter
- A sphygmomanometer, preferably with a digital readout facility
- Charts for recording pulse, respiration and blood pressure
- A watch with a second hand
- A thermometer for measuring body temperature; if possible an electronic thermometer, or some disposable, single-use thermometers.

3.1 Physiology and anatomy

The human body is made up of an enormous amount of tiny units of living material called cells. Groups of cells form tissues, and these tissues make up the organs that are concerned with the functions of our bodies. The organs, in turn, are grouped into systems, which function interdependently. The study of the form and arrangement of organs is called anatomy, sometimes referred to as structure. Physiology refers to the working of the organs and may also be referred to as function.

In order to know about control mechanisms in the body, you need to know about structures and how they function as systems.

The respiratory system

Respiration is the process whereby oxygen is obtained and used for the oxidation of food materials to liberate energy and to produce carbon dioxide and water as waste materials.

Internal respiration

Internal respiration is the chain of chemical processes that take place in every living cell to free energy for its vital activities.

External respiration

External respiration is the means by which oxygen is obtained from the environment and carbon dioxide released into it. This process is referred to as **gaseous exchange** and takes place in the lungs. The bloodstream carries oxygen away from, and carbon dioxide to, the lungs.

Air reaches the lungs through the respiratory passages. The system dealing with external respiration involves nasal passages, pharynx, larynx, trachea, bronchi and lungs, in addition to the muscles involved in making the breathing movements.

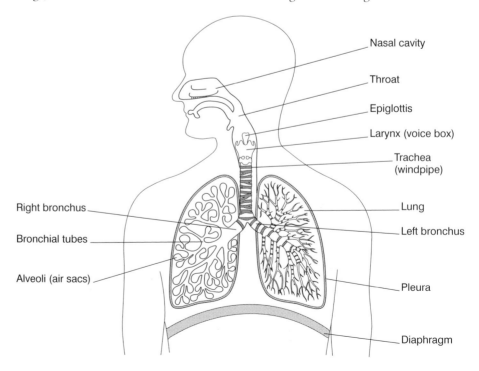

Right bronchus
Bronchial tubes
Alveoli (air sacs)

Nasal cavity
Throat
Epiglottis
Larynx (voice box)
Trachea (windpipe)
Lung
Left bronchus
Pleura
Diaphragm

Fig. 3.1   The respiratory system

The alveoli

Oxygen from the air in the lungs dissolves in the thin film of moisture on the cells lining the alveoli. The alveoli are small pouches situated at the ends of the bronchioles, which in turn are attached to the bronchi. They are close to a dense network of very fine blood capillaries which link the pulmonary arteries to the pulmonary veins.

Gaseous exchange

Oxygen diffuses through the cells lining the alveoli and through the walls of the capillaries into the plasma of the blood. From the plasma it diffuses into the red blood cells, combining with **haemoglobin** to form oxyhaemoglobin. In other parts of the body, the oxyhaemoglobin breaks down and oxygen diffuses out of the blood, while carbonic acid from dissolved carbon dioxide diffuses in. Carbonic acid combines with haemoglobin to form carbaminohaemoglobin.

When blood returns to the lungs, the carbaminohaemoglobin breaks down to liberate carbonic acid, which in turn liberates carbon dioxide.

Inspiration and expiration

Breathing is normally a reflex action, controlled by the respiratory centre in the medulla oblongata of the brain (see Nervous system, pages 87–91). Breathing involves a rhythmical inspiration and expiration without conscious thought, the rate varying with body activity. As energy use increases, so carbon dioxide levels increase and the demand for oxygen also increases. Small rises in the level of carbon dioxide in the blood cause a large increase in the rate and depth of breathing. It is possible, however, to voluntarily control the rate of one's breathing. **Tidal volume** refers to the air that passes in and out of the lungs in normal respiratory action. Inspiration, or breathing in, is brought about by contraction of the diaphragm and the intercostal muscles, which are situated between the ribs. Expiration, or breathing out, is brought about by elastic recoil when the muscles relax.

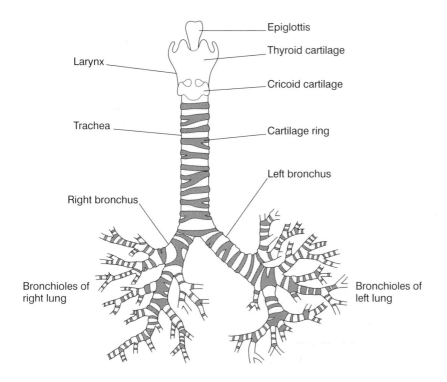

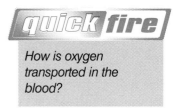

How is oxygen transported in the blood?

Fig. 3.2 The respiratory passages

The cardiovascular system

The heart is completely divided in order to keep oxygenated and deoxygenated blood separate. As a general rule, **arteries** transport oxygenated blood and **veins** carry deoxygenated blood, the only exceptions being the pulmonary arteries and veins (see Fig. 3.3).

Arteries have strong muscular walls, whereas veins have comparatively little elasticity or muscle. The pressure of blood in the arteries is therefore higher than it is in the veins. The force exerted against the walls of the arteries is referred to as **blood pressure**. Arterioles are the smallest arteries, which break up into a number of minute vessels called **capillaries**. These consist of a single-cell layer through which small-molecule substances can pass.

Blood in the arteries flows in spurts that are synchronous with the heart beat. The wave of contraction that passes along an artery wall is called a pulse, which can be felt in many places where the vessels are sufficiently superficial.

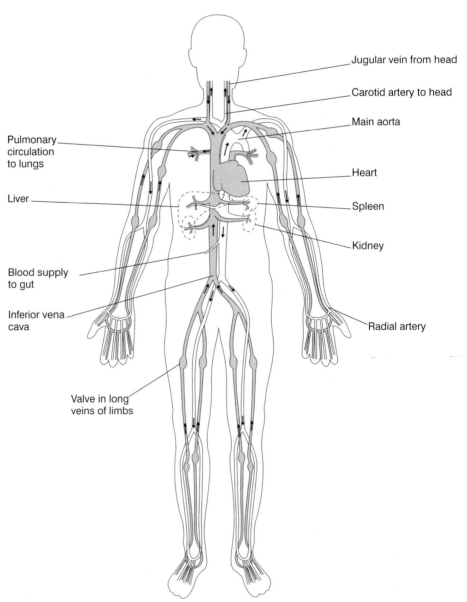

Fig. 3.3 The circulation of blood through the body

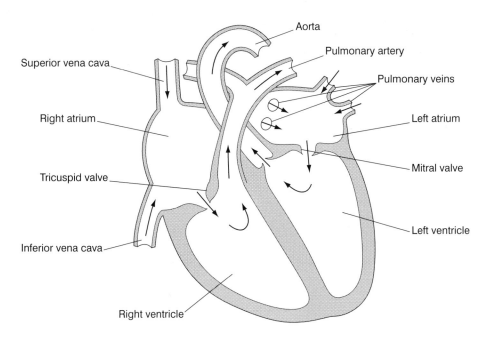

Fig. 3.4   The four cavities of the heart

The heart is divided into four chambers: two ventricles (lower chambers) and two atria (upper chambers) (Fig. 3.4). Blood vessels are connected to each chamber. The direction of the flow of blood is maintained by valves. The circulation of blood through the body is shown in Figure 3.3.

quick fire

Name the chambers of the heart.

The digestive system

The food that we eat is not in a suitable form for use as an immediate source of energy. It has to be broken down in order to be used. This work is carried out by the digestive system.

A healthy digestive system is essential for maintaining life. It converts food into the raw materials that build and fuel our bodies' cells. The digestive system takes in food, breaks it down into nutrient molecules, absorbs these molecules into the bloodstream and then excretes the indigestible remains not required by the body. The organs of the digestive system can be divided into two main groups:

- the alimentary canal
- the accessory organs of digestion.

The alimentary canal

The alimentary canal, also called the gastrointestinal tract, is a continuous, coiled, hollow muscular tube that winds its way through the ventral body cavity and is open to the external environment at both ends. The organs of the alimentary canal are:

- the mouth
- the pharynx
- the oesophagus
- the stomach
- the large intestine.

The accessory organs of digestion

The accessory organs are:

- the teeth
- the tongue
- the gallbladder.

83

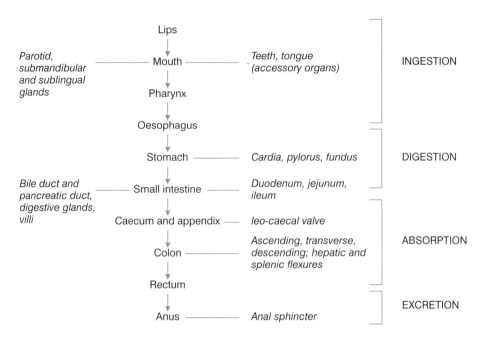

Fig. 3.5   A diagrammatic representation of the composition and functions of the alimentary canal

The digestive glands are:

- the salivary glands
- the liver
- the pancreas.

These glands produce saliva, bile (see below) and **enzymes**, which contribute to the breakdown of food

Digestive processes

Food is prepared for consumption by the digestive processes of ingestion, mastication and swallowing. Ingestion (the taking in of food) and mastication (the act of chewing) are functions performed by the mouth and teeth, aided by the tongue. In the mouth, the food is chewed and mixed with saliva. Chewing reduces the food to a suitable size for swallowing and increases the surface area available for enzymes to act upon.

Movement of food along the alimentary canal

Food moves along the alimentary canal by the process of **peristalsis**. The walls of the alimentary canal contain circular and longitudinal muscle fibres. The circular muscles, by alternately contracting and relaxing, squeeze the food steadily forward along the alimentary canal in a wave-like movement from one organ to the next.

The breakdown of food by mechanical and chemical processes

Mechanical digestion prepares food for chemical digestion by enzymes. Mechanical processes include chewing, mixing of food with saliva by the tongue, churning food in the stomach and mixing it with digestive juices. Chemical digestion is accomplished by enzymes secreted by various glands into the alimentary canal. This is a catabolic process, where large food molecules are broken down into chemical building blocks that are small enough to be absorbed into the bloodstream.

The liver

The liver is one of the supporting organs of digestion. It is situated on the right-hand side of the body just below the diaphragm. It is the largest organ in the body,

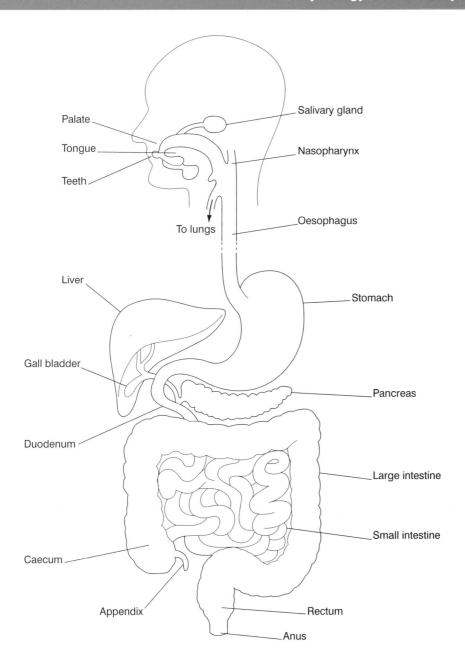

Fig. 3.6 *The digestive system and accessory organs*

measuring about 25–30 cm across and 15–18 cm from back to front. It is divided into two lobes: the large right lobe and the smaller left lobe. The liver has many functions, one of which is the formation and storage of bile, of which it produces up to 1 litre per day. Bile is passed to the gall bladder, where it is both stored and concentrated. Bile has a part to play in the breakdown of food substances.

What is peristalsis?

The renal system

The kidneys

The kidneys are two bean-shaped organs, approximately 10 cm long, 5 cm wide and 2.5 cm thick. They are positioned against the posterior (towards the back) abdominal wall at the normal waistline, with the right kidney slightly lower than the left.

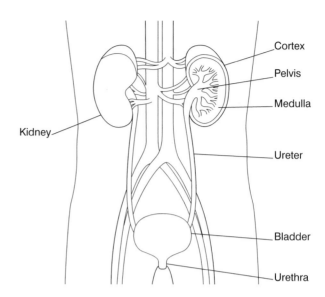

Fig. 3.7   The kidneys and associated structures

The kidneys consist of three principal parts:

- the cortex, or outer layer
- the medulla
- the pelvis; the hollow inner part from which the ureters (see page 87) open.

The function of the kidneys is to separate certain waste products from the blood. This renal function helps to maintain the blood at a constant level of composition despite what may be a great variation in diet and fluid intake. The functional unit of the kidney is a microscopic structure called a **nephron**. There are more than 1 million nephrons in each kidney. As blood circulates in the kidneys, a large quantity of water, salts, urea and glucose is filtered into the Bowman's capsules and from there into the convoluted tubules (see figure below). From here, all the glucose, most of the water and salts and some of the urea is returned to the blood vessels; the remainder passes via the calyces into the kidney pelvis as urine.

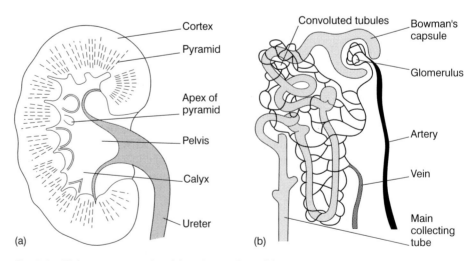

Fig. 3.8   Kidney cross-section (a) and a nephron (b)

It is estimated that 150–180 litres of fluid is processed by the kidneys each day, but only about 1.5 litres of this leaves the body as urine.

You can use Activity 1 to provide evidence for Key Skills Information Technology IT3.1.

> **Activity 1**
>
> Find out what happens to the fluid processed by the kidneys that does not leave the body as urine. You should aim for two alternatives. This information can be found from a chapter on the renal system in an anatomy and physiology text such as the one listed at the end of this unit. If you have access to an anatomy and physiology CD-ROM, you could use this.

The urine is carried from the kidney pelvis to the bladder by two fine muscular tubes, measuring approximately 25–30 cm long, called the ureters. The bladder is a very elastic muscular sac lying immediately beneath the symphysis pubis, the joint formed by the union of the two hip bones.

The urethra is a narrow muscular tube passing from the bladder to the exterior of the body. The urethra in women is 4 cm long, and in men is 20 cm long. In the male, the urethra is the common passage for both urine and semen. Also in the male, the urethra passes through a gland known as the prostate gland, which is the size and shape of a chestnut. It surrounds the neck of the bladder and tends to enlarge after middle life when it may, by projecting into the bladder, cause urine retention.

Where are the kidneys located?

The nervous and endocrine systems

The endocrine system and the nervous system are not entirely separate entities. There is a small area of the brain, called the **hypothalamus**, that helps to control homeostasis (pages 96–100) and provides the link between the nervous system and the endocrine system. The hypothalamus exerts control over the master gland of the body; the pituitary gland (pages 91–92).

The nervous system

Consider the following situations:

* You are driving home late at night and a fox runs out in front of you. You swerve to avoid it.
* You are busy studying with radio music playing in the background, which you are not really consciously aware of. A favourite song of yours is played; you suddenly 'listen in'.
* You are sitting doing a crossword, and puzzle hard over a difficult clue until you arrive at the answer.

What do these activities have in common? They are all examples of how your nervous system deals with everyday life. It is constantly buzzing with activity and, even when you are asleep, it will be alert to unusual activity or noise.

The nervous system is the major controlling and communication system of the body. Although it works alongside the endocrine system in the maintenance of homeostasis, it is far more sensitive, fast-acting and complex. There are three main functions of nervous tissue:

* The sensory nerves monitor changes in the environment; these changes are called stimuli.
* These changes are interpreted and decisions made as to what action needs to be taken; this is called integration.
* A response occurs – the contraction of muscles or the stimulation of glands. This is a motor response.

The central nervous system

The brain and spinal cord make up the **central nervous system** and are the control centres of the body. The brain has been compared to a telephone exchange – messages from all over the body being transported to and relayed from it. It has also been compared to a computer – when the messages arrive the brain interprets them and decides on what action to take.

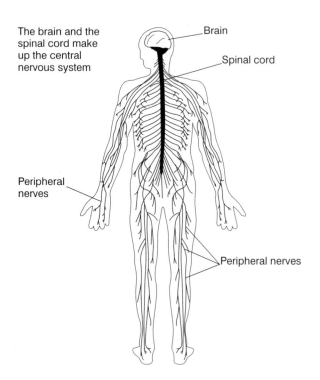

The brain and the spinal cord make up the central nervous system

Brain

Spinal cord

Peripheral nerves

Peripheral nerves

Fig. 3.9   The central nervous system

The peripheral nervous system

Sensory nerves

Sensory nerve fibres travel to the brain bringing information from all over the body. Some fibres are sensitive to temperature, some are sensitive to touch, others are sensitive to pain. The sensory fibres in the eye are sensitive to light and those in the ear respond to vibrations.

Motor nerves

Travelling away from the brain to our muscles are motor fibres. These carry messages away from the brain to the muscles and control body movement. This control is conscious; we are aware of what we are doing.

The autonomic nervous system

Another part of the **peripheral nervous system** is automatic and based on reflex action. We are not usually conscious of its effects and have very little, if any, control over it. This is called the **autonomic nervous system**. Nerve fibres of the autonomic nervous system go to and from the gut and control its movement. They control the rate of secretion of many glands as well as the acid secretion in the stomach. They also regulate our heart rate and control our blood pressure.

The autonomic nervous system is very important in the maintenance of **homeostasis** (pages 96–100). It keeps our internal environment constant while our external environment is always changing.

The autonomic nervous system has two opposing parts – the sympathetic nervous system and the parasympathetic nervous system. Normally there is a balance between the two systems. In an emergency, or when the body is preparing for action, the sympathetic nervous system takes over.

The sympathetic nervous system

The effects of the sympathetic nervous system are:

- increased heart rate and force
- increased breathing rate and depth
- dilated bronchioles (see Fig. 3.2, page 81) in the lungs
- increased sweating
- dry mouth.

Even without any more effects being listed you may realise what else you may associate these effects with: they are those produced by the **hormone** adrenaline. The action of the sympathetic nervous system is immediate, however, and does not last as long. The sympathetic nervous system stimulates the adrenal glands to produce adrenaline, which then prolongs the above actions. This may happen in an emergency, such as an accident, when a person is very frightened or in a lot of pain. If blood has been lost, the action of the sympathetic nervous system raises the blood pressure and helps to combat shock. If someone is in a state of shock or in a lot of pain they feel cold and clammy; a sure sign that the sympathetic nervous system is dominant. Their pulse rate will be increased and their breathing faster than normal.

The parasympathetic nervous system

This part of the autonomic nervous system is in control when the body is relaxing – for example, sitting in an armchair following dinner. The effects of the parasympathetic nervous system are to:

- slow down the heart rate
- steady the breathing
- increase peristalsis (see the digestive system, page 84) and secretion of enzymes in the gastrointestinal tract
- increase secretion of acid by the stomach
- allow the body to get on with its everyday activities, such as digesting the food just eaten.

The autonomic nervous system works with the endocrine system to maintain our internal environment in a steady state. It does this without us being aware of all the changes it is constantly making. People may only become aware of its actions when they are anxious, for example, and feel their hearts thumping away in their chests.

Reflex action

- A **reflex** is a rapid automatic response to a stimulus.
- It does not have to be learned, is not premeditated and is involuntary.
- The same stimulus always causes the same motor response.
- Reflexes are usually protective.

Activity 2

In a group, make a list of situations when you have reacted rapidly and automatically to a particular stimulus. Construct your list as three columns: stimulus, response and reason (for the type of response).

One example could be:

Stimulus	*Response*	*Reason*
A very hot plate	Dropping the plate	Pain

The sort of reflexes that you may have identified are triggered by the spinal cord without any help from the brain, so that you do not have to think about them. Some reflexes can be over-ridden. For example, if the hot plate that you picked up was a very expensive one, then you might think twice about dropping it!

Doctors text some reflexes to see if the nervous system is functioning adequately. An example is the 'knee-jerk', where a tendon hammer is used to tap the area just below the knee and the lower half of the leg then automatically kicks forward.

Nerve cells

Nerve cells are called **neurones** and are very specialised for the transmission of electrical messages. They use up a lot of energy and need a constant supply of oxygen and glucose from the blood. They cannot survive for more than a few minutes without oxygen. In a resuscitation attempt, if the circulation is not re-established within 3 minutes, neurones will die and permanent brain damage will result.

Neurones are not replaceable if destroyed, but with good nutrition they can live and function well for at least 100 years. However, the brain reaches its maximum weight

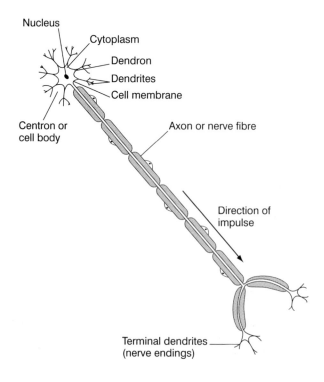

Fig. 3.10 The nerve cell or neurone

in the young adult, and for the rest of our lives neurones are damaged and die, and the brain weight decreases. Fortunately, the lost neurones are only a small percentage of the total and there should be very little change in thinking powers in the healthy adult until the age of 70 or well beyond.

The cerebral hemispheres

The part of the brain that is responsible for our conscious thought is called the cerebrum. It is divided into two halves: the cerebral hemispheres. Each half has several lobes, all with their own functions. This part of the brain is awesome in its complexity and staggering in its flexibility of thought. Some functions of the cerebrum are:

- maintaining consciousness
- integration of information
- memory and learning
- speech
- language processing
- personality
- perception, i.e. interpretation of vision, hearing and situations
- movement
- interpretation of feelings
- control of emotions.

What activities does the hypothalamus regulate?

The endocrine system

The **endocrine system** is a system of ductless glands whose secretions are called **hormones**. Hormones are released directly into the bloodstream from an endocrine gland and have their effect upon distant target sites. Endocrine glands differ from the other type of gland in the body, the exocrine glands, which do have ducts – tubes or vessels leading from them.

A salivary gland is an example of an exocrine gland: it releases its secretion, which travels to the mouth via a duct. The saliva then has an effect within the mouth itself, by lubricating food and commencing the digestion of starches.

The secretion of an endocrine gland does not act near the gland itself but travels in the bloodstream to its target cells. For example the adrenal gland, which releases adrenaline, is situated on top of the kidney, but the adrenaline works upon distant sites such as the heart and the lungs.

There are six main endocrine glands in the body:

- the pituitary gland
- the thyroid gland
- the parathyroid glands
- the adrenal glands
- the pancreas
- the gonads, i.e. ovaries and testes.

Certain diseases are caused by under-secretion or over-secretion from one of these glands; some of these will be referred to further on.

The pituitary gland

The **pituitary** is a small gland the size of a pea. It is situated at the base of the brain, attached to the hypothalamus by a short stalk. It exerts control over many of the other endocrine glands. Therefore, a disease of the pituitary gland would

91

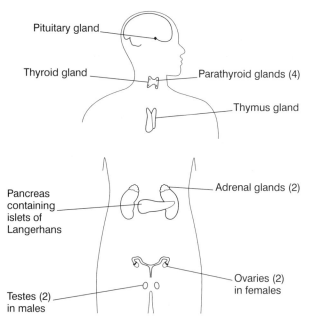

Fig. 3.11   The endocrine glands

affect other endocrine glands. The pituitary gland produces more hormones than any other endocrine gland, and is divided into the anterior and posterior lobes.

The anterior lobe
Three hormones are produced by this part of the pituitary:

* *Growth hormone* is produced mainly in childhood. Excess of this hormone leads to gigantism; a deficiency leads to dwarfism, which can now be treated by injections of growth hormone.
* *Melanocyte-stimulating hormone* affects the melanocytes, which produce melanin, and this colours the skin.
* *Prolactin* is produced in women after the birth of a baby and stimulates milk production.

These hormones are called stimulating hormones because they stimulate other glands – the adrenals, the thyroid and the gonads – to produce their own secretion.

The posterior lobe
This part of the pituitary produces only two hormones:

* *Antidiuretic hormone* concentrates the urine. More is produced when the body needs to conserve water, for example on a very hot day if insufficient fluids are taken.
* *Oxytocin* causes contraction of the uterus of women in labour and also controls the release of milk during suckling.

You can use Activity 3 to provide evidence for Key Skills Communication C3.1a.

Activity 3

Alcohol prevents the release of the antidiuretic hormone. In a group, discuss the implications of this fact, and the physical symptoms that result from drinking more than a moderate amount of alcohol.

The thyroid gland

This gland is situated in the neck, spanning the trachea. It produces thyroxin and controls the body's **metabolic rate** – the rate at which the body releases energy – which in turn controls the body's level of activity.

Activity 4

Make a presentation to your group, outlining a profile of the type of person who has a high metabolic rate. Aim for three characteristics. Use a diagram to effectively illustrate the identified characteristics.

Activity 5

To produce thyroxine, the thyroid needs an adequate supply of iodine in the body.

Find out which foodstuffs contain iodine. This information should be easily obtainable from a nutrition textbook or from one of the GNVQ texts that includes sections on diet and nutrition.

Key Skills

You can use Activity 4 to provide evidence for Key Skills Communication C3.1b

If the thyroid is overactive the symptoms include:

- loss of weight
- always feeling hot, even in cool weather
- fast pulse, even when sleeping
- hyperactivity; difficulty in relaxing
- an alert mind
- insomnia
- tremor.

If the gland is underactive, the opposite of these symptoms will occur. Underactivity of this gland is sometimes called myxodoema, and is more common in the older person.

The parathyroid glands

There are four of these small glands embedded in the four poles of the thyroid gland. They produce parathormone, which maintains the blood calcium at the correct level.

The adrenal glands

There are two of these glands, one on top of each kidney. They are divided into an outer part, called the cortex, and an inner part, called the medulla, both of which produce their own hormones.

The adrenal cortex
This produces:

- *Steroid hormones* – The most important of these is cortisol, which is essential to life. Among other things, it has anti-inflammatory properties and suppresses the immune system.
- *Aldosterone* – This helps to regulate the sodium and potassium balance of the body.

The adrenal medulla

Adrenaline is produced by the adrenal medulla to prepare the body for activity. It is important in the 'fight, fright and flight' response. In other words, it prepares the body for any of these three responses to a crisis; being released at times of acute fear or anger.

Key Skills

You can use Activity 6 to provide evidence for Key Skills Communication C3.1a.

/ **Activity 6** /

In a group, discuss situations when individuals were very frightened, received a sudden shock or had cause to be very angry. Your bodily responses to all three scenarios would be similar. List the physical changes that occurred, for example increased heart rate. There could be several others.

From this unit, and other sources, consider what these bodily responses are a result of.

The pancreas

The **pancreas** is situated in the abdomen and is both an exocrine and an endocrine gland. The exocrine secretions are enzymes released into the duodenum that help to digest food. Its endocrine function is to produce insulin and glucagon.

Insulin

The release of insulin is dependent upon the levels of glucose in the blood. Insulin is released when these levels are raised, commonly after a meal. The insulin enables the glucose in the blood to pass into the body cells and to be used for energy. If there is too much glucose, insulin allows the body to store the excess as fat. Without insulin, the body cannot utilise glucose, which accumulates unused in the blood. As the glucose level gets higher, some of it is excreted by the kidneys in the urine. This is the condition of **diabetes mellitus**.

Key Skills

You can use Activity 7 to provide evidence for Key Skills Information Technology IT3.1.

/ **Activity 7** /

Given this information, what do you think are some of the earlier signs of diabetes, and how do you think it may be detected by doctors? You could supplement your response by carrying out some further reading on the subject.

Diabetes mellitus can be treated by the administration of insulin by injection throughout life.

Whichever client group you care for, you are very likely to encounter people who have diabetes mellitus. If a person develops diabetes when they are young, it is likely that they will need insulin therapy. Some people who develop diabetes in later life do still produce some insulin, and control their diabetes by changing their diet and/or by taking tablets that stimulate insulin production by the pancreas.

Case study

Mrs Williams, aged 75 years, lives alone. She was admitted to hospital for stabilisation of her diabetes mellitus. The ward doctor ordered investigations of her blood to detect the levels of her blood glucose. On receiving the results of the blood test, the doctor ordered a special diet for Mrs Williams, in conjunction with medication that would stimulate cells in her body to produce more insulin, in order to promote utilisation of glucose. The nurses taught Mrs Williams to test her urine on a daily basis for the presence of glucose, so that her stabilised condition could be monitored.

ⓠ *In a group, discuss why this case study demonstrates that a basic knowledge of systems of the body (in this case the endocrine system), along with their functions, should enhance the work of carers.*

You can use this case study to provide evidence for Key Skills Communication C3.1a

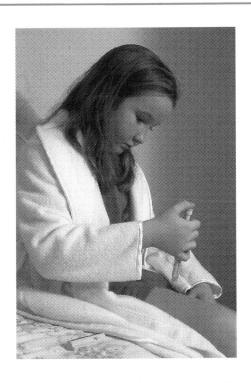

Fig. 3.12   Regular injections of insulin are necessary for many diabetics

The gonads

The **gonads** are the ovaries in the female and the testes in the male. They produce sex hormones necessary for the normal development of the body at puberty.

Female hormones

The most important hormone is called oestrogen, but progesterone is also produced. Oestrogen gives the woman a different bodily shape. Following the menopause, reduced levels of oestrogen can lead to various problems, most notably osteoporosis, and can be replaced via hormone replacement therapy (HRT). Oestrogen and progesterone regulate the menstrual cycle.

Male hormones

The male hormones are called androgens and include testosterone. Androgens are responsible for the muscular development of a young man, as well as body hair distribution and the deepening of his voice. Male hormones are also needed for the production of sperm.

The control of endocrine secretion

The secretions of some of the endocrine organs are regulated directly by feedback mechanisms; for example, insulin is secreted in response to a high blood level glucose. Others, such as cortisol (see page 93), are regulated by the pituitary, which is in turn influenced by the hypothalamus.

The hypothalamus

The **hypothalamus** is situated in the brain and is the link between the endocrine system and the nervous system. The hypothalamus:

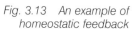

What is a hormone?

- is vitally important in the control of homeostasis
- controls the output of some hormones
- is the centre for control of body temperature
- regulates eating behaviour according to levels of nutrients and hormones
- regulates thirst; if a person's body fluids are too concentrated, they will feel thirsty.

3.2 Homeostasis

Our bodies are always interacting with a constantly changing environment. This includes both the external and internal environment. The internal environment refers to the mechanisms that regulate body functions and the fluids that surround body cells. Various physiological mechanisms within the body respond to internal changes in order to maintain internal constancy – **homeostasis**.

The essential chemical processes in the body cells are controlled by **enzymes**, which are biological catalysts made of protein. Enzymes can only operate within narrow temperature and acidity ranges. This means that the internal environment of the cell must be kept relatively constant to maintain normal body function.

To maintain this stability of environment in each cell, there has to be a good system of communication throughout the body. This communication involves the nervous system and the hormones. A simplified example of this is: if cells do not have enough glucose for energy, they have to ask for more. The glucose required may come from the liver.

Maintaining homeostasis

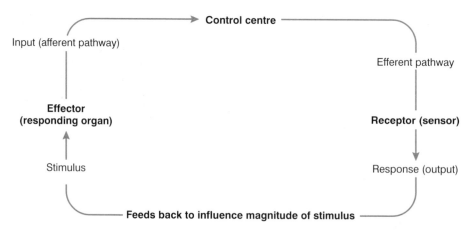

Fig. 3.13   An example of homeostatic feedback

The balancing process required to maintain homeostasis involves three functional parts:

- **receptors**
- a control centre
- a responding organ.

Receptors monitor the internal environment. They pass their information to the control centre, which initiates the correct response by sending out nervous or hormonal messages to the corresponding organ. This regulation can be compared to the central heating system in a house (Fig. 3.14). Most chemical processes in the body are controlled by this process of **negative feedback**.

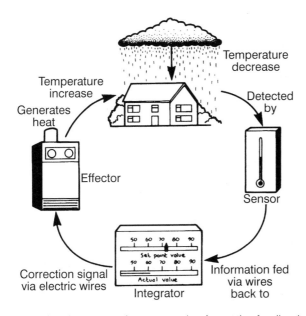

Fig. 3.14   A domestic heating system is an example of negative feedback

Feedback mechanisms in the human body

When the body is in homeostasis, the needs of its cells are being met and all is functioning smoothly. If homeostasis is disturbed this results in an imbalance, which may have serious consequences for the cells. Every body system has some part to play in the maintenance of internal consistency.

Communication and control systems in the body

The nervous system is the body's main communication network and is a system of control as well as communication. It works closely with the endocrine system, which produces chemical messengers called hormones. The vital role of the hypothalamus in the control of homeostasis, as a link between the nervous and endocrine systems, was described on page 96. These two systems regulate the body's responses to the internal and external environment.

Body systems control the homeostatic mechanisms for:

- blood glucose level
- body temperature
- heart rate
- respiratory rate
- fluid balance.

The processes involved will now be considered separately.

Maintaining blood glucose level

The homeostatic regulators that affect blood glucose level include the parasympathetic nervous system, which stimulates insulin secretion, that in turn has the effect of increasing uptake of glucose by the cells; the sympathetic nervous system, which stimulates the release of glycogen stores, that in turn has the effect of increasing blood glucose levels; and the adrenal glands, which secrete glucocorticoids, that raise glucose levels in response to the body's requirement for energy.

Maintaining body temperature

The nerve endings in the skin are the receptors that monitor temperature. If the temperature rises they send a nervous impulse to the brain – the control centre. The brain then sends a message to the sweat glands and stimulates them to function. Evaporation of sweat causes cooling, and homeostasis is restored.

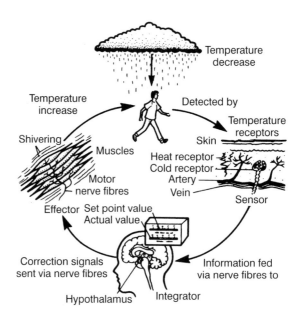

Fig. 3.15   The feedback control of temperature in the body

You can use this case study to provide evidence for Key Skills Communication C3.1b.

Case study

Mrs Jones, aged 83, complained of feeling cold, even in the summer. She reported that her memory seemed to be getting worse and friends observed that her mind was less agile. She put on quite a lot of weight but insisted that she was eating less than before. Relatives had noticed that she had become rather sluggish and her level of activity had fallen. One morning, after a very cold night in winter, Mrs Jones was found by her daughter sitting in a chair, staring into space. She touched her arm, which felt very cold. Concerned, she rang for an ambulance. The paramedics who arrived found Mrs Jones's temperature to be 33.5°C, and she was taken to hospital. Mrs Jones was suffering from hypothermia. Her body temperature had to be restored to within normal limits slowly. Tests revealed that Mrs Jones had an under-active thyroid. A disorder of the endocrine system had therefore affected her body temperature. Her earlier symptoms were also indicative of an underactive thyroid.

Ⓠ *Parallels are often drawn between the function of the hypothalamus and that of the thermostat in a car. How would you use this example of the thermostat to explain the function of the hypothalamus to your group?*

Maintaining heart rate

The homeostatic regulators in the body that have an effect upon heart rate include the parasympathetic nervous system, which regulates and slows the heart rate, and the sympathetic nervous system, which stimulates heart rate and force, increasing the rate, strengthening contractions and increasing cardiac output. During a 'fight or flight' situation, when the body needs to draw upon its reserves, the sympathetic nerves can boost the cardiac output by two or three times the resting value. Stimulation from the parasympathetic nervous system decreases the heart rate in order to restore homeostasis.

Maintaining respiratory rate

Regulation of respiration is a complex process that has to keep pace with constant changes in cellular oxygen requirements and carbon dioxide production. Regulation depends primarily on the respiratory control centres located in the medulla and pons of the brain stem. The main control centre in the medulla sets the basic pattern of respiration. This can be modified by centres in the pons. Breathing is regulated so that levels of oxygen, carbon dioxide and acid are kept within normal limits. Although it is possible for a person to consciously alter their breathing rate, for most of the time people breathe without being conscious of the process, which is being controlled by the respiratory centres in the brain stem.

Maintaining fluid balance

Homeostasis in relation to fluid balance is essential because constancy of **electrolyte** concentration is necessary for the transfer of water between blood, tissue fluids and cells. The **antidiuretic hormone (ADH)** secreted by the posterior lobe of the pituitary gland has a part to play in relation to fluid balance, by increasing the reabsorption of water in the kidneys, thus decreasing the volume of urine excreted. However, fluid balance is threatened when any organ fails to function properly.

Case study

Mrs King, aged 80, has recently been admitted to a residential home following the death of her husband, as she has problems with mobility. Within 3 weeks she has lost weight, about which the staff express concern. Because of the level of help that Mrs King requires, it has also been possible to observe that her urinary output is low. She is found to have a weak, thready pulse and to be suffering from postural hypotension (the systolic blood pressure (see page 105) drops when she is moved from a lying to a sitting position). When her urine is tested it is found to have a high specific gravity (it is very concentrated). Her body temperature has dropped to 36.7°C.

After her fluid balance is monitored more closely, it becomes clear that her fluid input is insufficient. Her symptoms are associated with electrolyte imbalance. A comprehensive assessment reveals that Mrs King's reluctance

Which two systems of the body are most involved with the maintenance of homeostasis?

to take fluids is associated with depression caused by her bereavement. Her care plan now details a holistic approach to Mrs King's problem, which includes encouragement to drink, identification of likes and dislikes in relation to fluids, monitoring of fluid balance, mouth care and bereavement counselling.

3.3 Physiological measurements of individuals in care settings

It is not always possible to tell if the body is healthy just by looking at a person. To help diagnosis and to attempt to detect disease at an early stage there are ways of taking physiological measurements. When learning how to take physiological measurements of individuals in care settings, it is necessary to do so within a safe environment, under supervision, using the opportunity to practise safely on yourself and other students.

Monitoring body temperature

Body temperature refers to the heat of the body, measured in degrees. The degree of body temperature reflects the difference between heat production and heat loss. As indicated on page 96, the core body temperature of a healthy person is maintained within a fairly constant range by the thermoregulatory centre in the hypothalamus. Core body temperatures reflect the temperature of the viscera and the muscles, which are insulated by the adipose tissue and skin to prevent heat loss. Heat is lost when heat from the body's inner core is transferred to the skin surface by circulating blood. Body temperature is often measured orally, but the axilla and rectum may be sites of choice, depending on individual circumstances, for example if a patient or client is uncooperative and might bite a glass thermometer. Temperature-sensitive patches or tape are often used with infants; these are applied to the forehead.

It is important to note that readings will differ according to the site used to record body temperature. A rectal temperature would be higher, for example, than the oral temperature taken from the same person.

You can use Activity 8 to provide evidence for Key Skills Information Technology IT3.1.

Activity 8

Identify and write about:

a the factors that affect body temperature
b the mechanisms of heat transfer (i.e. how the body loses heat when it needs to be cooler).

This information may be found in a nursing textbook, some anatomy and physiology textbooks, or CD-ROM.

Pyrexia is a term that is applied to an increase in body temperature. It is a common symptom of illness.

The expected body temperature of an adult, taken orally, would be between 36.6°C and 37°C. Body temperature can be measured in degrees Celsius or Fahrenheit, but Celsius (C) is generally the system of choice.

A glass thermometer has traditionally been used to measure body temperature. There are two types, one for the purpose of taking oral temperatures, and one for taking rectal temperatures. The shape of the bulb on the end of the thermometer indicates which is which; the rectal thermometer often has a blue bulb, which is blunter in shape than the longer, thinner bulb of the oral thermometer.

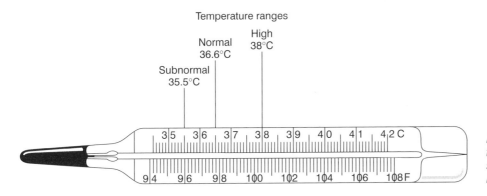

Fig. 3.16   A clinical thermometer showing subnormal, normal and high temperatures

However, these days concerns have been raised regarding the use of mercury in monitoring such as **sphygmomanometers** and thermometers, and alternatives have been introduced. Examples are: electronic thermometers and disposable, single-use thermometers.

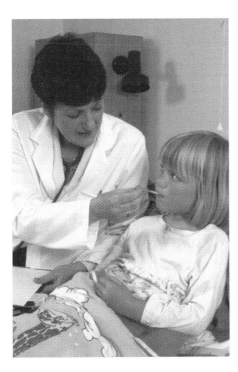

Fig. 3.17   Taking an oral temperature

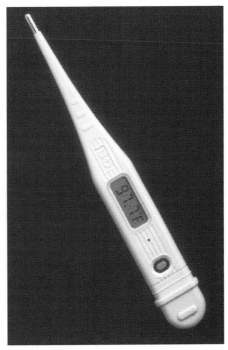

Fig. 3.18   An electronic thermometer

The principles of taking an oral temperature however, remain the same:

1 The equipment should be prepared (thermometer, wipes, chart, pen).
2 The patient/client should receive an explanation about the procedure.
3 The nurse/carer should wash their hands.

4 The thermometer should be cleaned; this will depend on the method of storage and type used. For example, a disposable thermometer will not need to be cleaned. With an electronic thermometer, a disposable probe cover is used.

5 If a glass thermometer is used, the nurse/carer should grasp it between thumb and forefinger (not at the bulb end) and shake the mercury down to at least 36°C.

6 The thermometer should be placed beneath the client's tongue, and the client should be asked to close their lips around the thermometer.

7 The thermometer should be left in place for 3 minutes; however an electronic thermometer will make a sound when the peak temperature has been reached.

8 The thermometer should be wiped once to remove saliva, and read.

9 The thermometer should be cleaned according to local procedure and according to the type used.

10 The temperature should be recorded.

Monitoring the cardiovascular system

Pulse rate

As described on page 82, blood in the arteries flows in spurts that are synchronous with the heart beat. The wave of contraction that passes along an artery wall is called a **pulse**.

The average resting pulse rate of a person varies throughout his or her life span. At birth, the heart beats about 130 times per minute, at 6 years old about 100 times per minute and in an adult between 65 and 80 times per minute.

Activity 9

Pulse rate is usually counted in the radial artery. Using three fingers (not your thumb), find your radial pulse, which you should be able to locate on your arm near the base of the thumb of the other hand (Fig. 3.19). Try timing your pulse by counting it for one minute.

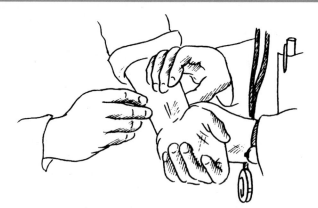

Fig. 3.19 Taking the radial pulse

Although the radial pulse is the most common one to record, there are several other sites in the body where a pulse can be found, i.e. where an artery is sufficiently superficial. Examples are:

- the temporal artery (at either side of your forehead)
- the carotid artery (at either side of your neck)
- the brachial artery (can be felt on the inner arm, between the forearm and upper arm).

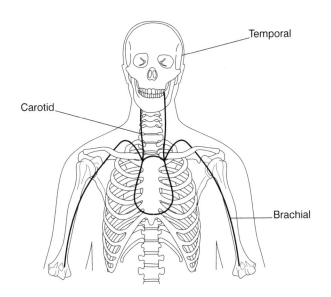

Temporal

Carotid

Brachial

Fig. 3.20   The location of the temporal, carotid and brachial arteries

Activity 10

Try to find the three pulse sites mentioned above. Take care not to press too hard.

Activity 11

Refer back to the section on the nervous system (pages 87–91). The body's 'fight, fright and flight' responses were described. These are enabled by the production of the hormone adrenaline. In your group, discuss the reasons why, in response to such a situation, one of the physiological effects would be an increased pulse rate, and the implications that this might have for taking physiological measurements of individuals in care settings.

Key Skills

You can use Activity 11 to provide evidence for Key Skills Communication C3.1a.

Activity 12

a Record your pulse rate for 1 minute, while you are at rest. Then, using an aerobic step, a suitable stair or a gymnastics bench, step up and down for 3 minutes. Record your pulse rate for 1 minute immediately following this activity. Stop this activity immediately if you experience pain or breathing discomfort.

b For the resting pulse, and after exercise, calculate the volume of blood pumped by each ventricle of the heart in 1 minute (each ventricle pumps about 70 cm^3/beat).

c Does the volume change? Why should this be?

Present your findings to your group, using graphs and diagrams to illustrate them.

Key Skills

You can use Activity 12 to provide evidence for Key Skills Application of Number N3.3.

What is the expected resting pulse rate for a healthy adult?

Blood pressure

Blood pressure is the amount of pressure that the blood exerts on the walls of the arteries as it flows through them. It is an important measurement because it can give significant clues as to the state of a person's arteries and can provide an early indication of cardiovascular disease. The pressure is often measured in millimetres of mercury (mmHg) using a sphygmomanometer. However, increasing use is now made of blood pressure monitoring devices that display a digital blood pressure reading. These are easier for people to use to monitor their own blood pressure.

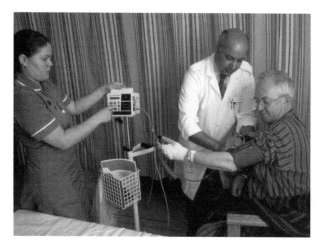
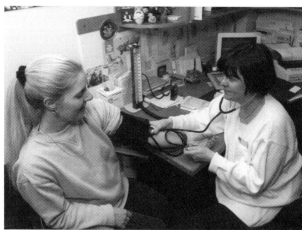

Fig. 3.21   A digital blood-pressure monitoring device, left, and a traditional sphygmomanometer, right

Using a traditional sphygmomanometer, the most common way to record blood pressure is as follows:

1 The bell of the stethoscope is placed over the brachial artery (see below).
2 The sphygmomanometer cuff is applied to the arm above the elbow.
3 The cuff is inflated and mercury rises up the manometer, from which the pressure is read. The cuff is inflated to approximately 20–30 mmHg (millimetres of mercury), above the last recorded reading, or until the pulse can no longer be heard or palpated (felt with the fingers).
4 There is a control valve to deflate the system. The pressure valve on the cuff should be released slowly. The point at which the first sound can be heard through the stethoscope is the **systolic** reading. The point at which the pulse that can be heard fades is the **diastolic** reading.

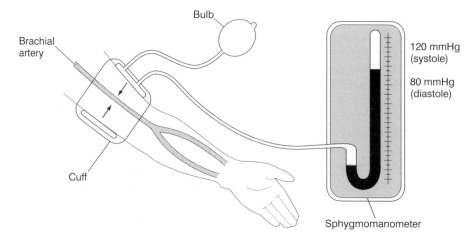

Fig. 3.22   Measuring blood pressure

These terms will now be explained.

Blood pressure is recorded as two figures. The upper figure, the systolic, is the pressure in the blood vessels as the heart contracts. The lower figure, the diastolic, is the pressure in the vessels when the heart is relaxing between beats. In healthy adults at rest, systolic blood pressure varies between 110 and 140 mmHg and diastolic pressure between 75 and 80 mmHg. This would be written down as (for example) 110/75.

Alternatively, on a blood pressure chart, the reading may be recorded as shown below.

When a person is in hospital, the doctor usually decides how often the patient's blood pressure should be taken and recorded. The frequency depends upon the person's condition. This could apply also to some clients in other care settings, for example an older person in a residential home, who requires regular monitoring of their blood pressure.

Indeed, about one-third of people aged over 50 have raised blood pressure. It is believed that, if these people were identified and their blood pressure was returned to within normal limits, the incidence of strokes would be reduced by about 30%.

Activity 13

Find out the meanings of the prefixes 'hypo-' and 'hyper-', so that you are able to define the terms 'hypotension' and 'hypertension' in relation to blood pressure. Anatomy and physiology texts often include a list of what are termed biological prefixes.

Atherosclerosis is a condition involving the narrowing and hardening of the arteries. This occurs because they become 'clogged up' as a result of plaques of a substance called atheroma building up inside the arteries. This process is associated with raised cholesterol levels and is made worse by such factors as smoking, stress and obesity. Eventually the lumen (the internal passage) of the artery becomes narrowed. Because the space through which the blood has to pass has been reduced, the pressure that it exerts on the walls of the arteries increases.

If increased blood pressure is thought to be an early indication of atherosclerosis, certain lifestyle modifications can be made by the individual in order to help slow down the process and to enhance the individual's health status generally.

Activity 14

Make a presentation to your group about health information that could be given to a person who shows early signs of developing atherosclerosis, including reference to appropriate, informative health promotion literature.

Activity 15

a Identify a range of factors that may have an effect upon an individual's blood pressure (e.g. age; there are several others).

b Given these variables, what do you think would be an important factor to bear in mind when measuring and recording an individual's blood pressure within a care setting?

Key Skills

You can use Activity 14 to provide evidence for Key Skills Communication C3.1b.

Key Skills

You can use Activity 15 to provide evidence for Key Skills Information Technology IT3.1.

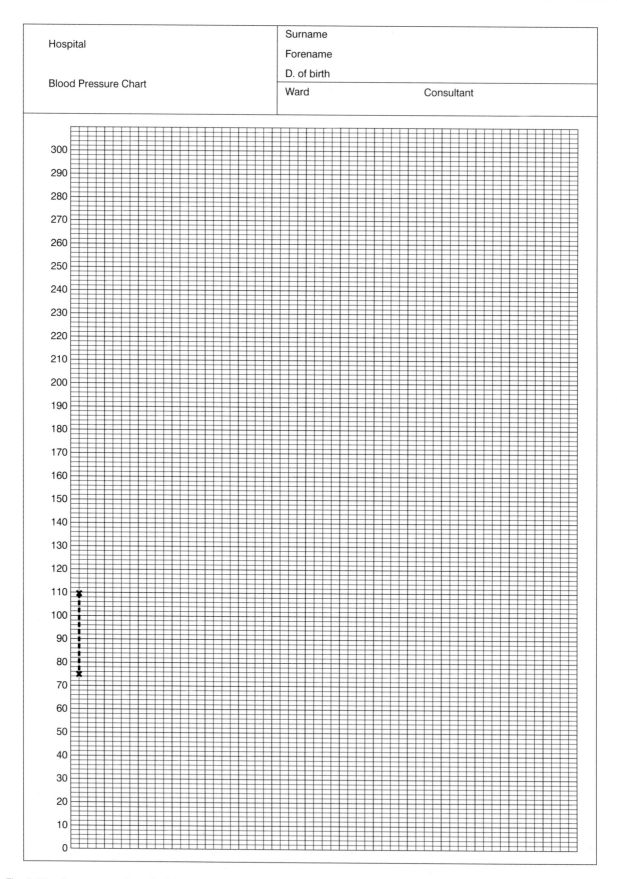

Hospital	Surname
Blood Pressure Chart	Forename
	D. of birth
	Ward Consultant

Fig. 3.23   *A representation of a blood pressure chart, indicating one way in which blood pressure may be recorded*

Monitoring the respiratory system

Respiratory rate

The control of breathing is normally undertaken by the respiratory centre in the medulla oblongata of the brain. It involves a rhythmical inspiration and expiration without conscious thought.

Tidal volume refers to the air that passes in and out of the lungs in normal respiratory action. It is possible, however, to voluntarily control the rate of one's breathing.

What is the name of the device used to measure blood pressure?

Activity 16

It is difficult to measure your own respiratory rate, as awareness of the intended activity may cause you to involuntarily alter the rate. Try to measure the respiratory rate of another person, preferably when that person is unaware! Count the rise and fall of the chest as one. Expect the rate to be between 16 and 22 per minute for a healthy adult.

What does the term 'tidal volume' refer to?

Lung volume

The measurement of air taken into and expelled from the lungs is known as **spirometry**. Changes in lung volumes provide the best measurement of obstruction to air flow in the respiratory passages.

A spirometer consists of a hollow drum floating over a chamber of water and counterbalanced by weights so that it can move freely up and down. Inside the drum is a mixture of gases, usually oxygen and air. Leading from the hollow space in the drum to the outside is a tube that has a mouthpiece through which the person breathes. As the person inhales and exhales through the tube, the drum rises and falls, causing a needle to move on a nearby rotating chart. The tracing recorded is called a spirogram.

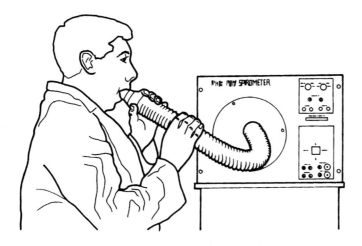

Fig. 3.24   A spirometer in use

Vital capacity refers to the volume of air breathed out after a person has breathed in as fully as possible. The normal capacity is 2500–3000 millilitres (ml). It is higher in males than in females. Forced vital capacity measurements are taken in the form of peak flow measurements. Vital capacity is reduced in obstructive lung diseases, such as bronchitis (inflammation of the bronchi; see page 81). A person suffering from asthma would also have a reduced vital capacity, because of difficulty in expiration caused by muscular spasm of the bronchi.

Activity 17

If possible, obtain a mini peak flow meter. This is a small tube-shaped structure with a calibrated measuring scale and disposable cardboard mouthpieces for hygiene reason. The more basic versions are fairly inexpensive and can be obtained from sports equipment suppliers. This is because they are frequently used as part of fitness assessments. Mini peak flow meters are simple to use. You should inhale and then forcibly and rapidly exhale into the mouthpiece. Normally the 'best of three' readings is recorded. Compare readings with other students.

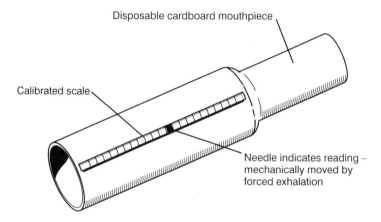

Disposable cardboard mouthpiece

Calibrated scale

Needle indicates reading – mechanically moved by forced exhalation

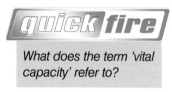

What does the term 'vital capacity' refer to?

Fig. 3.25   A mini peak flow meter

3.4 Safe practice

It is important to observe safe practice when carrying out physiological measurements of individuals in care settings. The level of knowledge and skill acquisition required prior to practising a procedure on another person varies according to the activity in question. With all procedures, however, correct and safe techniques must be used. If at any time during the implementation of a monitoring activity, pain, discomfort, breathlessness or any other difficulty is experienced by the subject, whether during practice or within a real situation, then the procedure must be stopped immediately and medical advice sought if the problem persists.

When students are undertaking exercise that involves exertion, such as in Activity 12 on page 103, they should stop the activity immediately if pain or breathing discomfort is experienced.

Being able to record a blood pressure reading is a fairly complex skill, and it is important that the student receives theoretical input, demonstration and the opportunity to practise before being allowed to measure and record the blood pressure of an individual within a care setting.

Also with reference to blood pressure measurement, consideration should be given to the fact that European legislation requires the phasing out of equipment containing mercury. If the more up-to-date digital methods for recording values are available, then these should be used. Reference to these blood pressure monitoring devices can be found on pages 104–105.

When using a peak flow meter, which requires forcible exhalation, if any pain or discomfort results, the activity should be discontinued. Also, a new disposable mouthpiece should be used for each person in order to avoid the risk of cross-infection.

In general, health and safety legislation should be considered by students when collecting physiological **data** from individuals within care settings.

What is now considered to be a safer alternative to a mercury manometer?

3.5 Accuracy of results

The student needs to be aware of potential sources of error that could occur when carrying out physiological measurements of individuals in care settings.

Potential sources of error – reading body temperature

A glass thermometer will need to be 'shaken down' by the carer using thumb and forefinger at the opposite end to the bulb prior to use, in order for an accurate reading to be obtained. The thermometer must also be left *in situ* for the recommended length of time to ensure accuracy.

Potential sources of error – pulse readings

The carer must use the first, second and third fingers to palpate (feel) the radial pulse; if the thumb is used for this purpose, the carer may feel his or her own pulse.

Moderate pressure should be applied in order to be able to feel the pulsation of the radial artery. Too much pressure will suppress the pulse. If too little pressure is applied, then the pulse will be difficult to locate.

Potential sources of error – blood pressure

When using a sphygmomanometer to measure blood pressure, it is important to select a cuff of the proper width to obtain an accurate reading. If it is too narrow, the reading could be falsely high because the pressure is not evenly transmitted to the artery. This could occur, for example, when using an average-sized cuff on a person who is overweight. If a cuff is too wide, then the reading could be falsely low, because pressure is being directed towards a proportionately large surface area. This could occur, for example, when using an adult cuff on the thin arm of a child.

Similarly, if the cuff is too loosely wrapped around the arm, an inaccurate reading may result.

Clothing that is too tight around the upper arm may also cause an inaccurate reading to be taken.

If using a mercury manometer, the blood pressure reading should be made with the eye at the level of the meniscus – the point at which the mercury stops. If the meniscus is observed above eye level, it appears higher than it really is. If the meniscus is lower than eye level, it appears lower than it really is.

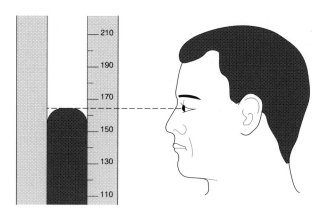

Fig. 3.26   A blood pressure reading should be made with the eye at the level of the meniscus

The mercury manometer should also be placed on a level surface, as tilting the manometer could lead to error.

The blood pressure reading may be misleading if the measurement takes place following physical activity, or if the person is emotionally upset. The person should be at rest, assuming a comfortable sitting or lying position.

Potential sources of error – respiratory rate

On page 107, reference was made to the fact that it is possible for individuals to consciously alter their own respiratory rate. It is important, therefore, to observe respiratory rate while the person is unaware, so that an accurate assessment can be made. This can be achieved by making the observation immediately after taking the pulse rate, keeping the fingers in place, so that the person is unaware that respirations are then being counted.

Potential sources of error – lung volume

Why should the thumb not be used to feel a pulse?

When using a spirometer (see page 107), the person should not wear restrictive clothing, which may affect their breathing and, therefore, the accuracy of the result. Any medication that they are taking concerned with the respiratory tract is usually withdrawn prior to the procedure, as again a true picture of the individual's lung volume may not emerge. This must not be done without medical advice.

3.6 Accurate analysis of results

Accurate recording of information

You can use Activity 18 to provide evidence for Key Skills Application of Number N3.1.

Activity 18

a Study the chart on page 112 to see how the measurements of a pulse would be recorded.
b Photocopy the chart so that you can use it for this exercise.
c Why is it important to maintain records of physiological measurements?
d Keep a record for one week of your resting pulse rate, using the photocopied chart to record your findings. You could also record the pulse of another student, friend or family member for one week.

e If there are any variations in pulse rate throughout the week, identify possible reasons for this.

f What factors may cause variations in pulse rate in an individual within a care setting?

g You could also compare records of the resting pulse rates among a larger group (e.g. your student group), monitored for one week.

The measurements of pulse rate and other physiological measurements that are then recorded become data, which is necessary for analysis of an individual's physiological status. Analysis of data involves the use of statistics. There are various methods of **statistical analysis** that could be applied to a set of data in order to make sense of it. However, in relation to analysis for clinical relevance, it is common practice to compare findings with a set of existing norms, for example, comparing a child's height to normal growth charts.

Activity 19

a How would the data for 'normal growth charts' be collected?

b What does 'normal' mean in this context?

Activity 20

It is possible that an individual in a care setting may have certain physiological measurements taken and recorded (e.g. pulse, temperature, respiration and blood pressure) when they first arrive. These recordings are baseline observations. Why do you think that these are important?

These baseline observations become the individual's own norms (or values that occur frequently in any group) against which any subsequent changes can be compared. Even though there are expected ranges (e.g. pulse rate) for a healthy adult, each individual may vary in terms of what is 'normal' for them.

Activity 21

Consider once more the chart used in Activity 18 (page 110). Why do you think that information is presented in such a way?

The recording of physiological measurements is often presented in a graph format, which assists with comparison of information. On the temperature, pulse and respiration chart it is easier to observe any changes that occur than if the readings had simply been written down.

The use of formulae

A formula is a rule or fact expressed by symbols or figures. In physiology, formulae have been devised in order to enable the calculation of certain values.

What is meant by a baseline observation?

Physical aspects of health and social well-being

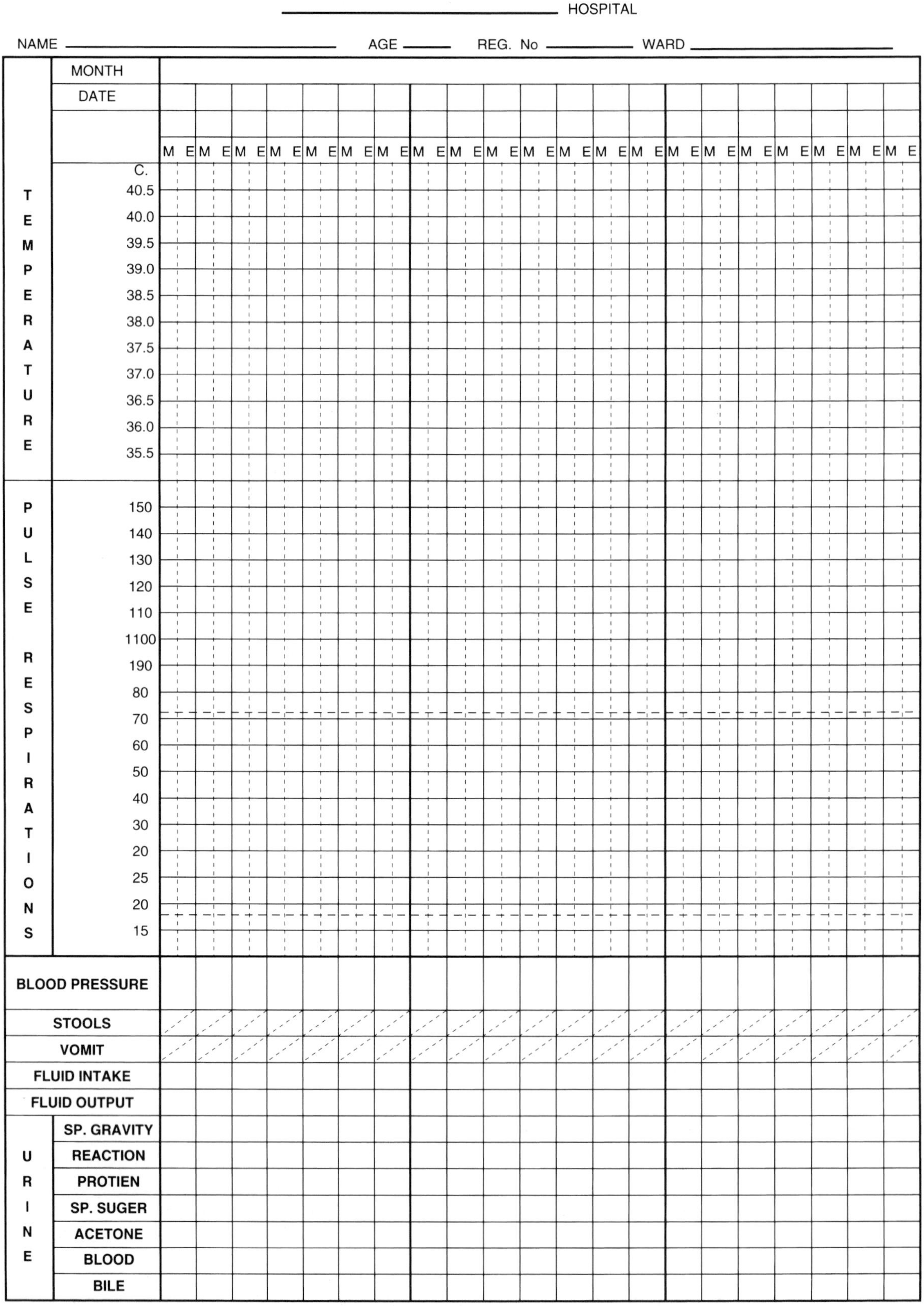

_____ HOSPITAL

NAME _____   AGE _____   REG. No _____   WARD _____

	MONTH	
	DATE	
		M E M E M E M E M E M E M E M E M E M E M E M E M E M E M E M E M E M E M E M E M E M E M E M E

TEMPERATURE

C.
- 40.5
- 40.0
- 39.5
- 39.0
- 38.5
- 38.0
- 37.5
- 37.0
- 36.5
- 36.0
- 35.5

PULSE
- 150
- 140
- 130
- 120
- 110
- 1100
- 190
- 80
- 70
- 60
- 50
- 40
- 30
- 20

RESPIRATIONS
- 25
- 20
- 15

BLOOD PRESSURE	
STOOLS	
VOMIT	
FLUID INTAKE	
FLUID OUTPUT	
URINE	SP. GRAVITY
	REACTION
	PROTIEN
	SP. SUGER
	ACETONE
	BLOOD
	BILE

Fig. 3.27   An example of a chart used to record temperature, pulse and respiration

Spirometry (see page 107) is used to measure lung capacity, volume and flow rate. Functional residual capacity is equal to the expiratory reserve volume (the amount of air that can be inspired beyond tidal volume; page 81) plus the residual volume (the amount of air remaining in the lungs after a maximum expiration).

The functional residual capacity in a young adult male is 2400 ml. Approximately 150 ml of this volume is dead space. Dead space constitutes the air in the smallest, terminal bronchioles (see fig 3.2, page 81), which does not exchange gases with the blood. If the next inspiration were to admit 450 ml of fresh air, then 150 ml of stale air would be displaced into the alveolar region (see fig 3.1, page 80) from the dead space, followed by 300 ml of fresh air, leaving the remaining 150 ml of inspired air in the dead space. Thus the percentage of air inspired that actually reaches the alveoli is:

$$\frac{300}{450} \times 100 = 66\%$$

In terms of a formula, this is:

$$\frac{\text{Inspired fresh air} - 150}{\text{Total amount of inspired fresh air}} \times 100 = \text{Percentage of air reaching alveoli}$$

This example represents a typical resting value. However, if the inspired volume is increased by physical effort, the percentage of fresh air reaching the alveoli would be greater.

Activity 22

Calculate the percentage of air reaching the alveoli, given an inspired volume of 1500 ml, using the above formula.

What is meant by the term 'residual volume'?

The accurate analysis of secondary source data

If you count and record a pulse rate, you are collecting primary source data. This is information that you have collected yourself. Secondary source data refers to data that has not been collected directly by you. It could still, however, be used by you as a source of information from which certain conclusions could be drawn.

The electrocardiogram (ECG)

Heart tissue is highly specialised and is capable of automatic, rhythmic contraction. The heart beat starts as an electrical impulse at a specific point in the heart, the **sinoatrial node**. From this point, the impulse travels through the conducting system of the heart (the Bundle of His), causing first the atria then the ventricles (see fig 3.28, page 114) to beat. The atrioventricular node is situated between the atria and the ventricles, and transmits impulses. The phase of activating the muscle membranes within a section of the heart is called depolarisation. The process of returning the muscle membranes in that area of the heart to its resting phase is referred to as repolarisation.

Electrodes applied to the skin can increase the currents produced by the electrical activity in the heart. The **electrocardiogram** records these electrical impulses in the form of waves on a graph.

An electrocardiogram can help to diagnose heart attacks and is a valuable tool for the observation of people with heart disease. In many disorders of the heart the electrocardiograph shows changes that can help the doctor to make a diagnosis.

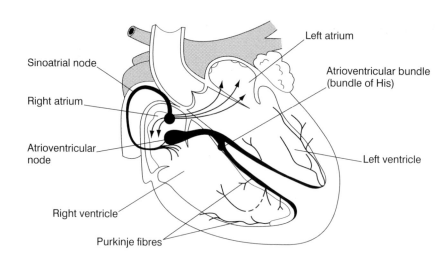

Fig. 3.28   The conduction system of the heart

If a person suffers a heart attack or lowered blood supply to the heart, the shape of some of the waves changes. Other abnormalities may occur in an infection of the heart or in heart failure, or when the heart can no longer pump efficiently.

The electrical activity of the heart may be continuously monitored using a cardiac monitor. Electrodes are placed on the client's chest and attached to a monitor. The monitor displays the ECG so that any changes can be noted. This is necessary if the person has an irregular beat or disorders of rhythm following a heart attack. These rhythm disturbances could be the first indications of possible problems that might lead to a cardiac arrest.

In Figure 3.29, the vertical axis is used to represent the amount of electrical activity in the myocardium (middle, muscle layer of the heart). A height of 10 mm (10 small boxes) is equivalent to 1 millivolt (mV). Therefore, if a wave is 10 mm high, this is the result of 1 mV of electrical activity.

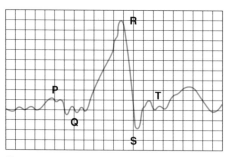

Fig. 3.29   A normal electrocardiogram

Key
P = Atria contract
QRS = Ventricles contract
T = Heart relaxes

Key Skills

You can use Activity 23 to provide evidence for Key Skills Communications C3.1b.

Activity 23

Study the figure above. Given that each small square represents 0.04 seconds (on the horizontal axis), make the following calculations:

a How long does the QRS complex last?
b How long does one PQRST cycle last?

Present an explanation to your group about your findings, using a diagram to illustrate your explanation.

Determining heart rate from electrocardiographs

Electrocardiographs are printed out on graph paper with large boxes divided into smaller squares (5 × 5 squares in each box). Examples are shown in Figure 3.30.

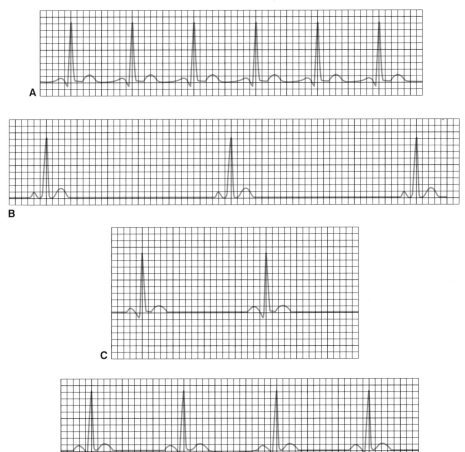

Fig. 3.30   Determining heart rate from electrocardiographs

Which phase of a heart beat does the QRS complex on an ECG represent?

Activity 24

a In Activity 23 it was explained that each small square on the electrocardiograph represents 0.04 seconds. How much time does each large square represent?

b What length of time is represented by 300 large boxes?

c The method for determining heart rate from an electrocardiograph is to count the number of large boxes between consecutive beats and divide this number into 300. So, if there are two large boxes between consecutive beats (as in A of the figure above), then 300/2 gives 150 beats per minute. Calculate the heart rates from B, C and D in the figure using this formula.

Key Skills

You can use Activity 24 to provide evidence for Key Skills Application of Number N3.2(d).

Blood cell counts

Investigations of blood are used as a method of screening to ascertain an individual's health status. The composition of blood reflects the function of many bodily activities and the results obtained from blood tests are always compared to a normal body range. The normal ranges are given in the following table. The next table explains the metric readings.

Normal blood ranges, including cell counts and electrolyte concentrations

	Men	Women
Blood count		
Haemoglobin	13.5–19 g/dl	11.5–16.5 g/dl
Packed cell volume	40–50%	36–47%

	Men and women
Blood count	
White cell count	$4–11 \times 10^9/l$
Platelet count	$150–400 \times 10^9/l$
Biochemistry	
Sodium	135–147 mmol/l
Potassium	3.8–5.0 mmol/l
Urea	2.5–6.5 mmol/l
Glucose	3.4–6.5 mmol/l
Cholesterol	< 5.2 mmol/l (desirable)
	5.2–6.2 mmol/l (borderline)
	> 6.2 mmol/l (high)
Serum albumin	35–55 g/l

NB 'Normal ranges' may vary slightly in different texts.

Metric measures, units and SI symbols

Name	SI unit	Symbol
Mass	gram	g
Volume	litre	l
Amount of substance	mole	mol

Standard prefixes are used for decimal submultiples of the units

Submultiple	Prefix	Symbol
10^{-1}	deci-	d
10^{-2}	centi-	c
10^{-3}	milli-	m
10^{-6}	micro-	μ
10^{-9}	nano-	n
10^{-12}	pico-	p

Activity 25

a Study the table above; it provides normal blood ranges. Haemoglobin (see page 81) is measured in g/dl. From the lower table, try to work out what is meant by this measurement.

b Given the information on page 81 about haemoglobin, what would be the implications for an individual who has a reduced haemoglobin level?

Haemoglobin is carried on the red blood cells, the erythrocytes. There are 5 million erythrocytes in every millilitre of blood. The average blood volume is 5–6 litres, depending on the gender and size of the individual.

Activity 26

Calculate how many blood cells there are in a person with a blood volume of 5.3 litres. If 1% of this person's red blood cells are replaced every day, how many red blood cells will need to be replaced, and therefore made, in one week?

An erythrocyte count of 3 million per millilitre would be an indication of anaemia in an individual.

quick fire

What is an erythrocyte?

Spirometer tracings

Spirometry was described on page 107 and was also referred to earlier in relation to the use of formulae (page 113). It may also provide secondary source data.

The figure below represents a spirometer reading that indicates the aspects of lung functioning described on page 107. Measurements from the spirometer reading are expressed as cubic centimetres (cm^3), or in litres. For example, 1000 cm^3 is equivalent to 1 litre.

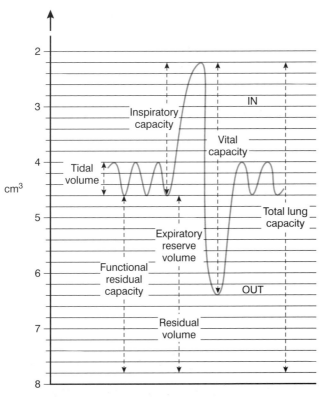

Fig. 3.31   A spirometer reading

Activity 27

Given that 1000 cm^3 is equivalent to 1 litre, how many litres would be equivalent to 2300 cm^3?

Activity 28

a From the figure above, estimate the following:
   i   tidal volume
   ii   inspiratory capacity
   iii vital capacity.
b If a man's respiratory rate is 20 per minute and his tidal volume is 300 cm^3, how much air does he breathe in one minute?

Key terms

After reading this unit you should be able to understand the following words and phrases. If you do not, go back through the unit and find out, or look them up in the Glossary.

Adrenal glands	Metabolic rate
Antidiuretic hormone (ADH)	Negative feedback
Artery	Nephron
Atherosclerosis	Neuron
Autonomic nervous system	Pancreas
Blood pressure	Peripheral nervous system
Capillary	Peristalsis
Central nervous system	Pituitary gland
Diabetes mellitus	Pulse
Diastolic	Pyrexia
Electrocardiogram	Reflex action
Electrolyte	Respiration
Endocrine system	Sphgmomanometer
Enzyme	Spirometry
Gaseous exchange	Systolic
Gonad	Thyroid gland
Haemoglobin	Tidal volume
Homeostasis	Vein
Hormone	Vital capacity
Hypothalamus	

Review questions

1 Identify two physical signs that may indicate that a client is in pain.
2 A client is sitting quietly in an armchair, after dinner. Which part of the nervous system is working to digest the meal just eaten?
3 Identify two symptoms that may be seen in a client who has an overactive thyroid gland.
4 Name two early signs that may indicate that a client could be diabetic.
5 With an older client, what may an alternative be to insulin injections, in order to control diabetes?
6 Name one sign that may indicate that a client has an inadequate fluid intake.

7 Explain why a client should be at rest when their temperature, pulse and respiration are being recorded.

8 When giving health promotion information to a client, identify two areas that could be addressed in relation to the prevention of heart disease.

9 Why is it important to take baseline observations when a client first enters a care setting?

10 How can secondary source data help a carer to gain information about a client?

Assignment

You need to carry out an investigation into the interaction of human body systems and how physiological status is measured.

To do this you must:

* investigate, make and record appropriate routine measurements to monitor two aspects of the physiological status of three different individuals
* explain how and why you have recorded the chosen measurements
* clearly explain how the immediate structures and the systems involved in each homeostatic mechanism interact to enable the body to function effectively.

Tasks

1 Find out the normal range of expected values for two routine measurements of physiological status.

2 Recognise and explain any deviations from the norm in relation to the chosen measurements.

3 Accurately interpret the data that you have obtained.

4 Recognise and describe potential health and safety risks when carrying out practical monitoring activities and explain how these can be reduced.

5 Explain the homeostatic mechanisms involved in controlling the physiological factors that you have monitored.

6 Evaluate the monitoring methods that you have chosen in order to identify any possible sources of error.

7 Explain how abnormal data would have indicated homeostatic dysfunction in relation to the chosen aspects of physiological status.

8 Analyse and clearly interpret the data obtained to show how systems are working together in order to bring about homeostasis.

9 Implement and explain procedures to ensure the accuracy of primary data collected.

10 Suggest and justify methods of improving the accuracy of collecting data to be used to monitor physiological function.

11 Relate homeostatic dysfunction to the potential care of clients within a care setting.

Get the grade

To get an **E** grade you must complete tasks 1–5

To get a **C** grade you must complete tasks 1–8

To get an **A** grade you must complete tasks 1–11

119

Key Skills	Opportunity
	You can use this Assignment to provide evidence for the following Key Skills
Application of Number N3.1, N3.2, N3.3	Record appropriate routine measurements to monitor two aspects of the physiological status of three different individuals.
Communication C3.2	Explain the homeostatic mechanisms involved in controlling the physiological factors that you have monitored.
Information Technology IT3.1, IT3.2	Investigate, make and record appropriate routine measurements to monitor two aspects of the physiological status of three different individuals.

Factors affecting human growth and development

What is covered in this unit

4.1 **Development from infancy to later adulthood**

4.2 **Skills developed through the lifespan**

4.3 **The range of factors that can influence growth and developing, including genetic, environmental and socioeconomic factors**

4.4 **Theories of development**

This unit builds upon the knowledge, skills and concepts developed in Unit Three, providing a base for exploring in depth how the human body functions. At the end of the unit you will be asked to produce a report covering the growth and human development of two individuals. This unit will guide you through what you need to know in order to put this report together successfully. If you would like to see further details of the tasks you are likely to need to carry out for assessment please refer to the end of the unit where an assignment has been set (see pages 185–186).

The unit is assessed through an external assessment. The grade you receive for that assessment will be your grade for Unit Four.

Materials you will need to complete this unit:

- *Our Healthier Nation: A Contract for Health*, Department of Health (1998), The Stationery Office
- *Report of the Independent Inquiry into Inequalities in Health*, Sir D. Acheson (1998), Department of Health, The Stationery Office
- *The Dietary and Nutritional Survey of British Adults*, The Stationery Office (1997)
- *The Health of the Nation: Low Income, Food, Nutrition and Health: Strategies for Improvement*, Department of Health (1996)
- Access to the government website where many publications on health are available – http://www.doh.gov.uk/hpss/index

4.1 Development from infancy to later adulthood

Introduction

Life is a process of change, some stability and more change. How a person changes will be determined by the significance his or her culture attributes to key events in that person's life, the person's view of themselves at any one time, in the past and in the anticipated future. Biological ageing will have an ultimate effect on a person, but the variation will be wide among individuals. The changing social norms and values will all influence how and if individuals develop.

The key life stages approach to human development illustrates the fact that as individuals age they go through periods that are separate and distinct from other periods with respect to rights, **roles**, responsibilities, capabilities and characteristics. As individuals grow older they move into and out of life periods as a result of physical changes, social changes and psychological changes. This approach illustrates that people in society develop and lose certain roles, responsibilities and privileges at certain points in their lives. Life stages break down into six phases:

- Infancy (0–2 years)
- Childhood (2–8 years)
- Puberty and adolescence (9–18 years)
- Early adulthood (19–45 years)
- Middle adulthood (46–64 years)
- Late adulthood (65+ years).

What is human development?

Human development means more than change – for a change to be developmental a movement towards a greater realisation of a person's potential to acquire new skills, increase self-awareness and clarify the person's values is needed. Development should involve a person being 'empowered', being less dependent on others and valuing the integrity of others as well as of the person. Change does not involve a progression from one theme in the life cycle to the next; development does. At critical points in a person's life the person may regress, 'ossify' or grow. Growth involves effort and risks, which can lead to greater creativity, awareness and openness to one's own potential and that of others.

Developing your potential can be seen as moving towards greater maturity. This is not merely moving from one stage to another; it also involves awareness and decision making, asking yourself where you are going and why, having control over direction and building on experiences as you achieve more of what you are truly capable of.

While growth and development are often tied together, it is useful to consider the two separately.

Growth, being related to size, can easily be represented graphically. On page 123 is a typical chart, known as a centile chart. This is used by health visitors and paediatricians to monitor children's growth. The chart shows typical growth curves for a new-born boy from 12 weeks premature to 2 years old.

The central line of the graph represents the 50th centile, or average for a child of that age, while the upper and lower lines show the boundaries within which 80% of children lie. A child's growth is plotted on such charts against the 'typical' growth curve. More detailed charts are used to assess growth against norms and identify

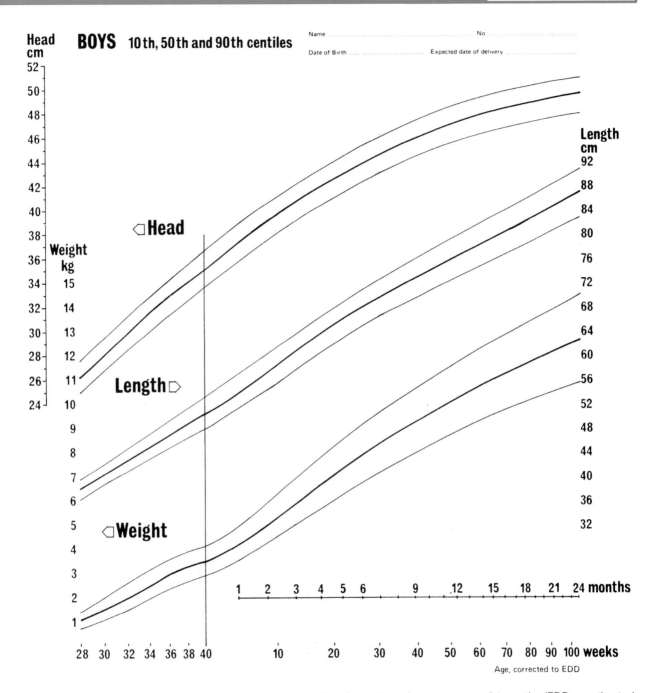

Centile charts showing typical growth curves for a new-born boy from 12 weeks premature to 24 months (EDD = estimated date of delivery)

children not following a normal pattern, particularly those in the top or bottom 3% of 'normality'. This does not mean that a child identified in this way is developing inappropriately but it does mean that the child may merit further investigation.

Similar graphs for height showing typical growth from birth to adulthood (16 years) are given in the figure on page 124. These graphs show a slight break at around 2 years because we are all slightly shorter standing up than lying down. There is a second feature occurring in girls between 11 and 12 and in boys about 2 years later. This is the growth spurt associated with puberty. Adult height is usually reached in the late teens.

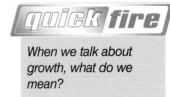

When we talk about growth, what do we mean?

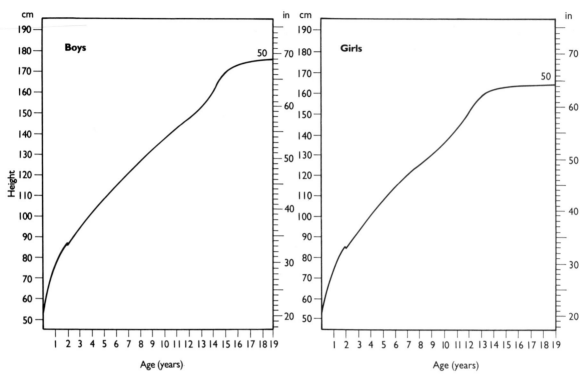

Note: The 50th centile for length is given from birth to 2 years, and for height from 2 years of age onwards.

Growth chart for boys and girls

Infancy

Infancy, more than any other developmental period, is highly reliant on physical development. Growth during this period is sequential and largely predictable. During this period, the child develops its central nervous system, which in turn allows the child to develop physical skills, such as prehension (the ability to grasp objects). The child learns to coordinate hand and eye movements and, by the age of 2, develops a preference for the use of one hand (handedness).

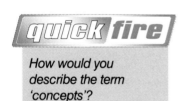

How would you describe the term 'concepts'?

The child's mental development during this period is rapid and pronounced, and is probably best described by Jean Piaget (see pages 180–182). Most important are the development of **motor skills**, anticipatory reactions and the understanding of object permanence. The child also begins to develop 'concepts', which is a mental image that represents an object or event. The sensory organs develop dramatically as the child learns to use them.

Most importantly, during the infancy period, the child begins to develop language. There is no one theory that explains the development of language, but there are three prominent theories – reinforcement theory, social learning theory and the innate theory.

The innate theory has proved to be the most influential theory of language development. The development of language is fairly predictable. At approximately 2 months, the infant begins to make 'cooing' sounds, which soon develop into 'babbling' at 6 months. The first word is likely to be spoken between 12 and 18 months, probably as a consequence of imitation. Following this, the acquisition of more words is quite rapid, as the child learns simple rules of grammar and begins to put sentences together.

Language is an organised system of symbols that humans use to communicate with one another. Every known human society has a language. This ability to use language is one of the main characteristics that separates humans from the animal kingdom. Humans are the only species that have the ability to use language. However, not every human brain is adequate for the acquisition of language.

There is no society in the world where the newborn baby immediately begins to imitate speech it hears. It is argued that in the first year the baby is maturing and developing some of the ideas that it may want to communicate using language in later years. Before a child can produce recognisable words, the child will produce sounds that will become steadily more varied and deliberate. Many children, before speaking recognisable words, pass through a stage of jargon. This is the stage at which an adult may feel sure that a child has said words but cannot make out what the words might be.

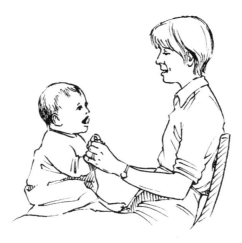

Activity 1

Talk to a mother with a very young child. Find out what sounds the child produces and discuss with the mother how she knows what the child is trying to communicate.

By the time babies are about 3 months old, if their attempts at communication are positively reinforced by adults, they will be producing a variety of sounds. The baby will vocalise – make sounds in response to others. The sounds that are reinforced are likely to continue to be used by the child, while those that are not are less likely to be repeated. By the time a baby is 6 months old, it has begun to listen and can distinguish familiar and unfamiliar voices. The baby also begins to understand some of the emotional tones in the speech heard. By 9 months, there are usually clear signs that the baby has grasped that making sounds results in action from others and by the time the baby is 12 months old, it will often show, by behaviour, that it understands a few familiar words in context. From around the first birthday, the words used are likely to be for people or things the child is most familiar with, such as 'mama', 'dada', 'cat' or 'teddy'.

Early in the second year, children begin to produce words and by the middle of the second year they start to make two-word sentences. By the end of the third year, the child is able to use a large part of the basic grammatical apparatus of the local language.

Some psychologists argue that the first 10–11 years are a critical period for language development. However, some studies indicate that the first 10 years may not be so important, as illustrated by the following two case studies.

Case study

Genie was confined to a small bedroom, harnessed to a potty seat and left, unable to move. She heard no sounds, saw no daylight, was force-fed and deprived of all stimulation until she was discovered when she was 13 years old. Essentially, she then had to learn her first language, which was constrained and lacked the spontaneity of normal speech. She had to be taught the rules of language long after a normal child would have picked them up, and it was more difficult for her than for a younger child.

However, the fact was that Genie did learn a language, which tends to contradict the argument of those who say that the first 10 years are critical in language and development.

Biology is critical for language acquisition, but a number of situations have made it quite clear that learning opportunities and environment are also important. There are a number of sad cases of children being deprived of stimulation that illustrate this.

Case study

Isabelle was found in America in the 1930s, hidden away, with no contact with anyone but her mother, who could neither hear nor speak. Isabelle was just over 6 years old when she was found, and she could not talk. After care and training she began to vocalise and 2 years later her speech could not easily be distinguished from the speech of other children of the same age.

Certain groups of children lag behind others in their speech development. Middle-class children have been shown to talk more and produce a greater variety of vowels and consonants than children from working-class backgrounds. Children also seem to have a tendency to develop language in some form or other. This is illustrated by the case of four children, all deaf from birth, who developed sign language, including grammar, even though their parents had no knowledge of sign language.

Activity 2

How important do you think contact with other humans is for the development of language? (Look back at the case study of Genie.) Discuss your views with your class colleagues.

What is social cognition?

During the infancy period, children are wholly dependent on their family. Through interactions with the family, children develop a **self-concept**, and also begin to understand something of the world around them. This awareness is sometimes referred to as social cognition. Children develop an attachment to their caregivers. The nature of that attachment has produced a huge body of research and many theoretical perspectives.

Another important development during this period is the acquisition of gender role. Gender role is a set of socially generated expectations about how men and women should behave. Parents have a major influence on the child's gender-role development.

What is meant by the term gender role?

The child's emotions are relatively basic, compared to the more complex emotions seen later in life. Infant emotional responses include laughter, crying, fear and anxiety, and anger and aggression.

Much development in the infant period depends upon play. Through play, the child learns to interact with its environment, so the nature of infant play is often exploratory and manipulative.

All of the theoretical perspectives found later in this unit address the infant period in more detail. In the appendix, you will find a table the first part of which summarises development from the ages of 0 to 3.

Childhood

Development during childhood is very rapid, and much of this development has been thoroughly researched. By the age of 5, birth length will have increased twice, and weight five times. Motor skills develop as a consequence of developing coordination skills and muscular growth, and by the age of 6 these skills are quite refined. However, during the middle years of childhood physical growth stabilises, with the child achieving approximately 90% of his or her adult height.

Piaget (see page 180) proposed that, in early childhood, mental development is characterised by egocentrism. This means that children are self-centred and cannot perceive any point of view other than their own. This is evident in the child's thought processes, and most importantly in the ways in which the child socialises, mostly through play. Also, children begin to handle concepts more effectively. Language development continues throughout early childhood, with the development of the ability to create multiword sentences. However, the rate of language development is greatly affected by socioeconomic influences, such as **intelligence**, gender and whether the child is bilingual or not.

What is meant by the term egocentrism?

As children reach middle childhood, they move through Piaget's stage of intuitive thought and into the stage of concrete operations. The essence of this stage is the knowledge that object properties always remain the same. Children develop the ability to categorise shapes, sizes and quantities, hence becoming capable of classifying concepts. The child's ability to process information notably improves.

By the age of 11, the average child has a reading vocabulary of nearly 50 000 words, although abstract word meanings are still difficult. Nevertheless, children learn to express themselves better and begin to understand and use the rules of grammar.

During early childhood, the child's gender role will begin to be formed, being influenced by peers, parents and play behaviours. This becomes even more deeply-rooted during school years. There is also a shift from physical displays of anger to vocal displays. Interaction with the family becomes more influential, with parental style of control deeply affecting the child's personality. Sibling relationships also influence personality development.

In middle childhood, the child's emotions become more sophisticated and expressed in more acceptable ways. The child also develops concepts of moral behaviour, which is dependent on the child's **cognitive skills**. Theorists such as Piaget and Kohlberg both emphasised the importance of moral development.

Social development is clearly affected by interactions with peer groups and family, but in more recent years there has been a great deal of interest on the effects of media such as television and films on children's development.

You will read more about the importance of childhood development in section 4.4 on Piaget, Freud and Erikson.

Puberty and adolescence

Adolescence describes the period of time during which a person passes into adulthood. It encompasses physiological, emotional and social development, a stage where the experiences of childhood will be re-evaluated and re-formulated in preparation for the new status of adolescence. In western culture adolescence normally coincides with the growth spurt and physiological changes of puberty. In other cultures this rite of passage is determined by age and is not necessarily related to an individual's physical development.

During puberty the sex hormones (gonadotrophins) are secreted and bring about the characteristic changes. Early signs in boys are axillary sweating in the armpits and groin, enlargement of the testes and growth of the penis. Later, facial, underarm and pubic hair develops and the voice deepens. In girls, breasts develop and axillary sweating commences. Later, there is the onset of menstruation (menarche), although few if any eggs are released in the first year. As with boys, underarm and pubic hair grows, although the distribution pattern of pubic hair differs between the sexes.

Changes in the composition of sweat, together with changes in hormones, can lead adolescent boys and girls to develop spots, which can develop into acne. While this is common, it should not be seen as acceptable, and is treatable. Acne has a secondary effect in that it often affects behaviour at a time when there is rapid psychological development.

Some of the issues related to adolescence are psychosocial in nature. It is a time when an individual's identity becomes established and moral, social and personal responsibilities are developed. Adolescent people often challenge accepted norms in order to test and establish their own mores (ideas of right and wrong). This is occurring at the same time as sexual awareness is developing and so establishment of intimate relationships, sometimes involving sexual experimentation, occurs. Unfortunately, this can lead to unwanted pregnancy, the prevention of which may well reflect the quality of learning and support given to the adolescent in the rite of passage to adulthood.

The 'classic' theory of adolescence sees the adolescent as a rebellious person rejecting parental authority. The adolescent is seen as substituting the authority of parents for that of the peer group. Some argue that the adolescent passes through unstable periods that are an inevitable part of development. Others argue that this emotional instability is due to the physical bodily changes that occur during adolescence.

Sorenson (1973) puts forward the view that boys, in particular, experience stress as a result of biological changes and developing sexual awareness, which produces tension, anxiety and a likelihood of confrontation with authority. The 'classic' theory has three main components:

- storm and stress
- identity crisis
- the generation gap.

Activity 3

Discuss with your colleagues the feelings that you experienced during your adolescence. Did you all experience the same feelings or experiences? Is it true that adolescence is a period of rebellion?

Key Skills

You can use Activity 3 to provide evidence for Key Skills Communication C3.2.

Psychoanalysts view adolescence as a period of emotional upheaval that stems from the sudden eruption of genital needs during puberty and the need to work through many of the sexual conflicts that have been encountered during childhood. Freud (1968) argued that this re-working of old conflicts results in mood swings from elation to suicidal depression. The balance within the personality of the individual becomes disturbed.

Erikson (1968) states that puberty and adolescence is a period of identity versus role confusion in which the individual has to develop a consistent sense of identity. Erikson believes that rapid body growth disturbs the previous trust in the body and mastery of its functions that were enjoyed in childhood. The individual has to grow into his or her new body. Erikson argues that adolescence is one period in a series of developmental stages that span the individual's life. The unsuccessful resolution of conflicts in earlier stages could produce lasting consequences by leaving unsettled conflicts to interfere with current psychosocial development. Healthy resolution of conflicts means that the individual is able to adjust to the demands of adolescence while still retaining a strong sense of personal identity.

Any conflict with parents during adolescence tends to centre on such things as clothes and hairstyle, homework and time of getting home at night. The majority of parents and adolescents report harmonious family relationships. Coleman (1990) sees adolescence as a time when individuals are active agents of their own development, managing the transitions of adolescence, choosing whether or not to confront parents, seeking or not seeking the acceptance of peers, or resisting the persuasion of others. As adolescents exercise choice they are not overwhelmed by the stresses of everything happening at once.

Early and middle adulthood

During adulthood most people reach a peak of performance. Skeletal growth ends in the late teens or early twenties and physiologically a person is also then at a peak. Intellectually, this peak may occur later and social development may also take longer.

From the age of about 30 years signs of ageing begin to show and physiological changes indicate a slowing down of many processes. This is often associated with increase in the bulk of adipose tissue and a loss of elasticity in connective tissues, resulting in the development of 'middle-aged spread' and wrinkles. Skeletal changes mean that joint strength and flexibility are diminished; cartilage becomes less resilient.

There is a clear stage of development in women (at any time from their mid-30s to late 50s) at which their natural ability to reproduce ends. During this period, called the menopause, the ovaries reduce production of the sex hormones. As a result, egg release is reduced and menstruation becomes irregular. Eventually, ovulation and menstruation cease. As we have already seen, these changes have significant effects on the skeleton. The reduction of oestrogen production also means that the balance between oestrogen and adrenal testosterone alters. An effect of this is often observed as increased facial hair. Changes at the cellular level are also noticeable. Some cells, such as nerve cells, die and are not renewable. Others function less well and accumulate toxic metabolites and other substances. Environmental effects can lead to damage to chromosomes, giving rise to gene mutations that occasionally lead to abnormal cell growth and cancers.

The range of individual differences is enormous and no physical change during adulthood can be exactly predicted from chronological age – the one possible expectation being grey hair (Fozard et al., 1972). Longevity and youthfulness run in families and are more class-related than age-related. People from lower socio-economic groups tend to age faster and die sooner than those from middle and upper socioeconomic groups; they also suffer from poorer health throughout their lives.

Physical development in adulthood

- Maximum height is attained at the beginning of adulthood
- Strength peaks at about 30 years, after which the muscles weaken somewhat, unless maintained by exercise
- Manual dexterity is greatest at 33 years of age
- Sight diminishes throughout adulthood
- There is a gradual hearing loss after 20, especially among men
- Sensitivity to smell and taste decreases and diminishes after 45
- Adults get fewer acute illnesses and more chronic ones than children
- Appearance alters at middle age – hair goes grey, skin coarsens and darkens, wrinkles appear
- Sexual potency reaches its peak in late adolescence for men and the mid-twenties for women
- Women cease menstruation at 40–50 years of age.

Later adulthood

Ageing may be defined as all the regular changes that occur in biologically mature individuals as they advance in chronological age (Birren and Renner, 1977). This change involves structural changes in the body and also the adjustment and behaviour of the individual. There are several important theories of ageing, for example:

- the phenomenological theory
- the age stratification theory
- the labelling theory
- the disengagement theory

- the activity theory
- the personality theory
- the subculture theory
- the role theory.

Some of these will be examined below.

As people age their roles change and new roles are added. The major role losses that characterise old age come with retirement, widowhood and institutionalisation. As a rule, the majority of retired people never return to the workforce as full-time workers and most widows do not remarry (Blau, 1981). When people suffer physical decline in later life they also lose roles, especially when they have to enter residential care. The types of role loss experienced by elderly people underlie the basis for two important theories of ageing, namely, the activity theory and disengagement theory.

When people suffer physical decline in later life they also lose roles, especially when they have to enter residential care

The disengagement theory

This theory has been persistent and controversial, emerging in the early 1960s as the first formal theory to try and explain the ageing process. Since then it has gone through a number of refinements. The approach is basically functionalist; in other words, for society to function properly, the 'old' must be gradually phased out of important roles or replaced by the 'young', thus causing minimal disruption to society when they die. Cumming and Henry (1961), the originators of the theory, contended that the individual and society prepare for death through a gradual process during which the individual and society withdraw from each other.

This theory is based on the tenet that the process of disengagement is inevitable but will vary from individual to individual because of differences in personality, physical or mental health, or opportunity. Life satisfaction for elderly people is connected with a reduction in the number and importance of their roles, and this suits the society that the old person lives in. So happiness in old age entails elderly people recognising the fact that they are no longer young and that there are more competent young people to fill their roles.

Activity 4

You have been appointed the manager of a residential establishment for elderly people. You believe in the disengagement theory of ageing. How would you organise the regime in the establishment to put the theory into practice?

It is supposed that both society and the elderly person concerned contribute to the disengagement process, although the level of 'voluntariness' may vary from individual to individual. The process is gradual and the theory supposes that disengagement is the norm, demonstrated by mandatory retirement laws.

The disengagement theory has been criticised because research findings have been contradictory. The theory is simplistic, as not all elderly people experience ageing this way. It can also be seen as a self-fulfilling prophecy, in that many elderly people have a lack of opportunity to be active because of health or economic factors.

The activity theory

This theory originated as the antithesis of disengagement theory, although the basic ideas had been postulated for some time. Activity theory is seen as the 'golden years' concept of ageing. The theory claims that to be happy in old age the individual must keep active. Although society withdraws from the individual, this is against the individual's desire. To minimise the effects of this withdrawal the elderly person must keep active.

Those who believe this theory state that if roles and relationships are lost they must be replaced by suitable alternatives. If roles are not replaced the activity level will fall and as a result so will the quality of life. Activity theorists acknowledge that this is a simplistic theory and is unlikely to explain the behaviour of all elderly people.

Mrs L has the typical 'stoop' of osteoporosis. She lost 15 cm in height and is now being successfully treated with HRT

Those who criticise activity theory point to findings that suggest that a few stable meaningful relationships are the key, not necessarily high levels of involvement.

To minimise the effects of society's withdrawal the individual must keep active

The personality theory

This theory attempts to explain the inconsistencies between activity and disengagement theory. The proponent of this theory (Havighurst, 1968) argues that activity and disengagement theory are inadequate to explain the research findings on ageing. Havighurst suggests that it is not the amount of activity but rather the personality type of the individual that is crucial. Different personality types need different levels of activity and involvement to achieve satisfaction. Eight basic personality types have been identified that encompass at one end 'reorganisers' (activity theory) and at the other 'disengagers' (disengagement theory).

Health rather than wealth becomes more of a status factor as one gets older

The subculture theory

Rose (1965) put forward the theory that elderly people form a subculture that defines and gives direction to their behaviour. The subculture has developed as a result of the growing numbers and percentage of the elderly population in society.

- This subculture has its own values, ideas and beliefs and now has an impact on society and the individual old person.
- Elderly people are 'excluded' by society, through retirement, ill health and the emphasis on youth. The elderly subculture has its own characteristics, different from the young.
- This developing 'age consciousness' has united elderly people as a group, which has led to the recognition of 'the elderly' by society as a 'peer group'.
- There are subcultures within the subculture based upon wealth, ethnic background, environment and health. These affect status and self-image, so that in old age 'health' becomes more of a status factor than wealth.

The role theory

A number of writers believe that behaviour in old age can be explained through role theory. A role is behaviour expected from individuals who occupy certain positions, e.g. father, mother, social worker or doctor. These roles call for certain types of behaviour that we should or should not be involved in. One major factor that determines how we view the different roles in society is the development of our personality and the process of **socialisation**. The role is also influenced by our expectations of self and society's expectations.

The implications of role theory for elderly people are that they will behave:

- generally within expected ranges (role prescription/expectation)
- individually differently from others (individual interpretation)
- differently with individuals according to their roles (e.g. daughter, doctor, social worker, child, manager, etc.).

Goffman (1961) put forward the proposition that, whenever we enter into a social interaction, we commonly seek information about those with whom we are interacting. We ask questions about what the other person looks like, observe their mannerisms and speech patterns, and form opinions about occupation, status and other variables. This information-gathering is the process that allows us to make a judgement about the situation and the other person, which in turn allows us to know how to behave in the interaction.

Goffman believes that we all have the ability to put forward any number of selves. The self is something that is malleable and can assume a number of different forms or roles. After analysing the situation we present the role (self) that we consider appropriate to the situation. Role theory can be used to explain the wide fluctuations in the behaviour of elderly people.

You can use Activity 5 to provide evidence for Key Skills Communication C3.2 and C3.3.

Activity 5

Discuss Goffman's theory in relation to residents in homes for elderly people. List the reasons how and why seemingly independent people can become dependent after some time in care.

The labelling theory

This theory focuses on the processes by which some people label other members of society as deviant. According to labelling theorists, people's labels rather than actions are important. One of the basic tenets of labelling theory is that through the process individuals are forced into acting out specific behaviours.

Sometimes a particular facet becomes dominant in how others see or relate to us

When other people give us a label such as 'old', 'senile' or 'confused', this has a significant impact on how we are seen by others. This in turn affects our identity or behaviours. Sometimes a particular facet becomes dominant in how others see or relate to us. For example, if people are labelled 'senile', this label will lead to their behaviour being seen in those terms (senile) and interpreted as such. The 'senile' reinforcing behaviour will be noticed and enhanced. People will respond to the 'senile' person in terms of the label. As a consequence, the person accepts the label, begins to see him or herself as deviant (senile) and then behaves in accordance with the label.

To integrate and relate effectively to his or her environment the person has to behave in a way consistent with the label 'senile'. The label proves to be a self-fulfilling prophecy.

You will read more about Goffman in the section on symbolic interactionism on pages 182–184.

The age-stratification theory

Just as most societies are stratified by social class they are also stratified by age, race, sex and ethnicity. Riley (1972) argues that age, like social class, divides society into categories on the basis of wealth, prestige and power. This theory is still in its formative stages. It puts forward the tenet that age is the determinant of behaviour because:

* it may limit an individual's ability to perform certain roles (biological, legal, social or sexual)
* society allocates rights and responsibilities, roles and privileges on the basis of age.

In essence, society is seen as being divided into age strata, each of which has a defined set of rights, roles, obligations and opportunities. As individuals move from one age stratum to another they acquire the expectations and roles of that new stratum. Each age stratum contributes to society in different ways from the others. Different sanctions exist and we are continually being socialised into the appropriate behaviour of the new age stratum.

As people move through the different age strata so individuals' attitudes, values and aspirations change in a way that is appropriate to their age stratum. In each age stratum we have an experience of life different from that in the others.

Summary of the stages of human development

Infancy

0–2 months

- Child mainly behaves in an instinctive, reflexive way – cries for food or if in pain.
- Begins to smile, may show interest in the world around.
- Probably no clear-cut attachment to a single individual.

2–8 months

- Child now coos and babbles.
- May show preference for one adult over another; vision improves; can sit up and reach for things.

8–18 months

- Child learns to crawl and walk.
- Can use a series of actions to gain what it wants.
- Speaks words and half sentences.
- Will show attachment to other caregivers and shows an interest in other children.

18 months–2 years

- More complex language.
- Transition time – possible disruption of sleeping and eating patterns.

Childhood

2–6 years

- Motor skills (walking, using hands, etc.) are refined.
- Co-ordination improves, so that games of bat and ball become fun.
- In terms of thinking, the child can use words or images to stand for things, develops a gender awareness, can put things into groups and can take other people's perspectives into account.
- Strong attachments to primary caregivers, especially if under stress (child always calls for Mummy or Daddy if frightened or under pressure).
- Play choice may begin to be with the same gender and be for traditionally gender-related toys – little boys may want trains, etc.
- Early friendships formed, evidence of sharing, generosity and aggression.
- Explores further from own base – growing independence.

6–12 years

- Physical growth steady until puberty. Girls may see the beginning of puberty.
- Gross motor skills improve – mountain bike for Christmas!
- Gross motor skills: riding a bicycle, climbing, jumping, etc.

- In terms of thinking, 'child' can subtract, order, add up, etc. Can perform tasks in the mind, e.g. reading and mental arithmetic.
- Friends or peers become important, usually same gender. Individual friendships become more important. Attachments to parents less obvious, but still very much needed. Continues to absorb gender roles.

Adolescence

12–18 years

- Puberty is completed in this period. Increase in physical strength and speed.
- Most adolescents can reason morally – what is right and wrong, and why.
- Need to seek out future career, as well as interest in opposite gender.
- A lot of conflict as peer pressure mounts, possibly against parental influence.
- Questioning of taught values, roles, ideas, mood swings, depression, elation.

18–21 years

- No significant physical changes.
- In relationships, idea of giving and taking is consolidated – mature response.
- Understanding that identity is a complex product of past experiences and background.
- Intimate relationships; possibly new self-concept through work; religious and political views may be worked through.

Adulthood

22–24 years

- Physically most people function at the maximum before the end of this stage; similarly with mental performance.
- Socially – possible marriage, parenthood, work peak.

40–65 years

- Physically and mentally, possibly some loss of abilities.
- May be demands from children and ageing parents.
- Marriage may be reassessed; friendships may increase in importance.
- Mid-life physical and emotional upheavals will occur in the early part of this stage.

Old age

65 years +

- Further decline physically and mentally.
- May experience loss of social contacts and gradual withdrawing or 'disengagement', cutting off from wider issues.
- Retirement: readjustment to post-retirement phase.
- Family may be more significant in terms of mutual help.

4.2 Skills developed through the lifespan

Language skills

As a community, we negotiate the meaning of words. This makes 'self' a difficult term to define. Much of its meaning will derive from personal experiences that are difficult to communicate and agree upon. The term 'self' refers to the way people would like to describe themselves, i.e. the kind of people they think they are.

One way of finding out how people see themselves is to ask, 'Who am I?'. This question usually produces two main categories of response:

- social roles
- personality traits.

We are continually measuring these traits and social roles against our own self-concept and seeing how they 'fit' with it. Each of us entertains a notion of our own separateness from others and relies on the essential privacy of our own consciousness. This idea of self-concept is wide-ranging. We know roughly how we would behave in a particular situation, what music we like, what clothes we wear, what food we like, what people we like – all these add up to what we call our 'self'. This self develops over the years. We change our likes and dislikes, and all our experiences contribute to our self-concept. As we grow during childhood, we develop a clearer sense of self, which includes the ways that we can influence the environment.

Gradually, the self-concept develops and forms a basis for our interaction with the rest of our environment. We extend the notion of 'me' into the notion of 'my world'. We think of events as more or less relevant to us. We distinguish between what concerns us and what does not concern us. In this way we can use the phrase 'my situation' to indicate the boundaries of our important experiences and the ways in which the various parts of it relate to make up our personal world.

Activity 6

Think about the changes in your personality that you have experienced over the years. Have these experiences contributed to the way you behave today?

Argyle (1967) argued that four main factors affect the way an individual's self-concept develops:

- other people's reactions to us
- comparisons we make with other people
- the roles we play
- the identifications we make.

Getting to know ourselves is a developmental process; it is something we learn in the same way that we learn to walk or to relate to others. Underlying our notions about ourselves are theories called 'trait theory'. Trait theory argues that there are, in each of us, characteristics that differentiate us from others – the notion that we are 'bad tempered', for instance, or that other people are 'anxious' or 'excitable'.

To try to understand ourselves is not simply an interesting pastime, it is a necessity of life. To plan for the future, we have to make choices and be able to anticipate our behaviour. This makes self-knowledge a necessity. In some situations, it is simple to anticipate what we would do, but others are far more difficult. How could you deal with a difficult manager? Could you live with another person in marriage? Could you live by yourself after living with a family for many years? The stranger the situation, the more threatening the prospect becomes and the more we realise that some degree of self-change is necessary. The more self-change that is necessary, the more we must rely upon our understanding of ourselves, our character and our potential.

At times of change we are acutely aware of the dangers of that change and may take a rigid approach to ward off any change in ourselves. We do not lightly abandon our theory of what we are, since doing so might threaten our identity. We may destroy a close relationship in order to 'prove' that we are independent, or some teachers may 'prove' that students are stupid in order to show that they themselves are clever.

Activity 7

Have you had any experience in the past that might now help you to deal with a client exhibiting challenging behaviour? Discuss it with your class colleagues and explain why you would find it helpful.

Key Skills

You can use Activity 7 to provide evidence for Key Skills Communication C3.2.

Personality development

As with other dimensions, although generalisations can be made, the range of individual variations is so great that it is dangerous to make assumptions about any individuals on the basis of their age. Bearing this statement in mind, some generalisations are given below:

- People change 50% of their interests (hobbies, vocational) between adulthood and middle age (Kelly, 1955).
- Middle-aged people (45–55) are more sensitive to themselves and aware of their ability and responsibility to make things happen for themselves.

Maximum height is attained at the beginning of adulthood

- Those in their middle age restructure time in terms of time-left-to-live rather than time-since-birth.
- Middle-aged people place more importance on reflection, introspection and the structuring and restructuring of experience (Neugarten, 1977).
- **Self-esteem** generally seem to increase with years.
- People who cope well with early life stresses seem to be able to cope well with later ones.

The analysis of adult development by Erikson (1951) reveals a richness and orderliness in the psychological stages and transitions of the adult life beginning between the ages of 20 and 65. Erikson proposes an eight-stage progression over the whole life span, each stage being characterised by a different crucial issue that is either resolved successfully or not. Failure to so impedes all later development. The first stages are infancy and childhood; the last four, beginning with adolescence, are:

- identity versus role definition
- intimacy versus isolation
- general activity versus stagnation
- ego integrity versus despair.

Selecting a mate

Some researchers (e.g. Gruen, 1964) have found some support for the sequential nature of these stages but found them unrelated to age, sex or social class. Havighurst (1953), on the other hand, proposes a universal stage theory involving developmental tasks. The tasks for early adulthood are:

- selecting a mate
- learning to live with that mate
- starting a family
- rearing children
- managing a home
- getting started in an occupation
- taking on civic responsibilities
- finding a congenial social group.

In later adulthood the tasks are:

- achieving civic and social responsibility
- establishing and maintaining an economic standard of living
- assisting teenage children to become responsible and happy adults
- engaging in appropriate leisure activities

- relating to one's spouse as a person
- accepting the physiological changes of middle age
- adjusting to ageing parents.

Engaging in appropriate leisure activities

Some theorists, like Havighurst, maintain that certain attitudes, behaviour and problems are highly correlated with chronological age. Others, like Neugarten, believe that it is the nature of the individual's experience that determines behaviour, etc. For example, it is not being 40 years old that causes people problems but the fact that reaching 40 has been emotionally charged by the culture – the person concerned may have been married for 20 years, have children leaving home, his or her career may have peaked and parents may be dying.

Collin (1977) concludes that the mid-life crisis is not a developmental stage of life through which everyone must pass, rather that it results from:

1 ineffective adjustment to the normal stresses of growth and transition in middle age
2 the reaction of a particularly vulnerable person to the normal stresses of growth and transition in middle age
3 attempted adjustment to the stresses of 'abnormal' growth and transition in middle age (Collin, 1977).

The mid-life crisis clearly manifests itself in extreme patterns of response to stress denial, depression, anger, regression and acting out.

Emotional development

One of the most common causes of illness and disease is stress. It is a major part of our everyday lives. Most of us realise that too much stress can be harmful; it can lead to acute or chronic ill-health. The term 'stress' is used in two distinct ways:

- external stressors – conditions in the world around us that induce feelings of discomfort, tension and pressure
- internal stressors – internally induced reactions.

A biological indication of stress is an increased level of the hormone adrenaline in the blood. This hormone is naturally released in preparation for fight or flight. It prepares the body by increasing the heart rate and breathing rate, and by increasing the production of muscle glycogen. The muscles are made ready for action. There is a heightened awareness as the senses are made more acute.

These reactions are natural and help in times of major emergency. However, many lifestyles now involve a constant background level of stress. There is a constant release of adrenaline at low levels, which keeps the muscles in a state of readiness without allowing them to actually make use of the heightened levels of glycogen. Over time this affects the heart muscle and also psychological wellbeing. A second, less well-understood effect is weakening of the immune system. People suffering from stress have decreased resistance to infection and take longer to recover from illnesses and other traumas.

There are now many people teaching stress management to employers, employees and the general public. They teach strategies for relaxation and reducing current physiological stress, as well as techniques to prevent high stress levels from developing. In supporting the promotion of wellbeing, it becomes important to identify the causes of stress and to develop strategies to deal with them.

It must be emphasised that some level of stress can be useful. It would be difficult to imagine an examination without pre-exam nerves, which can help performance. It is the long-term effects of a constant drip-feed of adrenaline as a result of prolonged stress that are physiologically and psychologically damaging.

Case study

Stress in the health service

In the latter half of the 1980s there was a dispute between two factions in a mental health unit in the Midlands. The dispute was over the setting up of community-based mental health care. One group was very strongly in favour of moving patients away from the hospital environment while the other wished to establish mental health units within general hospitals. The former group was advocating the development of care in the community some time before the ideas were put forward in the NHS and Community Care Act 1990.

There were two consultants on the anti-community-based-care side and one consultant, a head of psychology and the head of social work on the pro-community side. Acting as a neutral referee was the unit general manager. There then ensued a battle of wills that went on both in and outside meetings. The different factions were constantly pushing forward their own views and trying to 'sabotage' the other's position.

As a result of all of this, the participants were under a great deal of stress for over 2 years. The final decision was to set up a mental health team in the district general hospital and another in the community. Thus, neither viewpoint had prevailed and the original mental health unit had been split into two.

The effects on the personnel were more marked. Of the three consultants, one had a heart attack and two had nervous breakdowns. The head of psychology had a heart attack and the head of social work developed myalgic encephalomyelitis (ME). The unit general manager, who was neutral, also suffered a stroke. While none of these incidents can be proved to be a direct result of the conflict, all have been identified as linked to persistent high stress levels. It is reasonable to assume that the constant stress of the conflict contributed to the ill-health described.

Ⓠ *How might the participants have attempted to reduce their stress levels, given that their individual views were strongly held and, in their eyes, professionally justified?*

Stress: a definition

There is a potential for stress when an environmental situation is perceived as presenting a demand that threatens to exceed a person's capabilities and resources for meeting it.

In the 19th century, the emphasis of research into the causes of disease was on 'science'. Causes were sought in agents such as germs and pathological processes. As a result, social or psychological explanations for the causes of disease (such as stress) were ignored because they were unscientific.

Freud was the first to argue that certain illnesses could be explained in terms of the individual's response to internal psychological conflict. This anxiety is an emotional state that involves feelings of uneasiness, fear or apprehension. According to Freud, we develop a number of defence mechanisms to counteract this anxiety. Stress-related diseases such as ulcers, skin diseases and asthma began to be seen as the body's expression of unconscious tensions that the individual could not deal with in any other manner. We now know that psychological stress produces vulnerability to a wide range of diseases.

Measuring stress

Estimating stress is one approach to the examination of the impact of key life events and the extent to which stress may contribute to subsequent illness. In 1967, Holmes and Rahe published a table of stress factors (see below). It attempted to express, in quantitative terms, the amount of stress involved in a range of specified key life events. Events near the top of the list are highly stressful and often seem to produce adverse effects upon health. Those events near the bottom of the list are only mildly stressful and have less impact upon personal health. A score of 300 points or more, accumulated over a 12-month period, is considered high and a strong indication of ill-health. Most people can cope with up to 150 points over a 12-month period.

The impact of key life events

Life event (in the last 2 years)	Crisis unit score
Death of husband or wife	100
Divorce	73
Marital separation	65
Jail sentence	63
Illness or injury	53
Marriage	50
Loss of job	47
Retirement	45
Pregnancy	40
Sex problem	39
Major change of work	39
Large mortgage taken on	31
Starting school	26
Leaving school	26
Change in sleeping habits	16
Major change in eating pattern	15
Holiday	15
Christmas	12
Minor violation of the law	11

143

Job-related stress

Many jobs are more stressful than others. The most stressful occupations are:

- Advertising executive
- Journalist
- Actor
- Dentist
- Doctor
- Social worker
- Pilot
- Police officer
- Nurse
- Miner
- Construction worker.

The least stressful occupations include:

- Banker
- Nature conservancy worker
- Nursery nurse
- Beauty therapist
- Biologist
- Linguist.

Student nurses, for example, find certain aspects of their job more stressful than others: top of the list is care of the dying, conflict with other nurses, insecurity about competence and fear of failure. Engineers, on the other hand, put wasting time and interpersonal conflict as the top stressors.

Some jobs are more stressful than others

Reaction to stress

Events have different effects on different people. Certain changes in life, such as divorce, leaving school or change in residence may ultimately reduce stress, as such events may improve the quality of our lives. Why do some people readily succumb to the stress produced by traumatic life events? Why are some people quite resistant to this factor and continue to function effectively in the face of one personal disaster after another? What factors account for these differences in susceptibility? People who believe that they are in control of their lives and those with a sense of purpose and meaning seem not to let themselves be affected by stress factors. Those who perceive change as a challenge or an opportunity for development rather than a threatening burden are also less likely to suffer from stress.

Activity 8

a List as many situations or activities that cause you, as a student, stress.
b What factors in a person's lifestyle would lead you to believe that person is capable of dealing with intense levels of stress or pressure?

You can use Activity 8 to provide evidence for Key Skills Communication C3.2.

There are a number of times when we can go through overwhelming changes in our lives, such as:

- marriage
- giving birth
- unemployment
- starting a new job
- the loss of someone close
- the loss of a limb
- starting university or college.

These key life events can often cause us anxiety and stress. During these times of major life changes, the individual has to come to terms with a new status. Such changes force people to become aware of what they have lost – the old patterns and relationships. The anxiety that may be experienced can be influenced by a range of personal and social factors, but may be less where the change is expected and shared with others. Ceremonies, such as weddings and funerals, may serve to reduce anxiety by offering a formal, ritualistic set of responses.

Activity 9

List the reasons why you think that many societies have 'rites of passage' such as funerals and wedding ceremonies.

Bereavement and loss

A most devastating form of stress experienced by individuals is bereavement – a state characterised by loss. The most frequent, and obvious, example of loss is that occasioned by the death of a close relative or friend, but people may be bereaved by other losses, such as loss of job, loss of status, loss of a limb or loss of a home.

145

The bereaved person may have to learn new skills

Studies have shown that individuals who have lost a close relative have a much increased risk of sickness or mortality themselves as a result. In a study of widowers, Murrey Parkes (1975) observed an increased mortality, usually from heart disease, for 6 months following the loss. Men seem more vulnerable than women to ill-health or death following the loss of a close relative. It has been suggested that people become more vulnerable to stress following such loss because of the pathological effects of bereavement due to the loss of meaning in their lives and severe disruption to assumptions about the world created by the death. These effects combine to undermine basic coping abilities in the individual, including resistance to illness.

Coping with bereavement and loss

Grief is the individual's response to bereavement. It is a complex response, which may include 'symptoms' such as:

- fatigue
- anxiety
- loss of appetite
- withdrawal
- depression
- guilt
- sleep disturbance.

Other symptoms include:

- searching behaviour
- suicidal thoughts and panic
- heightened vulnerability to physical illness.

Stages of grief

The complexity and stress of grief is now appreciated by all professionals. Although everyone's experience of grief is unique, several studies suggest that most people experience a number of stages; these are also associated with people's reactions to serious illness. The most commonly observed stages are as follows.

Stage one: denial
Sometimes the bereaved person will behave as if nothing has happened, they may not believe that the dead person has died. Denial may be expressed by keeping all the dead person's belongings ready for use, or alternatively getting rid of everything that reminds them of the deceased.

Stage two: shock

The second stage begins when the bereaved person begins to feel the pain of loss. Some people may cry, but others may feel anger at the dead person for dying, or guilty for not having prevented the death. The bereaved may also feel a sense of rejection by the dead person.

Stage three: acceptance

The acceptance of the situation usually happens after a short period. Attending the funeral, for example, is part of accepting the loss and facing the pain of carrying on without the dead person. Once the bereaved person has accepted the reality of the situation, the person can begin to live life again. Most people will not return to their former levels of functioning – they may move on to a new level where the pain and loss of grieving are incorporated. Bereaved people may need to learn new skills: cooking, looking after themselves or living on their own.

The length of time that a person spends in each stage of grief will depend upon the circumstances of the loss, the relationship that they had with the animal or person they have lost and the cultural and religious background of the grieving person.

Most people agree that is desirable for the bereaved to give way to grief. Grief has to be worked through; if it is not, the bereaved person will continue to have troubles of some sort. The problems must be brought out into the open and confronted. The bereaved person should be helped and supported at his or her own pace until the loss begins to be accepted.

Activity 10

a How would you support someone who has lost a close relative?
b How would you try to alleviate the effects of stress on a bereaved person?

Loss can occur at any age, but we are only now beginning to appreciate the effect of loss in old age. Many people remain remarkably fit into extreme old age and stay strong and mentally agile. However, there are many losses that affect elderly people, including:

* loss of status and defined role as a result of retirement
* loss of income as a result of retirement
* loss of health and bodily function, leading to loss of mobility and independence
* loss of sexual function
* loss of company, e.g. spouse, friends or pets
* loss of independence and home by admission to a residential home or hospital
* loss of life.

Coping with change and transition

Despite the possibility of positive outcomes, change is often resisted by individuals. Resistance to change, or the thought of the implications of change, appears to be a common phenomenon. People seem to be naturally wary of change.

Resistance to change

Resistance to change may take a number of forms:

* *Selective perception* – An individual's own perception of stimuli presents a unique picture of the 'real' world and can result in selective perception. This

can lead to a biased view of a particular situation, which fits comfortably into the individual's own perception of reality. For example, lecturers may have a view of students as irresponsible and therefore oppose any attempts to involve them in decision-making about their own learning or course organisation.

- *Habit* – Individuals tend to respond to situations in an established and accustomed manner. Habits may serve as a source of comfort and security. Proposed changes to habits may be resisted.
- *Inconvenience or loss of freedom* – People will resist change if it is perceived as likely to directly or indirectly make life more difficult or reduce their freedom.
- *Security in the past* – People tend to find a sense of security in the past. In times of frustration or difficulty, individuals may reflect on the past. They may wish to retain old and comfortable ways.
- *Fear of the unknown* – Situations that confront people with the unknown tend to cause anxiety. People may resist a job change because of the uncertainties over changes in responsibilities.

People attempt to adapt to change by adopting what are commonly called defence mechanisms; these they are unaware of. People will react to change in individual ways. For example, some will become depressed while others may see it as a challenge.

Defence mechanisms

It is always important to remember that defence mechanisms are defences against anxiety and are always unconscious, which means that individuals are not aware that they are using such mechanisms: if people are aware of what they are doing, then it cannot be a defence mechanism.

Defence mechanisms are sometimes seen as protection against the pain of traumatic life experiences. Some of the most common forms of defence mechanisms are as follows:

- *Identification* – This occurs when an individual unconsciously copies the dress, behaviour or mannerisms of the person the individual admires or envies.
- *Repression* – People may repress from their consciousness any thought of a situation that causes anxiety. They may therefore refuse to come to terms with the change in their lives. For example, you may forget a dental appointment or some other unpleasant appointment.
- *Denial* – People often deny that some change in their lifestyle has happened. For example, after bereavement a person may carry on as if the dead person is still around the house.
- *Regression* – This involves a return to earlier modes of functioning. The most extreme form may manifest itself in the individual reacting to a traumatic shock by regression to childhood behaviour. For example, a previously toilet-trained child may revert to incontinence on the birth of a sibling.
- *Projection* – People use this, the most common form of defence mechanism, when they attribute their own feelings to another person. It may be as 'normal' as blaming someone else for some everyday incident, such as seeing all the problems on a ward or in a residential home as due to the shortcomings of the other shift, or it may be more serious, as in the individual who is suffering from paranoid delusions.
- *Introjection* – This is the global taking in of attitudes. The individual will tend to internalise the attitudes of those who may be creating a threat. For example, a child might pretend to be a ghost to cope with his or her fear of ghosts.
- *Reversal or reaction formation* – This is the transformation of feelings into their opposite. For example, a person tempted by unacceptable feelings of love may instead hate the object of such love.

- *Sublimation* – This is another of the most common forms of defence mechanism. To keep their minds off a situation, people may become obsessed with work or single-mindedly take up some new sport or hobby.
- *Displacement* – This is particularly applicable to people in institutions. Emotions stirred up by one situation are displaced and expressed in an inappropriate situation. For example, a senior member of staff shouts at a junior member who, instead of shouting back, shouts at a yet more junior member.

Activity 11

Mary, a residential care worker, has just experienced a serious telling off by her senior manager. On returning to the main day room she sees a resident spill some tea on the carpet. Mary shouts at the resident, who then goes into the garden and tries to take out her frustration on the establishment's cat.

What defence mechanisms have Mary and the resident exhibited?

Key Skills

You can use Activity 11 to provide evidence for Key Skills Communication C3.2 and C3.3.

Social skills

Social attitudes are learned through a process of association. We are all driven by basic **needs** that have to be satisfied. When we behave in ways that satisfy needs, the behaviour, or response, is rewarded, or reinforced. We are then likely to use the same behaviour again and again to satisfy the need. In a social context, if we behave in ways that meet with the approval and praise of those around us, those behaviours will be reinforced.

Many of our attitudes are also shaped by the responses of those around us. Thus, the attitudes of the social class we belong to are likely to be adopted by us because we are socially rewarded by the approval of others. Similarly, our gender, race and religion will all play a role in shaping our attitudes, as all of these constitute social groups that will reward certain attitudes and disapprove of others. For example:

- social class may determine our views about education and work
- gender may influence beliefs about roles within the family or safety in the streets
- our race may influence the realistic expectations we have about being treated fairly in employment, or our tastes in music and food.

Religion is a major shaper of attitudes, as it often constitutes an organised system of beliefs about right and wrong. Most of these attitudes will be learned within the context of the family.

Activity 12

a In small groups of three or four, define your own religious attitudes.
b How do you believe that these attitudes may help or hinder your activities in supporting a client?

Examples of issues that you may wish to consider are euthanasia and contraception.

Most societies tend to reproduce their social kind from generation to generation

The learning process described above is called socialisation. Our personalities are shaped and developed through social contacts with other people. The process starts when we are infants and progresses throughout our lives. We come to behave, to feel, to evaluate and to think similarly to those around us. Most societies tend to reproduce their social kind from generation to generation. However, the process is complex and not fully understood. We all know of examples of lack of socialisation – for example, the child who rebels and adopts a lifestyle completely different from the parents!

Sources of socialisation

Socialisation is influenced by two groups in society:

- membership groups, such as a person's culture and social class, where socialisation occurs through one-to-one contact with family (the strongest socialising influence, and the most studied), friends and neighbours
- reference groups, which are perhaps the most personally significant influence of attitudes.

Membership groups

Family

The family is the best-known and strongest socialising influence. Parents essentially want to guide the child's acquisition of values, behaviour and personality characteristics into what the culture considers appropriate. Parents direct the child's learning towards what the culture defines as desirable characteristics and behaviour. At the same time, undesirable behaviours and values are inhibited.

The inhibition of undesirable behaviours in the child is referred to as repressive socialisation. Repressive socialisation usually begins during the child's second year. The child is asked to stop making so much noise at dinner, to stop jumping up and down on the bed, and to curb tantrums. Repressive socialisation emphasises obedience and respect for authority.

Some parents, however, soon begin to move away from this socialising technique towards participatory socialisation. This gives children freedom to try things out for themselves and explore the world on their own terms.

Participatory socialisation is child-centred, rather than parent-centred. Children are more likely to be motivated by their desire to be like someone they respect, love and admire. This is called the process of identification.

Early socialisation is probably most readily accomplished through a combination of both techniques. Rewards and punishments are both effectively used. However, as the child gets older, the acquisition of values and behaviours is more likely to be the product of identification with a model.

Both types of socialisation are not quite randomly distributed in society, but are correlated with socioeconomic level and education. The evidence indicates that repressive socialisation is more characteristic of the working class, while participatory socialisation is found more commonly in the middle class.

The socialisation that occurs within the family develops notions of what is right and wrong. It also determines the level of importance put on traditional roles. Importantly, the family has a powerful influence on the value of education. Religious beliefs are also largely socialised through the family.

Culture

Culture is the set of beliefs and values that people regard as natural and normal in a particular society. For example, the expectations of people in Britain are very different from those of people in China. The values of our society are taught to us in the family and in school, and are communicated to us through television and newspapers.

Subculture

There are variations within a national culture that are determined perhaps more locally, or related to special interests or lifestyle. The attitudes of people from Yorkshire, for example, may differ from those of Londoners. Examples of lifestyle subcultures are punks, hippies and travellers. Race and religion may also be subcultural influences. For example, African and Caribbean culture will influence the attitudes of that subculture in Britain, and Chinese culture will influence the attitude of the British Chinese community. Religions such as Judaism and Islam rely on subcultural influence on an international level in order to remain intact.

Social class

Divisions in labour and education create other subcultures known as social classes. Social class is characterised by values and attitudes acquired through contact with others in a particular class. Some young people, for example, attend privileged schools with the intention of socialising them into particular class attitudes and behaviours.

Peer groups

Peer groups have a strong influence on attitudes, as they may be simultaneously membership and reference groups (see below). Peer groups are formed by individuals with a common interest or identification. A good example is the friends you choose when you are young. They are likely to influence your attitudes toward school work, the music you like, the way you dress and even the way you express yourself both verbally and non-verbally. Later in life peer groups may be identified more in relation to vocation or profession. Teachers, for example, may relate as a peer group, members often dressing alike and possessing similar views.

Activity 13

a In small groups, make a list of other peer groups that influence dress and appearance. Examples may be based on age, profession, or social group.
b Do you think that the groups you identified are stereotyped by their dress and appearance?

Imposed membership groups

These include elderly people, disabled people, unemployed people and mentally ill people. Health and social care services have been largely ignorant of the importance of reference groups (see below) to people's own sense of identity. Hence, access to care services is often determined by establishing the client as a member of a group with a negative label (i.e. imposing a membership group upon the client) that stresses the client's 'abnormality'. These are not likely to be the membership or reference groups that the individuals would choose for themselves.

Putting individuals into groups creates a language for us to describe them. Language determines attitudes. This has been well-documented by sociologists such as Goffman (1961), psychiatrists such as Laing (1960) and neurologists such as Sacks (1985). Sacks describes how we use a language describing deficit, shortcomings and problems for users of health and social care services, and how our language does not describe the capabilities, potential or hopes of clients.

Reference groups

Aspirational reference groups

These are groups with whom the individual may have little or no contact but whose standards and attitudes are aspired to. Individuals will have internalised the values of the group to which they wish to belong (i.e. to which they 'refer') and want to be perceived as a member of. Such aspirations are often associated with upward mobility through the class structure. For example, young medical students often quickly internalise the conservative values of the medical profession to which they hope to belong. Some people may value flashy cars and expensive clothes because they want to be rich one day.

Imaginary reference group

This is where people adopt what they believe to be either the values of the future or the past. They might fancy themselves as 'ahead of their time' or 'longing for the good old days'. The slow uptake of services and benefits by elderly people may reflect former cultural attitudes about self-reliance.

Dissociative reference groups

This is where the individual, in rejecting a group's values, makes choices that puts the individual at odds with the group. This phenomenon is seen in some people who offend; the challenging of cultural values is rewarding, as it reinforces the image with which they wish to be perceived.

The importance of reference groups

It is important to understand reference groups as, more than any other influence, they direct our decisions and choices. Individuals are fiercely loyal to their reference group and strongly influenced by particular people who represent its values. Such a particular person might be a teacher, an employer or a minister. It might be a politician, an actor, a sporting personality or a member of the royal family. We are socialised not just into who we are but who we would like to be.

/ **Activity 14** /

a Work in groups of three or four. Individually determine which social class you believe you belong to and how this has influenced your attitudes.

b Do the same for other membership groups, and then reference groups. Make sure that you understand the differences between these groups and how they affect you.

c Compare your answers with others in the group and draw conclusions. Make a note of the conclusions to contribute to a summary session involving all of the class.

The development of attitudes and values

How social constructs change over time

The family

The family is the smallest of the formal associations in society and as such it is one of the most influential and important in the development of the individual identity. Any account of how individuals develop should take account of the social context in which the person has been reared.

The family is, and has always been, the most important and most intimate of human groups. The human family is centred on the biological needs of mating, begetting, rearing children and providing for the physical and emotional needs of its members. It is a natural grouping rooted in fundamental instincts such as emotions, serving biological functions and regulating sexual and parental behaviour. For the child, therefore, the family is a vehicle by which it comes gradually to experience wider, or secondary, social groupings that influence the development of the individual. Through this introduction, most families provide the child with values and modes of behaviour that are appropriate for life. The experience of family life and wider groupings is therefore the means by which the individual is 'converted into the person'.

Sociologists make a distinction between sex and gender:

- sex refers to the biological differences
- gender refers to the social and cultural differences between men and women.

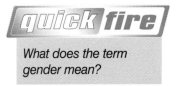

What does the term gender mean?

A person's sex is a fundamental part of his or her self-concept and interactions with others. How do children acquire gender roles? How do they learn what sex they are?

One of the first things that we may notice about someone is whether they are male or female. It seems that we need this information about a person if we are to be able to interact with them in a socially acceptable manner. It is argued that children pick up the appropriate sex role by imitating the same-sex parent and being reinforced for behaving in a manner that the particular culture expects of a boy or a girl. By reinforcing masculine behaviour in a boy, either parent could ensure that he showed masculine behaviour; similarly for feminine behaviour in a girl.

So, in the case of a single parent rearing children, provided the parent had an idea of normal male or female behaviour that parent would be able to reinforce any behaviour in children that corresponded to the sex of the child. Children tend to categorise certain behaviours as 'boy' or 'girl' behaviours and also learn that they should not cross the gender role lines if possible.

Activity 15

How might you use the theories outlined above to support a single male parent bring up his young daughter? What advice would you give him?

There are some myths about the behaviour of boys and girls. In the early 1970s, researchers spent 3 years examining the stereotypes about males and females, and came to the conclusion that the following may not be true:

- Boys are more 'analytic' than girls.
- Girls are more affected by heredity and boys by environment.
- Girls lack achievement motivation relative to boys.
- Girls have lower self-esteem than boys.
- Girls are 'auditory' while boys are 'visual'.
- Girls are more suggestible than boys.
- Girls are more 'social' than boys.

However, they did find some evidence for the following differences:

- Males are more aggressive than females.
- Girls have greater verbal ability than boys.
- Boys excel in visual–spatial ability.
- Boys have more mathematical ability.

Other researchers since the 1970s have suggested the following:

- Males take greater risks than females, or are conditioned into believing that they can.
- Boys are more active than girls.
- Girls tend to be more likely to comply with parental requests.
- Girls seem to be more interested in, and responsive to, babies than boys or men are.

Some research findings would tend to point to the fact that men and women, boys and girls are more alike than they are different.

4.3 The range of factors that can influence growth and developing, including genetic, environmental and socioeconomic factors

Environmental influences/genetic factors

The nature–nurture debate has been going on for centuries. Psychologists have carried out a number of practical studies to test if it is nurture or nature that affects the development of the personality. Galton, a psychologist in the late 19th century, looked at a number of families and found that parents with high intelligence quotients (IQs) tended to have children with high IQs, as did their children's offspring over a number of generations. Did the parents pass on 'intelligent' genes to their children or were the children of a high IQ because of the environment provided by the parents? Certain parents may have provided books and had more stimulating kinds of conversation with their children.

A more scientific way to argue this debate is to look at studies involving twins. The use of twins allows us to study and compare individuals with the same genetic make-up but different environmental experiences or those with different genetic make-ups but the same environmental experiences. This is possible because of the two types of twin. Monozygotic twins develop from the same fertilised egg; this means that they have the same genetic make-up. Dizygotic twins develop from two separate fertilised eggs and so are not genetically identical.

Monozygotic twins brought up together tend to have similar IQs. What happens when monozygotic twins are separated at birth? It would be reasonable to suppose that any differences would be environmental. Burt argued from studies of separated twins that IQ was 80% inherited and 20% due to environmental factors. However, Burt's studies must be treated with caution as they have been the subject of much criticism. The data used by Burt was used by others (McNemar, 1938; Kamin, 1974) to provide evidence that environment factors played a big part in the development of IQ. This would point to the fact that any evidence for the existence of a heritable gene factor must be taken as having a very limited value.

The so-called nature–nurture debate assumes that development is caused by either genetic or environmental factors. However, it may be that both together have an influence on personality development. Hebb (1949) tried to point this out by showing how both factors were essential for the development of an egg. He argued that if you take the gene (genetic factor) away you have no egg and if the environment is not warm (environment factor) then the egg dies. He states that it is not an either/or question: each factor is essential for growth.

At conception every person is provided with a mix of genetic material from his/her parents. This genetic make-up governs much of the person's later development. Many disorders of later life are a result of these inherited genes.

Inherited gene disorders

Just as we inherit characteristics such as eye colour from our parents, and a tendency to diseases such as asthma and heart disease, so we can also inherit defective genes from our parents that give rise to ill-health. Included in this category are single gene disorders such as:

- phenylketonuria
- cystic fibrosis
- Huntington's chorea
- sickle cell anaemia
- colour blindness.

Other inherited disorders involve whole chromosomes and cannot always be traced in families. These include:

- Down's syndrome
- Turner's syndrome
- Kleinfelter's syndrome.

People with Down's syndrome can enter the job market and become reliable employees

Single gene disorders

A person inherits two copies of most genes: one from the mother and one from the father. (In sex-linked disorders, such as red–green colour blindness, a male child inherits a copy from his mother only.) If one of the genes is defective, it is likely that the second is 'normal' and so normal function is achieved. However, if two 'abnormal' genes are inherited, then the function of the 'normal' gene is lost. With phenylketonuria the lack of a normal copy means that the metabolism of the amino acid phenylalanine, controlled by the gene, does not occur and so the disorder develops. The 'abnormal' gene is masked by the 'normal' gene, and so people can carry the defective gene and pass it on without showing any effects themselves. In this way so-called recessive disorders can skip generations in families.

With some disorders, the presence of the 'abnormal' gene always has an effect. If the gene is sufficiently dominant just one copy brings about the full abnormality. An example of this is in the relatively rare bone disorder inherited multiple exostoses. This gene, if present, must express itself and so the disorder cannot skip generations.

Some genes do not exhibit full dominance and so the presence of one copy brings about a reduced effect compared with the full effect from two copies. A disorder in this category is sickle cell anaemia. A person with 'normal' and 'abnormal' copies of the gene exhibits sickle cell trait. The trait creates problems for the person during times of physiological stress because of the abnormal haemoglobin produced by the gene. A double dose of the gene is normally a lethal condition, with children not surviving to adulthood. Again, this disorder does not skip generations.

Sickle cell disorder is interesting because, in some cases, the disorder has a positive advantage. People with the sickle trait are less susceptible to some forms of malaria and so natural selection has favoured the gene in areas where malaria is endemic.

Chromosome abnormalities

Occasionally, the meiotic cell division to produce gametes goes wrong and a gamete receives too much or too little chromosome material.

Case study

Down's syndrome

In the case of Down's syndrome, a gamete from either the mother or the father contains an extra chromosome number 21 as a result of a genetic 'accident', either when the gamete was made or during the initial cell division following fertilisation. The child produced as a result has three copies of the chromosome 21 and therefore 47 in all, rather than the normal 46. About 95% of cases of Down's syndrome are a result of this 'accident'. The effect is to produce characteristic physical features and a characteristic level of mental incapacity. Most people with Down's syndrome have a reduced life expectancy and a reduced level of fertility.

It is not fully understood why the abnormal gametes are produced but it is known that the older a woman is the greater the chance that a pregnancy will result in a child with Down's syndrome. However, the majority of babies with Down's syndrome are still born to younger women, simply because the overall birth-rate is higher in that group.

Approximately 1 in 100 people with Down's syndrome have inherited the condition from their mother or father because of a genetic abnormality called translocation. There is a third, equally rare, type of Down's syndrome known as mosaic Down's syndrome.

Source: Information supplied by the Down's Syndrome Association

---

Control and cure for inherited disease

Should we say that people from families with genetic disorders should not have children? Should we test for genetic disorders in the womb and then abort the fetus?

It is easy to identify simple ways in which people with genetic disorders could ensure that they do not pass on the genes. Some extreme regimes have even tried to cleanse the population of people they consider to be genetically inferior. Nazi Germany was an extreme example of this. It has not been, and never can be, a viable way of 'controlling' inherited disorders. Apart from the very clear moral issues, biology is also against any such programme. A simple example in the case study of phenylketonuria can identify the weakness.

Case study

Phenylketonuria

Phenylketonuria is controlled by a single gene, the defective one being recessive. A test is available for babies born in the UK, soon after birth, to identify if they have inherited two defective genes and have the disorder. About 1 in 25 000 babies do. Surely, if people carrying the gene could be persuaded not to have children, then the disorder could be eliminated and the cost of 24 999 wasted tests could be saved? The question then arises, 'How many people would have to be asked not to have children?'.

The Hardy–Weinberg equation can be used to calculate the number of people carrying the gene in the population. It relies on several issues but at its simplest it can be expressed thus:

Assume that there are two versions of a gene that occur with frequency p and q, where $p + q = 1$. Any person can have a double dose of either gene or one of each. The frequencies of these is related by the formula:

$$p2 + p2 + p2 = 2.$$

So, for the gene controlling phenylketonuria we can say that the normal version, K, has a frequency of p, while the abnormal one, k, has a frequency of q. The frequencies of each combination of genes are expressed thus:

$$KK = p^2$$

$$Kk = 2pq$$

$$kk = q^2.$$

We know that $q^2 = 1/25\ 000$. Therefore:

$$q = 1/25\ 000$$
$$= 0.0063.$$

As we know $p + q = 1$ and we also know that q is very small; for easier calculation we can say that p = 1.

By putting these figures into the Hardy–Weinberg equation we can calculate the frequency of people carrying the abnormal gene:

$$2pq = 2 \times 1 \times 0.0063$$
$$= 0.0126.$$

This means that the frequency of 'carriers' in the population is 0.0126, or 1 in 80.

So, to get rid of phenylketonuria, 1 in 80 people would have to give up having children. This may seem almost possible, but everyone carries at least five versions of genes that could give rise to inherited disorders. To follow this to its logical conclusion, i.e. to eliminate all genetic disorders, everybody should stop having children. There would then be no problem of inherited disorders in the next generation. But who would form the next generation?

Obviously from this case study it can be seen that eliminating defective versions of genes is not easy. However, the understanding of inherited disorders does mean that people can be advised by trained counsellors about the risks and can make informed decisions about having or not having children.

Role status

When considering the role of wife as a carer, we usually think of a wife as having childcare responsibilities. However, at any one time in Britain there are more women caring for elderly and handicapped dependants than for children (Briggs, 1981). Most carers do not have a choice regarding having to look after a dependent relative; spouses can be seen as having the least choice of all.

When a member of the family becomes ill or disabled there is universal expectation, from the health and social care services, that the wife will take on the role of carer. Professionals hardly ever ask or consider the wishes of the female carer. They assume that the ability to cope is bestowed by taking on the role of wife or mother. For the average wife there is conflict – she is under pressure from every side to care for the dependent members of society. She sometimes may feel that she exists only in her caring role and receives no support from doctors, social workers or other health or care services.

The state gives implicit support to the sexual division of care – men are not expected to look after themselves and are not able to look after dependent relatives. The fact that there is a conflict between men and women in the care of dependent relatives is demonstrated by the inequality between them. Men spend very little time carrying out care activities. A woman's identity is still organised around the home, domestic work, child-rearing and caring for dependent members. Women have been assigned a lower status than men in today's society and women are seen as having a role only within the home, while the male is perceived as the breadwinner.

There is still a substantial and unequal division of labour between men and women in western families, which is a vehicle for conflict. Carers in minority ethnic communities may not get support because of the stereotyped attitude that says that families in those groups 'look after their own'.

Local and global influences

People have a right to know as much as possible about the causes of ill-health and social problems, and to know what they as individuals may be able to do to reduce the risks. This basic human right was affirmed by the World Health Organisation in 1978. The provision of information on health care, health and safety, and social issues enables individuals both to influence political decision-making on a broad scale and to make personal decisions about their own health and lifestyle. Knowledge is power; it is the basis on which people can make informed choices.

Risks to health

Most accidents occur in the home. About 6000 people a year die on roads in Britain. Many others are injured and die because of accidents at work. We all take risks: we smoke, drive cars, drink alcohol and work in situations that cause ill-health. All these activities present health risks of varying degrees; all have been the subject of media attention; all have been related to health promotional activities. Modern health and social well-being promotion is not just about saying what is good for people, it is also about assessing risk.

Activity 16

a List as many risks to health and social well-being as you can.

b From this list select and rank in order of importance the five risks that concern you most and the five risks that you feel are most worrying in society in general. Keep these lists – you will need to refer to them again.

c Use your personal list to begin to develop an individual action plan for your own health and well-being Discuss this action plan with your class colleagues. Continue to develop your action plan as you work through this unit.

It is likely that your list from Activity 16 will have included concerns about specific diseases, accidents, assault, drug abuse, cancers, heart disease and poverty. The precise nature of your five main concerns will vary according to your current circumstances and issues currently being highlighted by the media. They will reflect some of your perceptions of risk. Other people will have different priorities. For example, with many elderly people the fear of assault ranks high because of stories in newspapers and on television about elderly people being mugged, while people from certain parts of the world would have more pressing concerns about obtaining sufficient water and food.

It is clear that promotion of health and social well-being is not an absolute, but is based on the perceived needs of the individual within the wider contexts of the needs of society. We all see risks in different ways. There is a massive industry gathering information to support decision-making; to provide the facts that contribute to the assessment of risk. In this part of the unit we will help you to identify the factors that affect health and social well-being, and give you the opportunity to assess risks using as much evidence as possible.

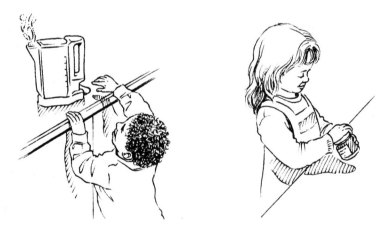

There are many areas of potential risk to young children in the home

Children at risk: accidents in the home

As children develop they become more capable of injuring themselves. The changes are rapid and need to be planned for in order to avoid putting the child at risk. What seemed impossible one day becomes easy the next. As the child's skills develop, the risks increase.

Developmental stages and potential risks

Developmental age	Abilities	Risks
3 months	Wriggles and waves limbs	Can move sufficiently to fall from raised surfaces Head can be trapped in badly-designed cot
5 months	Puts objects in mouth	Choking from small objects, e.g. buttons and pins
8 months	Crawling	Falling down steps Cuts from contact with and grasping sharp objects Climbing/falling out of buggies and high chairs
12 months	Opens lids and tins	Choking and poisoning from things put in boxes
18 months	Imitates, climbs and explores	Climbing on to window sills May be able to open medicines without child-resistant containers May be able to undo child restraint in cars
2 years	Turns on taps	Risk of scalding from hot water system

Why look at risks?

To talk of risk is to talk of the chance that something will happen. When flipping a coin, probability theory tells us that half the time a coin will land showing tails and half the time it will show heads. To gamble £5 on heads, yet have to pay £10 if the coin turns up tails, incurs a high financial risk.

Assessing risk

There is a massive industry based on taking risks related to health – life insurance. The insurance industry makes use of statistics to judge the chance of almost any occurrence and uses this to determine the premiums to be paid. Data gathered from millions of individuals is used to predict the potential risks associated with insuring the life of, for example, a 30-year-old, non-smoking man with those of a 30-year-old woman who smokes.

Activity 17

The figures in the table below show, for example, that the premium per £10 000 of insurance for a man wanting insurance for a 25-year term varies from £0.73 to £3.64 according to his age if he is a non-smoker, and £0.96 to £5.73 if he is a smoker. What would be the figures for a woman wanting a 10-year term?

Life insurance premiums, monthly contributions (£) per 10 000 insurance

| Term | Age next birthday (years) | | | | | |
| | 19 | | 30 | | 40 | |
	Non-s	Smoker	Non-s	Smoker	Non-s	Smoker
Women						
5	0.28	0.46	0.36	0.46	0.65	0.98
10	0.28	0.46	0.44	0.56	0.86	1.36
15	0.34	0.53	0.44	0.67	1.17	1.89
25	0.55	0.65	0.75	1.09	1.97	3.08
Men						
5	0.51	0.77	0.66	0.88	1.26	1 82
10	0.63	0.87	1.32	1.36	2.74	3.92
20	0.65	0.88	1.50	2.03	3 17	4.76
25	0.73	0.96	1.57	2.26	3.64	5.73

Source: Figures adapted from Allied Dunbar tables

Health statistics

The study of patterns of ill-health, mortality and the causes of disease is not a new science. You may think that the link between tobacco and cancer has only recently been established. In fact, the link between snuff-taking (inhaled powdered tobacco) and cancer of the nasal lining was described in the early 1900s. Another chemically induced cancer, cancer of the scrotum, was known in the 18th century. This was common in chimney sweeps and was caused by soot. Links between sunlight and skin cancer have also been known since the last century.

When John Snow identified the source of a cholera outbreak as the water from a pump in Broad Street, London, in 1844, the organism that caused it, *Vibrio cholerae*, was not known. His later work, using data gathered by William Farr about the source of water supplies to houses of cholera victims relative to a sewage outflow, led to the identification of sewage pollution as the source of cholera infections.

It is easy, with hindsight, to say that the link is logical and that pathogens (disease-causing organisms) and drinking water should not be allowed to mix. What in many ways is more important is to recognise that the results were an almost immediate success for the new science of epidemiology.

Gathering statistics

Both Snow and Farr had a powerful friend in Edwin Chadwick, the Secretary of the Poor Law Board. In the mid-19th century, Chadwick instigated the legislation requiring the gathering of statistics relating to birth and death, which helped in Snow's analysis. This work still continues and much of the data used today has its origins in statistics gathered by the Office of Population Censuses and Surveys.

Live births in the UK

Year	Total	Male	Female
1900	1095	558	537
1920	1018	522	496
1940	723	372	351
1950	803	413	390
1960	946	487	459
1970	880	453	427
1978	687	353	334
1979	735	378	356
1980	754	386	368
1981	731	375	356
1982	719	369	350
1983	721	371	357
1984	730	371	351
1985	751	385	366
1986	755	387	368
1987	776	398	378
1988	788	403	384
1989	777	398	379
1990	799	409	390

All figures in thousands with earlier ones representing an annual average from a 3-year period

Source: OPCS

Activity 18

a Using the table above, plot a graph with the birth rate on the *y* axis and the year on the *x* axis.
b What trends do you notice?
c Try to predict how many births there will be in the next decade. Remember that the number of births is related to the birth figures of 25 years previously.

Save the graph to help you when you do Activity 19, about life expectancy.

From such data, health risks can be analysed and health promotion developed. There is an increasing knowledge and understanding of people, not only from a sociological but also from biological and psychological points of view. Putting all of these data together it is possible to assess risk and propose actions, taking into account the broader context within which the risk is based.

What are life tables?

Life tables provide information about statistical life expectancy and are produced and used by insurance companies when they determine the risks for life insurance. In this crude form (see below) they give no indication of cause of death and so cannot be used to show increased risk factors.

Life expectancy

Age	Males I	Ex	Females I	Ex
0	100 000	72.4	100 000	78.0
10	98 710	63.4	99 086	68.8
20	98 238	53.6	98 786	58.9
30	97 396	44.1	98 442	49.1
40	96 240	34.5	97 723	39.4
50	93 451	25.4	95 858	30.1
60	85 361	17.2	90 828	21.4
65	77 087	13.8	85 705	17.6
70	65 369	10.8	78 242	14.0
75	50 075	8.3	67 536	10.8
80	32 993	6.3	53 154	8.0
85	17 410	4.7	35 317	5.8

I = the number of people out of 100 000 who would survive to the exact age on the left if the death rates do not change over their lifetime. Ex = the average future lifetime of a person of the age on the left if the death rates do not change over their lifetime.

Source: OPCS. Figures based on the interim life tables for 1987–9 produced by the Government Actuaries Department

Example
- Of every 100 000 men born in the years 1987–89, 96 240 will live to their 40th birthday at least.
- A woman at birth has an average future lifetime of 76.4 years. However, if she were already 75, she would have an average life expectancy of 10.4 years.

Activity 19

It is important in planning provision for health and social care to be able to predict the demand for services. In this activity you will have to use the data from the birth tables and the life tables to predict some of the market need for care.

a Using data from the two tables, plot graphs of the number of people born in the years 1981–1990 who will live to be 20. (To do this you will need to assume that the life table data in column 1 can be applied throughout the range of years 1981–90.) This graph represents the potential number of people entering the workforce.

b What use do you think these data might have in terms of planning care services?

c Using the birth data from the birth table for 1980, 1985 and 1990, together with the life table data, predict the number of 75, 80 and 85-year-old men and women who will be alive in 2065. (Assume the life table data apply to all of these birth years.)

d If it is assumed that these people will be in need of some level of social care, use the figures you have calculated to make predictions about possible demand.

The inter-relationships between socioeconomic factors, demographic characteristics and development

Personal situations and ill-health

There are many facets of ill-health that have no causative organism or that are made worse by the situations in which people find themselves. In this section we will try to identify some of the factors related to ill-health where the environment contributes to the nature of the health.

Mental and physical disabilities

This broad group contains:

- people with identifiable inherited disorders, such as Down's syndrome
- people damaged at birth, such as those with cerebral palsy
- people who have become ability-impaired during their lifetime, such as accident victims and those with Alzheimer's disease.

The common feature of all these is that the ill-health (with current knowledge) is permanent – there is no cure. However, for many people it is the disability that is recognised by society and not the ability. This is often expressed by other people communicating with a carer rather than the person. A failure to recognise abilities can have a very powerful demotivating effect. The stigmata characteristic of many of these 'handicaps' prove a handicap themselves.

Down's syndrome is most easily recognised externally by characteristic facial features. Some children with Down's syndrome have been offered surgery to alter these facial features. This in no way changes the biological nature of the syndrome but it does affect society's attitudes. The children are not automatically seen as disabled and so their abilities come to the fore.

This stereotyping of ability by identifying an infirmity is true across a wide range of people. Those with cerebral palsy may be classified as unintelligent because of their spastic movements. The effect of this can be to reduce the level of educational input to young children so that they do not reach their full potential.

At the other end of the scale, it is all too easy to accept that a person with Alzheimer's disease is in need of physical care only. However, when the person is presented with appropriate stimuli through such things as reminiscence therapy and reality orientation, the progress of the disease can be slowed and so the person remains more able for longer. These examples show how the disability brings about a double-jeopardy situation. Not only do the sufferers have to work against the problem, but they also have to fight the handicap imposed by society's stereotypes.

Psychiatric ill-health

This area of ill-health includes disorders of mood, perception and thinking. These can be classed as mental illnesses but, as Clare (1980) suggests, 'the concept of mental illness appears to permit a bewildering number of interpretations'. The complex inter-relationship between mind and body often makes it difficult to differentiate between mental and physical ill-health.

Mood

Illness related to mood, such as depression, may well have a biochemical origin. There can be obvious physical changes, such as childbirth, that are linked to depression. Depression can also follow physical illnesses such as glandular fever.

However, it is not known whether one is the cause of the other. In some people there is evidence that depression may be linked to low levels of serotonin, a brain neurotransmitter.

A hormone linked to mental illness is adrenaline. This hormone is released at times of stress but, in situations where there is a constantly raised level of stress, the level of the hormone is constantly higher than would be normal. This can lead to physical illnesses or mental illness – one cause with many effects.

Perception

Disorders of perception occur when one or more of the senses misinterpret stimuli. Most of us, especially as young children, have interpreted shadows as monsters. We may also have interpreted random sounds as speech, especially if we were expecting to hear something. These are cases of the brain trying to interpret stimuli by matching them to an already known pattern. When the stimuli are totally internally generated they are called hallucinations. Some drugs have the effect of causing these internal stimuli and their use has been linked to cases of mental illness. In controlled doses, some of these drugs have been used therapeutically to support treatment of other illnesses. In particular, some hallucinogens are used to ease the effects of chemotherapy for some cancer patients.

Two illnesses in which changes in perception are symptomatic are chronic alcoholism and schizophrenia. In the former, the cause is chronic drug abuse (alcohol), while in the latter the cause, or more probably causes, are not well understood.

Socioeconomic and environmental factors

A child brought up in a block of damp, draughty, high-rise flats with no other children to play with may have damaged emotional and physical development. A lack of contact with other children would clearly affect social development and may give rise to behavioural difficulties relating to interacting with peers when starting school. The lack of peer group stimulus could lead to depression, which tends to reduce the efficiency of the immune system. This in turn makes the child more prone to infection.

Poverty and ill-health go together. A study of ill-health related to family or personal finance would show increased episodes of ill-health in low-income families. This closely matches the relationship between social class and ill-health. The Black Report of 1980 highlighted the inequalities in care, relating them to social class. Included in the Report was epidemiological evidence that some diseases are more common further down the social class scale. It also highlighted the fact that access to health care and ill-health prevention was also related to class.

A variety of explanations have been put forward relating to such factors as education, access to health care, nutrition, family size and housing – you will be able to add other examples. Clearly, the example of the young child given above indicates how the immune system can be compromised by the way a person is feeling. It is also easy to identify how poor nutrition has a direct relationship to ill-health. It should also be possible to see how health levels alter in relation to more indirect causes such as the development of the welfare state and, more recently, the increased number of unemployed and homeless people.

Cancers

Cancer is a layperson's term to describe a variety of specific diseases. The common feature of all of them is that they involve inappropriate growth of cells, which is often rapid and uncontrolled. The cause of this growth varies and, while it is possible to link some cancers with specific causes, there are normally other factors involved.

The table below gives some examples of different cancers and major factors in their development. Clearly prevention, where possible, is easier with some of these and so individuals should reduce their exposure to the risk. However, some factors, such as an inherited tendency, cannot be removed and so it is not possible to remove all risk.

Examples of causes of cancer

Type of cancer	Possible causative link
Lung cancer	Tobacco smoke
	Radon gas (radioactive) from certain building materials
Cancer of the cervix	Infection with herpes virus causing genital warts
Bowel cancer	Lack of dietary fibre
Skin cancer	Exposure to ultraviolet light, in particular from the sun (melanoma)
Scrotal cancer	Exposure to soot and tar products of burning. This was particularly common in 19th-century chimney sweeps

---

The list is not exhaustive but gives examples from a range of types of cause.

Health improvement without an obvious medical reason

A feature of many of the indirect causes of ill-health is that not all people in similar situations develop the same levels of ill-health. The 'feel good factor' is often used to describe an unquantifiable state that can lead to reduced ill-health. If a person, while in an 'at risk' situation, has a level of confidence and happiness, then the level of illness is reduced. This may be related simply to an improved immune system, but it may also be related to maintaining the body systems in a natural biochemical balance. It is an interesting thought that feeling good about yourself may help improve your health.

Case study

Using the 'feel good factor' to promot

The Starlight Foundation is an organisation founded in the UK. This organisation makes the dream of cri terminally ill children come true by granting them wishe trips to Disney World, swimming with dolphins and ap comic. The original concept was to provide a experience for the child and family. However, there has surprising effect in that granting the wish appears psychological but also physical well-being. This has use fewer painkillers or shorter treatment periods. T evidence, although not scientific proof yet, that some granted a wish, receive a boost to their compromised light of these positive effects the Foundation is try rooms in hospitals, which will contain computer ga which will be off-limits to medical and nursing staff.

As ma
habitatio
repairs to th
They are also l

The case study of the Starlight Foundation is just one example of a whole series of stories that could be described as 'mind over matter'. Other examples that appear to work but have limited scientific support in western medicine include homeopathy and acupuncture. The latter has been shown to increase levels of brain endorphins and encephalins, which act, as do artificial opiates, to reduce pain and increase the person's 'happiness'. It may be that many of the alternative therapies work in similar ways to promote health.

Socioeconomic factors and development

The association between social class and health shows that death and disease are not randomly distributed throughout the population – there are indeed inequalities in standards of living. The conventional wisdom that the introduction of the National Health Service would prevent disease has received a sudden jolt with the discovery of the existence of systematic and widespread social inequalities in health. In particular, in 1980 the Black Report drew together evidence that demonstrated:

- that members of the 'lower' social classes suffered increased rates of nearly every category of disease
- that such differences affected them over the whole of their life span
- that, particularly since the 1940s, these differences appeared to be on the increase (see the table below).

A considerable percentage of the population moves from one social class to another at some time and it is possible that health influences this mobility. Those with good health move up the ladder and those in poor health are likely to move down the hierarchy. Another explanation for inequalities in health is the different rate of access to medical treatment.

Housing

Housing conditions are in a number of ways associated with health status. An obvious indicator is inadequate heating which can give rise to hypothermia in the old and very young. Overcrowding may cause respiratory diseases and may also contribute to mental illness. The homes of managers and professionals are likely to possess more amenities than unskilled workers.

Possession of amenities in the home

	Professional/managerial	Unskilled manual
Central heating	87%	44%
Refrigerator	99%	90%
Telephone	96%	50%
Car	93%	33%

Source: OPCS General Household Survey (HMSO, 1982)

...ny as 2 million dwellings in England are considered unfit for human ... because they lack basic amenities such as showers or bath, or require ...em. These dwellings are likely to be inhabited by unskilled workers. ...kely to be in areas where the air is polluted by industrial waste.

Social improvements have cleared the air of the more visible pollutants such as smoke, removed the most serious contaminates from food and the water supply, and provided for the hygienic disposal of waste. As a result, the diseases that affected people in the past, such as tuberculosis and cholera, have now been replaced by heart disease and cancer.

Diet

Diet is an important lifestyle factor affecting health (WHO, 1988). Some argue that social class differences in health may result from differences in exposure to factors such as poor diet, which may contribute to illness and disease:

- Studies have shown a clear decline in vitamin intake with rising family size and declining income.
- Protein consumption rises with income, but calcium intake shows no such trend.
- Poor families tend to consume more sugar in the form of sweets, biscuits and soft drinks.
- The quality of a child's diet tends to be class-related, falling with declining occupational class.

However, it should be borne in mind that people who eat certain types of food may make up for the disadvantage this might cause in some other way, for example, by obtaining food, such as sugar, from drinks or sweets.

Inadequate diet has been implicated as a factor in poor health and infant mortality. The theory of 'transmitted nutritional deprivation' suggests the existence of a cycle of nutritional deprivation that leads to low birth-weight and congenital malformation. It is difficult to break this cycle because it originates in the nutritional deprivation of the mother, not at the time of the birth of the child but at the time of her own birth.

However, the chances of becoming ill and surviving as a child are at their greatest during the post-neonatal phase of life. It is during this period that class differences play a large part. Factors that have been found to increase the child's chances of survival are the level of material resources in the family, household income, warmth and hygiene, and such things as a car or telephone, which are a means of rapid communication with services.

Activity 20

Why do you think that a middle-class child's chances of survival are greater than a working-class child's?

Diet can be crucial in both preventive and curative health. All countries, including the UK, have regions that have developed their own local diet based on the availability of foods and on such social factors as religion, culture, class and lifestyle. Each usually contains a balance of essential nutrients. Problems arise when people move area or migrate and take their diet with them. The climate, agricultural patterns, economics and food technology may be different and so traditional foods may not be available.

/ **Activity 21** /

List as many reasons as you can why income or capital might affect a family's or a person's ability to cope with ill-health.

Accidents to children

Unskilled workers' homes are likely to be lacking gardens, which means that their children are more likely to have to play in the streets or in an already overcrowded house or flat – conditions that are likely to contribute to the number of accidents that children from this social group experience. The increased risk of death faced by children in the 'lower' classes in ordinary everyday activities such as play and travelling to school by foot or bicycle has to be seen against a background of the differences in the environment to which children from different levels of society are exposed. The risk of death from accidents with motor cars is seven times greater for children from middle-class families compared to working-class families. Children from the lowest social class are nearly five times more likely to die before reaching school-leaving age.

The Black Report (1980) commented on the sex differential in each social class (apart from professional households). Boys were more likely to suffer a higher risk of accidents than girls – a fact that might reflect the greater range of careless risk-taking behaviour among boys and also, in part, reflects cultural practices in socialisation. Class differences between children regarding the risk of accidental death appear to be in part a manifestation of distinctive patterns of child-rearing. However, the report does point out that such patterns must be seen in the light of the differences in the material resources of parents, which place constraints on the level of care they are able to provide for their children.

/ **Activity 22** /

a Write down as many reasons as you can think of why children from middle-class families are less likely to have accidents.
b What part does socialisation play in this?

Health of children

One of the most important causes of death among children aged 1–14 is as the result of infection. This does not seem to vary as much between social classes as do accidents, poisoning, violence, respiratory disease and congenital abnormalities. The principal cause of respiratory symptoms is the extent of air pollution in the child's area of residence. For example, younger children in families where the parents had respiratory problems or smoked were most likely to have respiratory problems. For older children, the social class difference is larger. As the child gets older, the difference between the social classes becomes more pronounced for death from accidents, poisoning and violence.

Activity 23

Discuss with your class colleagues why the difference in social class affects a child's chance of suffering from accidents or violence.

Smoking and health

Smoking-related diseases kill about 100 000 people every year. The role of smoking in heart disease and in causing respiratory illness is well documented. If smoking is so bad for people, why does the government not ban it? This would seem to be a legitimate question to consider in a discussion of health promotion.

As stated earlier, the links between tobacco and ill-health were known in the 19th century. Further links with lung cancer and circulatory disorders have been established in the 20th century. There has been more recent evidence that the pollution of the air by tobacco smoke can induce cancers in non-smokers by so-called 'passive smoking'.

Activity 24

a   Do smokers have the right to smoke – after all, it's their health they are damaging?
b   Do non-smokers have the right to breathe smoke-free air?
c   What is the real risk of smoking (look back at the life-insurance data in the table on page 162)?

It is possible to find out the mortality figures for cigarette smokers, but an easy exercise is to look at some of the 'junk mail' that is delivered to your home. Insurance companies often send out details of insurance policies and quote premiums for both smokers and non-smokers.

It is interesting to note that life insurance companies do not usually 'load' premiums for those who drink alcohol or who are overweight in relation to height. (On the other hand, car insurance companies will give reductions for non-drinkers.) The figures indicate that insurance companies rate a non-smoker as having a significantly better chance of living for longer than a smoker. Between 13% and 24% of all deaths are smoking-related.

Are children at risk from smoking?

The Health Education Authority has identified evidence of the risks of passive smoking in children. The effects start with the unborn child and it has been estimated that there are 4 million children under 10 years old at risk in the UK. The simple statistic is that 48% of pregnant women are either smokers themselves or live in a house with a smoker. The possible effects of parental smoking include:

* an increased risk of spontaneous abortion (4000 per year)
* an increased risk of lower birth-weight
* an increased risk that babies are born earlier and suffer more infections
* an increased risk of death in the first week of life (1 in 10 infant intensive care beds are filled by babies affected by smoking)
* an increased risk of cot death – 25% of such deaths could be related to parental smoking

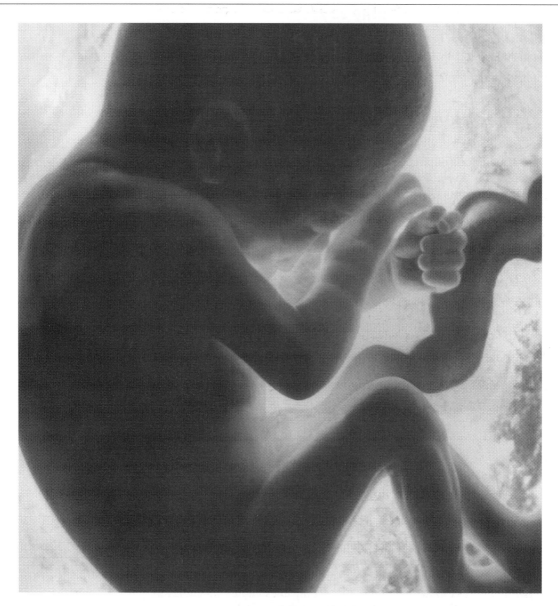

SHE CAN SUCK HER THUMB, HICCUP AND SWALLOW. UNFORTUNATELY SHE CAN'T ASK HER MOTHER NOT TO SMOKE.

Giving up smoking is not easy, especially when you're pregnant.
If you'd like some sympathetic advice call the Quitline on 0800 002200.

© Health Education Authority 1992 ISBN 0 7521 0488 6

Printed in England 10m 3/96

The anti-smoking campaigns use effective images such as these to put over the effects of passive smoking on unborn babies and young children

- a 30% chance of the child developing glue ear (a normally temporary hearing impairment)
- an increased risk of the child developing asthma – those from smoking households are twice as likely to develop asthma as those from non-smoking households
- an increased tendency for children to be shorter than average and to have lower intelligence.

The risks associated with passive smoking are such that many fostering and adoption agencies will not place children in families where there are smokers.

Alcohol

Alcohol is implicated in a wide range of health and social problems, and physical and mental disorders. Approximately 40 000 people die from alcohol abuse each year. We have considered one drug that if it were discovered today would almost certainly be banned because of the health risks – tobacco. We will now consider alcohol, a drug that is widely accepted in society and is readily available. The effects of alcohol have been acknowledged in the licensing laws, the minimum age for its purchase and areas relating to driving.

Health education reflects society's general views on drinking alcohol. The message is clearly one of moderation, with guidance on what constitutes 'safe' drinking (see below).

The effects of the drug are normally short-term and it is not strongly addictive. However, for those who do develop an addiction there is no cure. Abstinence is the only way to deal with the addiction.

Recommended alcohol consumption (units per week)

	Maximum recommended	Increased risk	Harmful	Recommended number of alcohol-free days
Men	21	50	50+	2–3
Women	14	35	35+	2–3
Pregnant women	Ideally no alcohol, at most 4 units			5–6

Typical values (units):		
a pint of beer or lager	= 2
a pint of extra strong beer or lager	= 5
a small glass of wine	= 1
a small glass of sherry	= 1
a measure of vermouth or aperitif	= 1
a standard measure of spirits (in the UK)	= 1

Source: Health Education Authority

Activity 25

While alcohol is socially acceptable and contributes to the economic status of the UK, it is also linked to many deaths. It may not be the drug itself that kills but it has a contributory effect.

a Make a list of the positive and negative ways in which alcohol contributes to the economy.

b Try to quantify these contributions.

4.4 Theories of development

There are many theories of development. Theories provide a conceptual framework that helps us to develop understanding. A theory organises and gives meaning to facts that have been observed. By developing a theory, researchers are providing a springboard for further research.

Theories of human development have raised a number of key issues, which need to be addressed.

The inter-relatedness of psychological, social and biological perspectives

We have stressed throughout this unit that these three perspectives are inter-related. No one perspective on its own can explain human development. These three perspectives are summarised below:

- *Psychological perspective* – This consists of self-perception, which comprises cognition (thought), self-esteem, motivation and feelings. It also includes the behavioural responses we make to ageing. For example, a biologically young person may feel psychologically old and vice versa.
- *Social perspective* – This looks at how society interacts with the ageing process. Society has considerable impact on how we should be at different stages of our lives: the roles we adopt, the status we assume, our style of dress and what constitutes acceptable styles of language. Have you noticed how differently individuals of different generations express themselves?
- *Biological perspective* – Our bodies physically change over time, and this comprises a major aspect of what we consider to be development. Our skeletal composition, heart rate, tissue structure and sensory capabilities all change as we age. We have already reviewed some of these changes earlier.

The important thing is that these three types of development interact. For example, a 14-year-old girl may be experiencing puberty (biological), but mentally appears to be a mature woman (psychological). However, her parents believe her to be too young to stay out late and place restrictions on her behaviour (social). Another example may be a 75-year-old man (biological) who is content with his life and welcomes old age (psychological). He is active and enjoys his retirement (social).

Heredity and environment

We have already discussed the complexity of the nature–nurture debate. Those who believe that behaviour is dependent on one's genetic endowment are called Nativists. Those who believe that the environment is the dominant force are called Environmentalists. Interactionists believe that genetics and environment interact in a complex way. Evidence is on the Interactionists' side.

Developmental theorists use some key concepts, which need to be understood. Nativists refer to **epigenetics**. This means that everything develops because of genetic programming. There are blueprints or sets of directions built into every individual. Epigenetics does, however, recognise the interplay of genetics and environment because, although the blueprint provides a master plan, environment both fills in the gaps and often makes things happen. Epigenetic theories are often referred to as discontinuous. A discontinuous theory stresses the role of heredity by claiming that development occurs through a series of sequential stages that are predetermined. The stages are not usually equal, as growth occurs in spurts.

A continuous theory, on the other hand, argues that growth is acquired through interaction with the environment, rather than from genetic blueprints. Continuous theories are characterised by stability through the life cycle rather than change. Maturity is acquired by a subtle flow. This issue of stability versus change is one of the key concepts in understanding theories of human development.

There are two models that address the issue of stability versus change. The active model claims that individuals actively control their own development. Humans are not passive creatures. We purposefully seek out environments that arouse our interests. The reactive model, on the other hand, stresses the importance of the environment, which shapes us into what we are. Humans are passive or malleable – i.e. wholly shaped by their circumstances.

These varying perspectives make understanding human development confusing, but that is the point. All theories of human development must explain behaviour in terms of developmental dynamics, and demonstrate how these dynamics make us all similar as well as all individual. Therefore a good theory describes and explains common behaviours but also highlights individual differences. Hence, we are interested in males versus females, urban versus rural and black versus white. A good theory stands up to tests and is logical. Most importantly, a good theory is evolving. More and more research will provide us with more and more information to develop newer theories.

It is important to bear in mind that the science of lifespan development is less than 100 years old, making it a small baby in the world of knowledge. The theories are primitive and probably ridiculously oversimplified. No lifespan development theory is anywhere near complete. Below, we review some of the more major perspectives.

Social learning theory

Social learning theory is based upon the principle that people learn by observing and imitating others.

Major influences upon this theory are the works of Skinner and Bandura. Observational learning, the basis of social learning theory, describes how behaviour is learned not by direct reward or punishment for particular behaviour, but by watching others behave and observing the consequences of that behaviour for the individuals concerned. With children, as well as adults, the other person is a model whom the child identifies with and whose behaviour the child imitates. The behaviour of the model provides crucially important information about the consequences of behaving in that way. Social learning theorists accept that people learn a great deal from **reinforcement** and punishment, but the theory also leaves room for the belief that children also learn by observation and by imitating others.

Activity 26

In a small group, discuss which is the most relevant to how children develop – observational learning or punishment? Give examples to illustrate your argument.

Social learning theory emphasises the effects of the consequences of our actions on our later behaviour and applies the rules of reinforcement and conditioning discussed above. It takes into account the expectations of reward and punishment in modelling a person's behaviour. The person is not, however, a passive recipient of reinforcement and punishment but will modify his or her environment and choose to do particular things that will have a greater expectation of pleasant rather than unpleasant outcomes.

It is important for children, for example, that the right or correct behaviour is reinforced if a child's performance is to improve. Learning is an active process and is done by the child. You cannot make a child learn; you can only provide the best situation possible for learning to occur. For example, if a child's behaviour results in a kiss, hug or other form of pleasant behaviour, then the child has good reason to carry on doing the same thing. On the other hand, if good behaviour does not result in a reward then the child may have no incentive to improve that behaviour.

In addition to reinforcement, the social learning theorists also stress the role of observation learning or imitation to guide behaviour. The child will not simply copy some actions: the relationship of the person to the child is also important – children are more likely to copy someone who is important to them. They will model their behaviour on these important people. Learning by watching someone else is much more effective than learning by trial and error or waiting until some reinforcement is given.

As all families are not identical and behave in different ways towards children (e.g. some will be more strict than others), each child's personality will inevitably be quite different. This process does not produce an individual with set characteristics that will be displayed in all situations. Rather, individuals' personalities are controlled by the situation they find themselves in. One classic example of this aspect of social learning theory was demonstrated by Hartshorne and May in 1930.

A sample of 11 000 children were given the opportunity to cheat, lie or be dishonest in different situations. In one situation children were given a multiple choice test and requested to circle the right answer. Later they were given the correct answers and asked to mark their own work. As a copy of the original paper had been taken without the children's knowledge, it was possible to see if a child cheated in the second test. The children took part in a number of tests varying in type, in the rewards for being honest and in the likelihood of being caught. There was no consistency of honesty in the results – the honesty of the children seemed to be governed by the situation, rather than characteristics of honesty or lack of it. The work of other psychologists supports the view of Hartshorne and May.

Summary of social learning theory

Social learning proposes that moral behaviour is learned from observation of others – mere exposure may be sufficient. The consequences of the behaviour for the other person determine whether the child is likely to imitate that behaviour or not. Parents or other significant persons serve as models for children. However, television as a socialiser is also increasingly considered to be an important influence.

Activity 27

Think about your own upbringing and list the events or relationships that you feel have shaped your personality.

Psychoanalytic theory (Freud and Erikson)

Psychoanalytic theories stress the importance of unconscious motivation and early experiences in development. Freud (1914), working in Vienna at the turn of the 20th century, was one of the first writers to emphasise the importance of the first years of a child's life in determining the personality for the whole of life. Freud's theory is one of the most influential and is normally regarded as an instinct theory. How children develop emotionally will have some influence on how their identities will develop. Freud claimed that children's personalities are to some extent formed through identifying with their parents and that deep instinctive urges direct much of human behaviour. Social learning theorists do not emphasis the early years as much because they believe that the effects of these years may be changed by experiences in later years.

Freud argued, however, that development through the first few years, which he considered very important, followed a particular pattern, with the phases overlapping one another. The phases are:

- the oral phase
- the anal phase
- the phallic phase.

The oral phase

During the first year or so, children gain satisfaction from putting things in their mouths. At this age, pleasure is gained through the mouth, the 'feeding instinct' that must be satisfied. Children at this stage are only interested in their own needs and will only do things that give them pleasure – the 'pleasure principle'. Too little or too much satisfaction at this stage will result in the child becoming arrested or fixated. For example, some see smoking or nail-biting in adult life as evidence of frustration or overindulgence during this very early period. A child who is frustrated by too little stimulation at this stage may become aggressive, depressed and often unable to develop personal relationships. Too much stimulation may lead to people having a high opinion of themselves and being dependent on others.

The anal phase

During the second and third years of life, children become more capable of control over their bowels and are said to obtain pleasure from the retention and expulsion of faeces. Potty training starts during this period and if parents approach this training in too strict a manner, Freud argued, it could result in the formation of what he called the 'anal personality' in adulthood. People with an 'anal personality' may become excessively concerned with order and cleanliness, and be unable to bear unpredictability or untidiness. They become overpossessive, obsessive, sadistic or generally miserable.

The phallic phase

This is the last of the important phases in child development in Freudian theory. During this phase, between 3 and 5 years, the genitals become the area of the body from which the child gets most pleasure. Freud saw this stage as the most important one in personality development. During it, children will be socialised into learning what is right or wrong and learning sex roles. Girls unconsciously want their fathers (what Freud called the 'Electra complex') and boys their mothers (what Freud called the 'Oedipus complex'). It is at this stage that the sex role develops – masculine behaviour in boys and feminine behaviour in girls – through the process of identification that involves the adoption of the father's or mother's whole range of attitudes, values and beliefs. After this stage, a child may act as the child thinks the mother or father would in a given situation.

Problems with the psychoanalytic theory

Freud's theories have been criticised because he worked as a therapist and gained most of his experience and insights from the behaviour of patients. It is argued that his experience was limited and his sample biased because it was middle-aged, middle-class and mostly female. His theory is said to be unscientific, cannot be repeated and has too many hypothetical notions that are not directly observable.

Summary of psychoanalytic theory

- *Oral stage, 0–2 years* – According to Freud this is the first stage of personality development. The baby has the instinct to take pleasure from feeding. Fixation at this stage can occur because of too little or too much stimuli.
- *Anal stage, 1–3 years (the stages may overlap)* – At this stage the child continues to derives pleasure from its mouth. During the anal phase the child starts to learn to control the body, arms, trunk and anus. Fixation at this stage may be caused by lax or too strict potty training.
- *Phallic stage, 3–6 years* – Freud argued that at about three years of age the child begins to experience sexual feelings about its parents. Boys develop such feelings for their mothers and girls towards their fathers. Children begin to develop feelings of guilt because of these sexual feelings and so begin to 'identify' with the respective parent to solve the feelings. Boys begin to act like their fathers and girls like their mothers. If this stage is not successfully negotiated, then problems may develop later with sexual relationships.

Activity 28

Chose two individuals (at two different life stages) and relate two main theories of development to them.

Erik Erikson

Erikson was a Freudian by training but developed his own theory of development, which differed from Freud's in several key respects. While Freud believed that personality is fixed by the age of 5, Erikson believed that development continued throughout the lifespan. Erikson believed that there were eight innately determined sequential stages of development (this is known as epigenetics) and that these stages were not strictly related to specific ages (although ages are provided as a reference). Central to Erikson's theory is the development of the ego. Ego strength accrues one quality at a time, and each of Erikson's stages develops one ego quality. Each stage of life has a crisis for the individual, which must be resolved in order to progress to the next stage.

Summary of Erikson's theory

- *Stage One: Basic trust versus mistrust* – This stage occurs between the age of 0 and 1, and is focused on the child's relationship with its parents. Through this relationship the child will learn either trust or suspicion and fear. The outcome for the ego is HOPE.

- *Stage Two: Autonomy versus doubt* – This stage occurs between the ages of 1 and 3, and still focuses on the child's relationship with its parents. The child is developing motor and mental abilities, resulting in increasing independence. The child will either develop confidence or doubts about its own adequacy. The outcome of this stage for the ego is WILL.

- *Stage Three: Initiative versus guilt* – The social focus of this stage (age 3–5) now expands to the whole family. The child engages in considerable environmental discovery and exploration, and will either develop purposefulness or guilt for seeking discovery. The outcome of this stage for the ego is PURPOSE.

- *Stage Four: Industry versus inferiority* – This stage occurs roughly between the ages of 6 and 11, and the social focus for the child now expands to its immediate neighbourhood and school. The child is interested in learning how things work and tries to develop a sense of order and rules. If adults are troublesome to the child in achieving this, the child can develop a sense of inferiority. The successful outcome for the ego is COMPETENCE.

- *Stage Five: Identity versus role confusion* – This stage is Erikson's famous adolescent crisis, where the person's focus is primarily on peer groups. The adolescent is attempting to develop an integrated sense of self that is personally acceptable yet distinct from others. Failure to achieve this results in role confusion, indecisiveness and a sense of inadequacy. Although most individuals resolve this stage by early adulthood, for some this role confusion can last for many years. The successful outcome for the ego is FIDELITY or, in other words, being trustworthy and reliable.

- *Stage Six: Intimacy versus isolation* – This stage would normally occur in young adulthood, focusing on relationships with friends and spouse. The individual is attempting to learn how to share him or herself with others on a moral, emotional and sexual level. Success in this will result in the establishment of warm and nurturing relationships, while failure will result in loneliness and isolation. The successful outcome for the ego is LOVE.

- *Stage Seven: Generativity versus self-absorption* – This stage usually occurs in middle adulthood, focusing on interactions both within the family and also at work. Individuals either attempt to look beyond themselves, becoming concerned about society and others, or become preoccupied with their own personal well-being and material gain. The successful outcome for the ego is CARE, or the ability to have compassion for others.

- *Stage Eight: Integrity versus despair* – This stage is normally associated with late adulthood, and focuses on the relationship between the individual and all others. The individual will attempt to resolve previous psychosocial crises and, in doing so, develop dignity, satisfaction and personal fulfilment. If unsuccessful, the individual will see the past as a series of disappointments, failures and misfortunes. It is perhaps the worst end to a life, to die with such regrets. The successful outcome for the ego is WISDOM, which represents the highest level of ego development.

Erikson's theory is typical of a stage theory, or a discontinuous theory – discontinuous because it is broken up into stages. This theory has unquestionably been the most influential of all developmental theories and, although more recent research has modified it somewhat, Erikson is still the most commonly used model of lifespan development.

Piaget – cognitive development theory and its relationship to personality development

Cognitive development theory refers to the ordinary changes that occur in the way children understand and cope with their world. This theory focuses on the cognitive aspect of morality and, hence, on moral development. The approach offers a progressive view of morality. It differs from Freud's approach because it views morality as developing gradually throughout childhood and adolescence into adulthood. During the 1930s and 1940s Piaget developed a theory of how children learn about things. His theory is concerned with how the child's knowledge and understanding change with age. He did not believe that intelligence was fixed at birth. His theory is concerned with how our senses take in from our environment information that we store in our brains; as we process this information our behaviour changes as a result. His theory emphasises the importance of imitation, imaging and symbolic representation during the period 2 to 7 years.

Piaget claimed that human thinking develops in a fixed sequence of stages and that it is not possible to skip a stage. He stressed that children think in a different way to adults. Over a number of years and numerous experiments, he came to the conclusion that the morality of the 5 to 9 year old is subject to another's laws or rules, and that the child of 10 years or over is subject to his or her own laws or rules.

Piaget was particularly interested in how children understand the world. The child's development takes place through the development of what he calls schemata – mental representations or ideas about what things are and how we deal with them – which can be likened to a set of rules about how to interact with the environment. The first schemata are for reflexes: thinking in the young child is only concerned with the information it picks through the senses, which are mostly concerned with the child's needs and wants. These 'reflexes' allow a young child to survive during the first few months of life. The reflexes are stimulated by any stimuli. For example, a child touching a hot object will pull its hand away. It is not until about the age of 7 that children begin to think about their own actions and their effect upon other people.

As children reach 10 to 15 years, they start to develop logic and reasoning, and to think about what things 'ought' to be like. Piaget stresses self-motivation and emphasises self-regulation, which he calls the 'process of equilibration'. This process has two aspects:

- *Assimilation* – children absorb experiences into structures that they already possess through the process of 'assimilation'.
- *Accommodation* – structures within the child have to be modified and adjusted to take in experiences that do not fit into the structures already in existence. For example, John, a 2 year old, has established that wheels are round. When he is given a wooden truck with squared wheels that moved when pulled by a string, he has to adjust his thinking to take in this new fact.

Essentially, Piaget shows that the child's thinking moves from a stage of egocentricity in early childhood to reversible reaction in early adolescence. Although he was primarily concerned with intellectual development, his theory has important implications for personality development.

A child in the egocentric stage is intellectually able to see the world only from its own point of view. For example, a mother told her 6-year-old daughter off for wandering away while playing on the swings and getting 'lost'. The child was quite unable to understand her mother's anxiety and said, 'But I knew where I was'. In other words, the child could not see or appreciate that the situation could look different from the mother's point of view.

One could argue that the primary consequence of personality development is to be able see a situation from another person's point of view. According to Piaget, this is quite a late development and in many cases it is not until adolescence that the logical ability to 'go back to the beginning' (i.e. reversible reactions) develops, enabling a child to look at the same situation from different viewpoints.

Piaget devised many simple but elegant experiments to illustrate this progression. For example, he had a piece of cardboard that was blue on one side and red on the other. He sat opposite the child and showed both sides of the cardboard to the child so the child could see each side was a different colour. He then placed the cardboard vertically between himself and the child, asking the child, 'What colour can you see?'. The child would answer, 'Red'. He then asked, 'What colour can I see?' and younger children would answer, 'Red'. They were unable to see that the piece of cardboard looked different from his point of view, even though they had been shown both coloured sides beforehand.

In this way, Piaget showed that the process of development is inextricably linked with the developing brain and intellect of the child. Furthermore, at different ages the thinking of the child operates according to different rules from those of the adult. Piaget claimed that children spend the first 10 years unable to use the rules of logic that most adults would use. He argued that logical thought develops from about puberty.

One criticism of Piaget's work was that he was always looking for what the average child could do at various stages. By doing this, he ignored the great variations in the ways individuals think. Others thought that Piaget underestimated the ability of younger children.

Summary of the cognitive development theory

- *Adaptive stage: 0–1 year* – This is often referred to as the 'sensory motor stage'. Piaget believed that children were born with reflexes that helped babies to survive and adapt to their environments. As the child adapts to the environment it has different kinds of experience and cognition. This cognition, in Piaget's terms, is not something that can be measured as it is individual to each child. Piaget calls this process of organisation and adapting invariant functions. These functions are individual to each child, as are the schemata (mental representations of how to deal with things, e.g. cross the road or eat bread) and operations that allow the child to order schemata in a logical way. This allows children to imagine what might happen if they take a particular course.
- *Pre-operational stage: 2–7 years* – During this stage the child sees the world only from its own point of view (egocentric) and also believes that everyone else holds the same view. The child also believes that everyone holds the same way of thinking about right or wrong (moral realism). Seeing things from other people's point of view can begin when the child develops the ability to

imagine this – known as 'decentring'. During this stage the child also believes that all objects have consciousness and feel emotions (animism).

- *Concrete operational stage: 7–12 years* – During this period the child begins to think logically and can think about objects without the object being present. The egocentric stage declines, as does the belief in animism. Children begin to see situations from other people's points of view.
- *Formal operational stage: 12–16 years* – The teenager begins to think in an abstract manner, to work things out in his or her head. Young people begin also to consider moral and philosophical matters.

Activity 29

What explanation would you give to parents to explain why their child always seems to get lost if not watched every moment?

Genetic and biological processes of development

How do we explain the differences that do occur between the sexes? There are two approaches to this question:

- *The biological approach* – This would argue that sex differences are innate; males and females are programmed for certain types of activity that are comparable with male or female roles. Bowlby (1951) argued that some differences in the behaviour of children are genetically transmitted. He believed that mothers must have maternal instincts to form bonds with their babies and that these show themselves some time after puberty. This theory is not well accepted now: many women today choose not to have children or to have them later in life. These facts are put forward to argue that the maternal instinct is not as strong as Bowlby thought.
- *The social approach* – This takes social factors into account in relation to biological ones. This theory emphasises how children of different temperaments or social conditioning contribute to their own development by influencing how others treat them. Parents or adults prefer to spend time with children who respond to them and the more demonstrative or demanding children tend to get most attention.

Activity 30

You are working in a playgroup as a helper. How would you use the information you have gathered to help you support a child in the playgroup who is unresponsive to adults?

Potential conflicts within a multicultural society

Symbolic interactionism

Symbolic interactionism is one of the most influential fields of study in modern sociology. It was built on foundations developed by John Dewey, George Mead and Charles Cooley early in the 20th century. The central premise of symbolic interactionism is that human psychological development is constructed in a social process. That means that who we are and how we develop is the result of intimate personal communication with other people. The self, or self-concept, is developed by each person in respect of how they believe they are perceived by others. The ways we act toward others have the intention of preserving the existing or desired image we have of ourselves. Desired image may be as important as existing image, because of our orientation to specific reference groups (see pages 152–153).

Interactionists believe that our sense of self – who we are and how we develop – is wholly dependent on interacting with others. This process begins in infancy, when the child relates to its parent and develops a sense of self through that relationship. Interactionism was an influence on Erikson's theory, which, although epigenetic, highlighted a primary role for this interactive process. For this reason, Erikson indicted for each of his eight stages a focus for this interaction. From a purely interactionist perspective, however, stages are less obvious, as our sense of self, our values and attitudes, and our development are wholly dependent on social interaction with others.

The most influential interactionist theorist is Erving Goffman, whose book *The Presentation of Self in Everyday Life,* published in 1959, made a profound impact on the social sciences and placed interactionism in a high-profile position, particularly in social work theory. Goffman employs a 'dramaturgical approach' in studying the development of individual identity. This means he views interaction as a performance that both communicates self-concept and adjusts self-concept to the relevant audience or environment. Goffman describes this presentation of self as 'front', which the individual will attempt to present in a consistent manner. Goffman's theory, therefore, is a continuous and environmentalist model of development that presents stability as the major force.

In presenting a front to others, the individual creates a role, which he or she attempts to preserve. There are different roles that the same individual can use in different circumstances. We all have what Goffman describes as a 'frontstage' presentation for formal environments and a 'backstage' presentation that we use in situations with which we are more familiar. The pressure to develop the proper front – an idealised concept – can create problems for individuals who are marginalised in society (see Unit One). Those individuals who are different and do not easily fit into mainstream society must adopt roles that assume the character of being discredited in some way. Goffman studied this aspect of interaction in some detail and wrote about it in his books *Stigma* and *Interaction Ritual,* both of which have had enormous influence on social work theory. Goffman describes, for example, the behaviour of individuals with mental illness as a presentation of themselves in order to fit in with the expectations of others. Goffman's concepts of stigma, institutionalisation and the 'sick' role make interactionism one of the developmental theories of particular relevance to health and care work.

Activity 31

Try to think of all of the different roles you have in differing situations, such as brother, student, friend, etc. Sketch out the many roles you have in the form of a spider diagram. In pairs, discuss how different these roles are, and try to identify which role is the 'real' you.

Goffman's work was largely anecdotal and observational but intensely rigorous in his analysis. There is still considerable scope to explore the concepts of interactionism and one of the methods used is known as ethnomethodology, which is the study of how people maintain the social order. Some interesting research done by Harold Garfinkel has shown that social order cannot really break down because, when rules are removed, individuals quickly replace them. This means that, because rules are directly and actively created by individuals, the concept of society is perhaps more robust than some sociologists believe.

The implications of interactionist perspectives, and the proposal that reality is actually socially constructed, has had a major influence on our understanding of human development. It means that we all continuously adjust what we perceive as real by sharing subjective meanings with others. Our self-concept is included in this and must, through interacting with others, pass a test of acceptance. This constant re-adjustment of who we are is progressive and constitutes what interactionists perceive as human development.

Maslow's hierarchy of needs

Abraham Maslow was an American psychologist who developed a theory in 1970 that proposes that human development is governed by the pursuit of basic needs. His theory, based on motivational theory, has been immensely influential and is known as Maslow's hierarchy of needs.

The important point about this theory is that it proposes that our needs as human beings are organised in a hierarchy, some needs being more essential than others for survival. We are anchored by our most basic biological needs, called primary

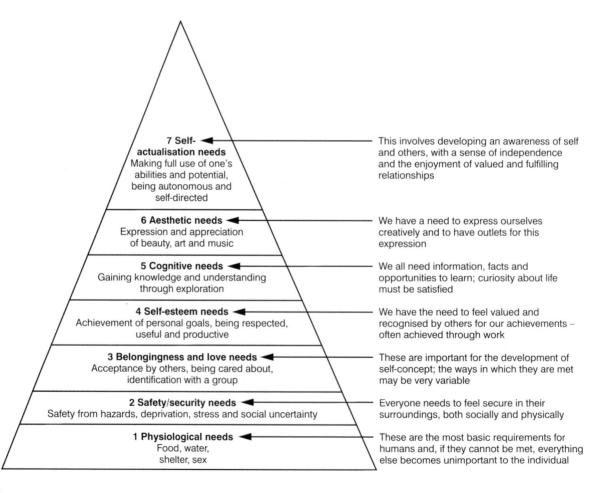

7 Self-actualisation needs
Making full use of one's abilities and potential, being autonomous and self-directed

This involves developing an awareness of self and others, with a sense of independence and the enjoyment of valued and fulfilling relationships

6 Aesthetic needs
Expression and appreciation of beauty, art and music

We have a need to express ourselves creatively and to have outlets for this expression

5 Cognitive needs
Gaining knowledge and understanding through exploration

We all need information, facts and opportunities to learn; curiosity about life must be satisfied

4 Self-esteem needs
Achievement of personal goals, being respected, useful and productive

We have the need to feel valued and recognised by others for our achievements – often achieved through work

3 Belongingness and love needs
Acceptance by others, being cared about, identification with a group

These are important for the development of self-concept; the ways in which they are met may be very variable

2 Safety/security needs
Safety from hazards, deprivation, stress and social uncertainty

Everyone needs to feel secure in their surroundings, both socially and physically

1 Physiological needs
Food, water, shelter, sex

These are the most basic requirements for humans and, if they cannot be met, everything else becomes unimportant to the individual needs. If these needs are not met, we cannot survive. Only when these basic needs are met do we focus on higher needs, called growth needs. Maslow suggests that the course of each life is dominated by attempting to satisfy each level of need and then moving on to the next. Maslow's hierachy has provided a really useful framework for exploring the importance of motivation to human development. His theory is summarised in the box on page 184.

Key terms

After reading this unit you should be able to understand the following words and phrases. If you do not, go back through the unit and find out, or look them up in the Glossary.

Cognitive skills   *Reinforcement*
Epigenetics   *Role*
Intelligence   *Self-concept*
Motor skills   *Self-esteem*
Needs   *Socialisation*

Review questions

1   Explain the concept of life stages.
2   How does personality develop?
3   What is the basis of social learning theory?
4   Write a definition of language. Why do humans use language?
5   What does the term 'self-concept' refer to?
6   What does Erikson have to say about the life-stage of adolescence?
7   What are the physical and psychological manifestations of the menopause in women?
8   List four theories of ageing and write down brief details of each one.
9   Discuss the nature–nurture debate.
10 List as many environmental factors as you can that may influence the physical and psychological development of children.
11 How do roles influence our development?
12 Identify the different theoretical perspectives of human development.

Assignment

Produce a report based on a study of the human development of two individuals at different life stages (the youngest must be under 8 years old and the other at least 19 years old). You will need to show that you understand the way the individuals have developed and why this has been the case.

To gain a merit or distinction you are asked to analyse and/or evaluate certain situations or tasks. Analysing means breaking the task down into detailed parts and discussing the pros and cons of the situation. To evaluate you must present facts to support your opinions or findings and you must also determine the value of your findings and appraise them.

To get an **E** grade you must complete tasks 1–4

To get a **C** grade you must complete tasks 1–7

To get an **A** grade you must complete tasks 1–10

Tasks

1 Clearly describe the growth and development of two individuals at different life stages.

2 Trace the development of two major skill areas in each individual.

3 Describe the range of factors that may have affected the development of the two individuals.

4 Describe four main theories of development, relating them to the individuals.

5 Compare and contrast the development of the two individuals.

6 Explain accurately the influence of the skill areas on the development of the two individuals.

7 Use appropriate theories to analyse the influence of the range of factors on development and present well-considered conclusions.

8 Present coherent arguments based on a comprehensive analysis of the relative importance of the factors that affected the development of the individuals.

9 Explain how the effect of the factors may have been enhanced or minimised.

10 Reflect on how the use of different theories might influence your interpretation of the development of a chosen individual.

Key Skills Opportunity

	You can use this Assignment to provide evidence for the following Key Skills
Communication C3.2, C3.3	When reviewing relevant literature and research.
Application of Number N3.1	When recording appropriate measurements to monitor the human development and growth of two individuals.
Application of Number N3.3	When carrying through at least one substantial activity that includes straightforward tasks relating to N3.1 and N3.3.
Information Technology IT 3.1, IT 3.3	If you use a computer to analyse data and statistics to illustrate findings.

Health, social care and early years services

What is covered in this unit

5.1 **The origins and development of health, social care and early years services**

5.2 **National and local provision of services**

5.3 **Access to services**

5.4 **Funding of services**

5.5 **How services are organised today**

5.6 **Informal carers**

At the end of this unit you will be asked to produce an investigation into one local health, social care or early years service that is part of a national framework. This unit will guide you through what you need to know in order to put this report together successfully. If you would like to see further details of the tasks you are likely to need to carry out for assessment please refer to the end of the unit where an assignment has been set (see pp. 251–252).

This unit is assessed through your portfolio work. The grade you achieve for your research project will be your grade for the unit.

Materials you will need to complete this unit:

- A local authority Community Care Plan
- Reports of local Community Health Councils
- Annual reports of Local Health Authorities
- Recent government documents (these can be obtained from the Department of Health website, http://www.doh.gov.uk)
- Access to websites of local, voluntary and national health care and early years organisations, e.g. the National Children's Bureau (http://www.ncb.org.com), Disability Net (http://www.disabilitynet.co.uk), the Imperial Cancer Research Fund (http://www.icnet.uk/index.html), the Disability Information and Support Centre (http://www.intadisc.demon.co.uk), NSPCC (www.nspcc.org.uk)
- Social Trends, Office of National Statistics statistical information
- Regional Trends, Office of National Statistics regional statistics
- The latest General Household Survey (published by HMSO).

5.1 The origins and development of health, social care and early years services

The formation of the National Health Service

The National Health Service (NHS) came into existence on 5 July 1948 as a direct result of the National Health Services Act 1946. The legislation was preceded by an influential report from the British Medical Association on health insurance and the Beveridge Report on Social Insurance and Allied Services. The minister who piloted the legislation through Parliament and oversaw the formation of the NHS was Aneurin Bevan, Minister of Health 1945–51.

It is important to recognise that this legislation built on a series of earlier plans, arguably started in 1808 with the County Asylums Act. Subsequent legislation included the Public Health Act 1848, the Metropolitan Poor Act 1867, the National Insurance Act 1911 and the Local Government Act 1929. In other words, there had long been a recognition of the weakness in the pattern of health care services and their availability to all.

The 1946 Act brought the health services and, in particular, the hospitals (most of which had previously been controlled by charities or voluntary organisations) under the control of the Ministry of Health. It expanded the provision of the National Insurance Act, which had provided for general practitioner care for working people, to cover access to health care for all, free at the point of delivery. Prior to the 1946 Act the funding for this care had been by private insurance through, for example, friendly societies. After the Act the funding came from general taxation, national insurance contributions and charges made to private patients. The Beveridge Report that preceded the Act had made the assumption that there was a fixed quantity of illness in the community, which the introduction of a health service, free at the point of consumption, would gradually reduce. (Funding of the present services is considered later in this unit.)

On what date did the NHS come into existence?

'Stuffing their mouths with gold'

One of the major difficulties in the setting up of the National Health Service was to get the agreement of doctors and consultants. Clearly, for the service to work, there needed to be co-operation from the medical profession. Members were, however, divided in their views.

- At one extreme were the consultants, who were able to command high fees for their work and feared that they would lose money and autonomy within a national service. They were at the top of their profession and had the greatest power.
- At the other extreme were general practitioners working in areas of poverty and unemployment. In such areas the opportunities to collect payments were limited and most insurance schemes were for people in employment. For these practitioners the **contracts** under the NHS would provide opportunities to plan health education and provide higher levels of care. There was still a fear of the loss of highly prized professional autonomy.

In order to persuade the consultants to join the NHS, the Minister of Health allowed them to maintain their private practices and to make use of NHS hospitals for consultancy and practice. In this way they were not becoming part of the NHS but were working within it while maintaining their work outside. The accusation was made that in order to form the NHS the Minister had had to 'buy off' the opponents in the medical profession by 'stuffing their mouths with gold'.

The legacy of these concessions to doctors still exists, although the funding arrangements in terms of **purchasers** and **providers** has blurred the distinctions.

The government had effectively nationalised the health services in an attempt to provide fair access to all.

In 1980 the Black Report (an official report of the investigative committee on inequalities in health in Britain, chaired by Sir Douglas Black) indicated that, after 40 years of the NHS, this provision was still not being made. In part, the recognition of this has been evident from the number of changes in the management of the NHS over the years. We will be looking at these changes in an attempt to identify some of the underpinning issues. The structure set up at the inception of the NHS (see figure below) was in place for almost 26 years. However, weaknesses began to appear almost from the start. In particular, there were three problem areas that were highlighted in the 1960s:

- The Gillie Report in 1963 recognised the greater emphasis being placed on **primary health care teams** and the integration of health and care services.
- In 1967 the poor quality of care given to certain patient groups was highlighted.
- The administrative control of the NHS was becoming ever more cumbersome. In particular, the need to provide balanced packages of care for all people in the community was being distorted by demands from acute specialities (surgery and general medicine) being favoured over long-term geriatric and psychiatric provision.

What three major problems were experienced within the NHS in the 1960s?

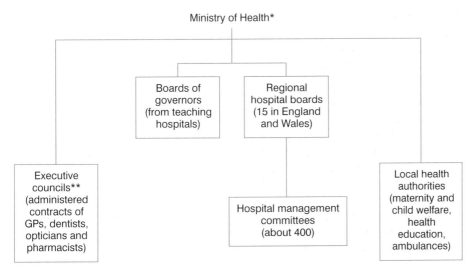

Ministry of Health*

Boards of governors (from teaching hospitals)

Regional hospital boards (15 in England and Wales)

Executive councils** (administered contracts of GPs, dentists, opticians and pharmacists)

Hospital management committees (about 400)

Local health authorities (maternity and child welfare, health education, ambulances)

*Later the Department of Health and Social Security (1968)
**Executive council members appointed by local professionals, local authorities and the Ministry

Structure of the NHS 1948–74

189

The tripartite structure of the health services under the National Health Services Act 1948

The National Health Service Act 1973

As early as 1962 the weaknesses of the **tripartite structure** had been identified, and in 1968 and 1970 the government produced papers proposing reforms in the NHS. It was another three years before the National Health Service Act 1973 was passed and it came into operation on 1 April 1974. The structure in England from 1974 to 1992 is shown in the figures on pages 191 and 192.

- *Wales*: The structure in Wales was similar, with the Welsh Office combining the functions of a central government department and the regional health authority.
- *Northern Ireland*: In Northern Ireland there were four health and social services boards linked to the DHSS (Northern Ireland). Each board was split into several districts and was responsible for personal social services as well as health services.

The three main aims of the reorganisation were as follows:

- *Unification* of health services under one authority. This was not total as GPs maintained independent contractor status and some postgraduate teaching hospitals retained separate boards of governors. Independent contractor status means that GP independently contract with the Health Authority to provide services – they are paid directly when these services are provided. GPs are not employees of the Health Authority unlike nurses or consultants.
- *Co-ordination* between health authorities and related local government services. To this end, the area health authority boundaries were to a large extent the same as local authority boundaries. Joint consultative committees were set up between the two types of authority to discuss the delivery of services and common issues.
- *Improvement* of management. A key feature was the introduction of multidisciplinary teams and **consensus management** (a style of management where all managers agree on a course of action; no one manager is usually in direct control of services). It is no coincidence that the management structures borrowed ideas from the private sector, as they were devised with the help of the management consultants from that sector.

All the changes reflected the need to pursue national priorities at local level and a movement of resources towards neglected groups such as the elderly and mentally ill. The new structure meant that by 1977 16 400 extra administrative posts had been created to cope with the bureaucracy. The decision-making procedures were long indeed, meaning that the costs of reorganisation were high and staff morale in all areas was low.

As early as 1979 the then Conservative government produced proposals for reform, which were revised and finally published in July 1980. In essence these proposed the removal of one management tier by amalgamating the functions of District Management Teams and Area Health Authorities within a new body, the

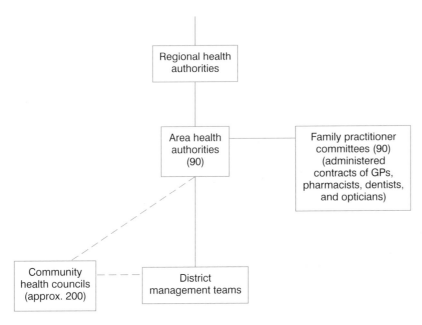

Structure of the NHS 1974–1982

District Health Authority. In 1981 the proposals were extended to give Family Practitioner Committees a level of independence with the status of employing authorities.

Health and Social Security Act 1984

The Health and Social Security Act 1984 encompassed these changes and recognised the structure that had been in place from 1982 (see figure on page 192). In Wales the structure was similar to England, again without a specific regional health authority. In Northern Ireland the Health and Social Services Boards were retained.

One important effect of this reorganisation was the loss of boundary links with local authorities in England and Wales, and hence integration of health services and personal social services became more difficult.

From 1982 increased emphasis was placed on devolving management of districts down to units, each with a general manager. These could be made up of a physical entity, such as a large hospital or group of hospitals, or a more diverse unit such as a 'community health unit'. The latter would have responsibility for services such as district nursing, health visiting, chiropody, community psychiatric nursing, etc.

It is these units (hospital or community-based) that have more recently become self-governing trusts.

The move towards a mixed economy of care

A mixed economy of care means the provision of health and or care services from a variety of sources and funded in a variety of different ways

Since 1983 it had been recognised that there were weaknesses in the general management of the National Health Service. Accordingly, the Griffiths Report

Why did integration of the health and social care services become difficult after the introduction of the Health and Social Security Act 1984?

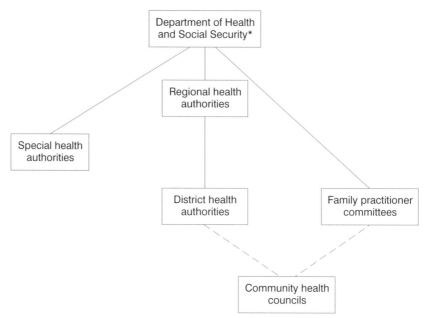

*The DHSS became the Department of Health in 1988

Structure of the NHS 1982–90

recommended that general managers should be appointed at all levels in the NHS to provide leadership, introduce a continual search for change and cost improvement, to motivate staff and develop a dynamic management approach.

There was also a recommendation that management be streamlined at the centre with the establishment of a Health Services Supervisory Board and an NHS Management Board within the then Department of Health and Social Security (DHSS), with the chairperson of the Management Board being drawn from outside the NHS and civil service.

Further change was instigated in 1989 with the government White Paper *Working for Change*, which proposed the creation of competition between hospitals and other service providers.

It introduced the concept of a distinction between purchasers and providers of health care. District health authorities (DHAs) would have the responsibility for purchasing services for patients, using funds based on the population (taking into account factors such as age, sex, etc.). Hospitals would then have to contract to provide services. The aim was to make the providers more responsive and more efficient as money would follow patients. DHAs could purchase services from public, private and voluntary providers. An example might be for a DHA to purchase 100 tonsillectomy operations from a local hospital. The money for these would be paid to the hospital, be it NHS or in the private sector.

- Hospitals (and any other units) were be able to opt out of health authority control and become self-governing NHS trusts.
- DMUs or directly managed units, usually hospitals, were managed directly by the district health authority.
- Family practitioner committees (FPCs) were to become family health service authorities (FHSAs), which were to be accountable to the regional health authorities rather than directly to the Ministry of Health. An FHSA had a general manager, together with four health professionals, five non-executives and a chairperson.

FHSAs

The Family Health Service Authority, which replaced the Family Practitioner Committee, was responsible for providing information to the public and developing health promotion activities over and above its existing responsibilities for screening programs for cervical cancer. FHSAs were involved, for example, in co-ordinating the call and recall of women for breast cancer screening and also in encouraging GPs to give priority to health promotion. FHSAs no longer exist.

Purchasers and providers 1990–99

At the same time as health care trusts were able to move towards direct control of their own affairs, there was also a move to take some of the purchaser roles from the DHAs. GP practices with a large number of patients were able to receive funding directly from the regional health authorities to purchase a defined range of services for their patients. (These were known as fundholding GP practices.) The services they purchased included outpatient services, diagnostic tests and inpatient and day-care treatments, for which it was possible to choose the time and place of treatments.

Activity 1

Find out and list how many NHS Trusts operate in your locality. What services do they provide? Present your findings to your colleagues.

Objectives of these changes

One of the objectives of these changes in the organisation and management of the public sector was the control of the cost to the taxpayer. Funding to the NHS by the government was achieved in two ways:

- open-ended funding for most of the primary care services provided by family practitioners
- cash-limited allocations to DHAs for expenditure on hospital and community health services and FHSAs for a limited range of expenditure. Cash limited allocations are distributed to DHAs on a 'capitation' model which uses death rates and the age structure of the local population to calculate how much funding the DHA should get. This money is distributed through the RHAs.

Activity 2

Visit your local library and gain access to the local health authority strategic plan. Find out what services are provided under the following headings: primary, secondary, and tertiary, care.

Key Skills

You can use Activity 1 to provide evidence for Key Skills Communication C3.1.

Key Skills

You can use Activity 2 to provide evidence for Key Skills Communication C3.2.

The structure evolved and the number of Regional Health Authorities was reduced in 1994 to 8 (from 14) in England. The role of the RHAs was altered to became more focused on the purchaser aspects and administration. The number of NHS Trusts rose rapidly and there are now very few directly managed units under the control of the District Health Authorities. The DHAs came together with the Family Health Service Authorities to take on a powerful position of purchasers of care. This emphasised the split between the purchaser and provider roles. Ironically it also made the role less clear for fundholding GPs as their numbers increased. Whereas the FHSAs and the DHAs undertook both roles when they had direct control of units and GPs, they fell firmly in the camp of the purchasers. The fundholding GPs had the role of providers of primary care and purchasers of care at other levels.

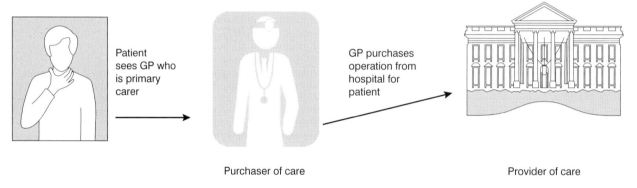

Patient sees GP who is primary carer

GP purchases operation from hospital for patient

Purchaser of care

Provider of care

Fundholding GPs as purchasers and providers

Case study

Fundholder GPs and access to care

Early experience of the implementation of the NHS and Community Care Act 1990 was that several hospitals had completed their contracts before the end of their financial year. Newspapers had highlighted the fact that, in some hospitals, routine surgery was only available to patients of fundholding GPs. What had happened is that the hospitals had contracted with the District Health Authority to carry out a certain number of the routine surgical operations. Once that number had been completed, there was no funding available to carry out more.

This meant that people still requiring such operations had to wait until the next financial year. It was a problem created at the district level, where the original number was determined. It might also have been that the hospital was charging more than others and so was allocated fewer operations.

The situation was complicated by the fact that the hospital could still accept contracts to fill the empty places but the only funds available were from fundholding GPs. These doctors contracted with hospitals to carry out routine procedures for their patients and had some control over with whom and when the contact was to be carried out. This explained the newspaper headlines highlighting queue jumping by the patients of fundholding GPs.

Key Skills

You can use Activity 3 to provide evidence for Key Skills Communication C3.2.

Activity 3

In your own area, establish which organisations deliver health care. Identify where they fit within the structure of the new NHS.

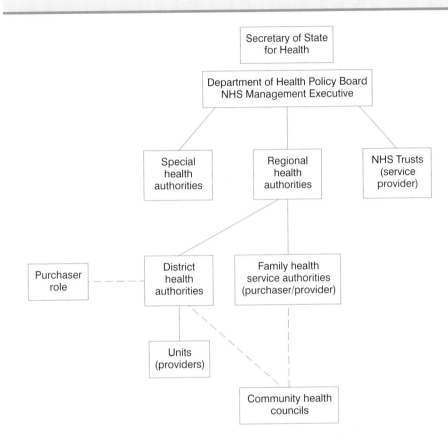

Structure of NHS 1990–99

The most recent changes in the National Health Service, resulting from the Health Act 1999, are discussed in detail in section 5.5 below.

Activity 4

Analyse how the NHS's practices were influenced by external factors such as:

a clients
b public
c government policy
d the work of other agencies.

Key Skills

You can use Activity 4 to provide evidence for Key Skills Communication C3.2, C3.3.

Local authority welfare and care services

The Ministry of Health was in 1948 responsible for local authority services under the National Health Service Act 1946 and the National Assistance Act 1948. These responsibilities covered nurses, home helps, residential care and social work.

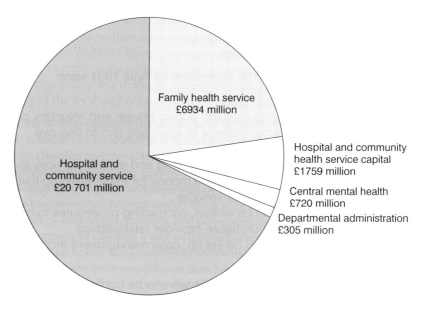

Where the NHS funding was spent, 1993/4

What were the founding principles of the NHS?

You can use Activity 5 to provide evidence for Key Skills Communication C3.2.

Activity 5

Make a list of all the key personnel involved in delivering both health and social care. Identify if they are providers or purchasers of care or both.

The responsibilities of social services departments

The Social Services Committee, established by the Local Authority and Social Services Act 1970, has responsibilities in four areas:

- childcare under the various children's acts and adoption acts, including the Children Act 1989
- provision and regulation of residential accommodation for older people and people with disabilities under the National Assistance Act 1948 and the Registered Homes Act 1984
- welfare services for older people, people with disabilities and those who are chronically ill, and statutory powers under the various Mental Health Acts
- power to delegate some responsibilities to other organisations and to provide necessary assistance.

The ways in which local authorities manage their roles and responsibilities through social services committees varies across the country. An example of the organisational structure for one local authority Social Services Department is given in the figure on page 238.

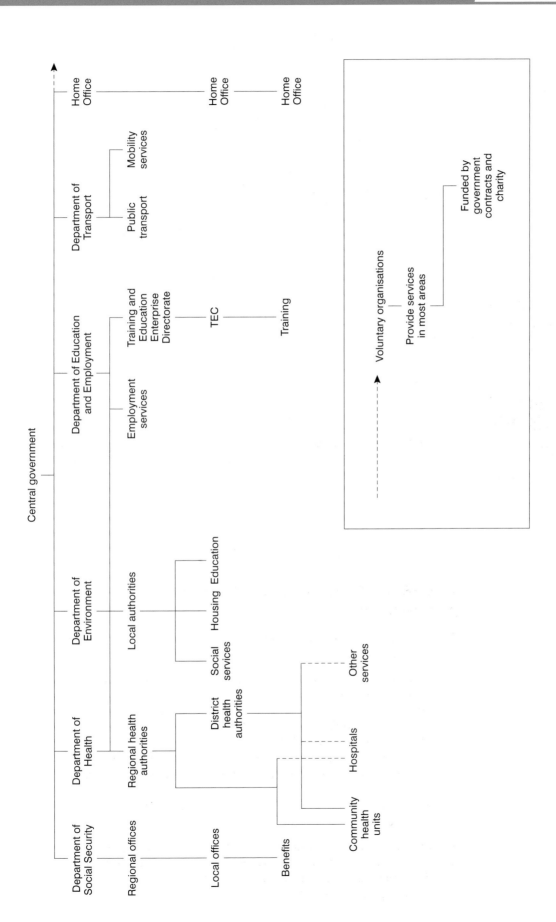

Present relationships of organisations involved in health and social care

> ## Case study
>
> ### Social care and children
>
> One area of local authority care that has received attention and has been the subject of significant legislation is care of children. It is no coincidence that many early charities that are still working today had their roots in working with children. Children are very vulnerable and so their protection has long been seen as a priority. The care of children is governed by many laws. Since 1969, for example, there have been at least 20 Acts passed by Parliament relating to children.
>
> The legislation can be broken down into two areas:
>
> - Specifying where public authorities can intervene in children's cases, for example the Foster Children Act 1980 and the Children and Young Persons Act 1969.
> - Those Acts that do not initially involve public authorities but define the position of children within families, for example the Guardianship Act 1973 and the Family Law Reform Act 1987.
>
> This mixture of legislation has more recently been brought into focus, and has been largely replaced by the Children Act 1989.
>
> Social services have responsibilities to children as follows:
>
> - Supervision of children placed in day care – nurseries, playgroups, childminders, etc. – which includes the need to register such provision and define the acceptable standards.
> - Preventing children having to be received into care or appear before the courts.
> - Receiving into care children whose parents are unable to care for them – legislation describes appropriate circumstances.
> - Initiation of court proceedings in respect of children and looking after the interests of children subject to certain court orders.
> - Supporting the best interests of children in their care, providing accommodation for them and maintaining them.
> - Supervising children placed for adoption – many departments also act as adoption agencies and arrange for children to be adopted.
> - Supervising children in foster care.

Individual entitlement to social services

Within a welfare state the expectation is that the state will provide for the health-care needs of the individual. In an ideal world that would be the case, but to do this would require infinite resources. Instead, there are certain services to which you are entitled and others that may be made available at the discretion of the purchaser or by paying for them yourself. This divide is present within the **statutory services** and has meant that charities are still necessary within a welfare state.

Entitlement to a service comes as a result of legislation, which identifies that something is a statutory right and that the statutory sector must make provision for it. This does not mean that the service must be provided by the statutory sector; it may be provided by the independent sector but paid for by the statutory sector – for example, meals on wheels may be provided by the local voluntary organisation but paid for by the local authority. In some cases the entitlement to a service may mean that a fee has to be paid by the client, with provision being made for those unable to pay.

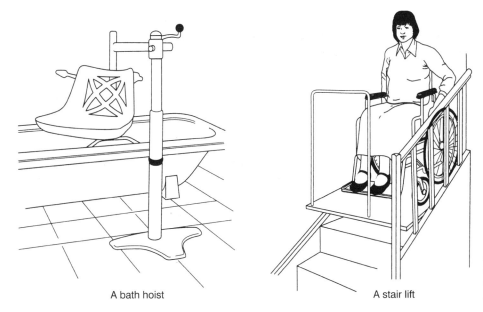

A bath hoist   A stair lift

Expensive pieces of equipment, such as a bath hoist or stair lift, are usually subject to payment

Each local authority can make its own decisions regarding what charges, if any, to make for a number of services (Section 17 of the Health and Social Services and Social Security Adjudications Act 1983). The government encourages authorities to recover the full economic cost of providing home-care and day-care costs where possible. However, the charges should not cause hardship to the client and should take into account the client's ability to pay.

Although the government's care reforms encourage people to live in their own homes, there is no absolute right to equipment to enable them to do so.

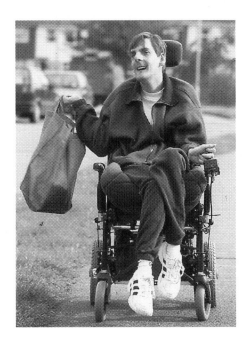

An electronically controlled wheelchair

People can approach social services departments directly for advice on, and the provision of, aids to daily living and other types of equipment. Such aids as wheelchairs, bath aids and aids to eating and dressing are usually provided free or on loan. More expensive pieces of equipment such as hoists, lifts and ramps are, however, subject to payment. The local authority may contract out the provision of some specialist equipment services, such as the services for deaf people or those with sight problems.

Residential care services

The provision of residential care also has to be paid for, but people who need such support can receive financial assistance with the cost of independent sector residential care through local authority social services departments. The local authority must pay the full fees for anyone placed in a residential or nursing home who needs help with the cost. The social services department will usually collect a means-tested contribution from the client towards the cost.

Most health-care services are free, but such services as dentistry, provision of glasses and prescriptions are subject to a charge.

People have a statutory right to services provided by the National Health Service (NHS) and local authorities. However, just because the services are provided on a statutory basis does not mean that the client is entitled to the services if the authority feels that, after assessment, they are not appropriate services. There is no statutory right to services from voluntary, independent or private organisations such as Barnardos, MIND, Scope, Mencap, Age Concern or many of the small local organisations.

Increasingly, the statutory services are becoming purchasers of services, and many independent organisations are providers of services. This means that some statutory services may be contracted out by the local authority to independent organisations.

Statutory services

NHS	Local authority
Hospital services	Day care
GP services	Residential care
Community nursing	Domiciliary services
Nursing homes	Aids and adaptations
Accident and emergency services	Meals on wheels
Approved social worker (mental health)	

Non-statutory services

Local authority	Private/Voluntary/Independent
Luncheon club	Residential care
Transport	Nursing homes
Holidays	Home help
Meals services	
Specialist adaptations	
Aids to daily living	

You can use
Activity 6 to
provide evidence
for Key Skills
Communication
C3.2.

Activity 6

a Investigate, through looking at local literature, the health and social care services to which you are entitled.

b Also identify services that are not part of statutory requirement but are provided by the statutory services.

c If possible, discuss with a care provider any changes that have taken place in the last 20 years.

5.3 Access to services

The resourcing of services is largely controlled by central government. There is direct resourcing of health care through the NHS. Social care (not nursing care or nursing residential care) is most often the responsibility of local authorities, which receive an allocation of money from central government and also raise money through the council tax. The NHS and Community Care Act 1990 requires local authority social services departments to manage the funds available for community care. This is done by assessing two criteria: need and wealth.

It has been the philosophy of governments in Britain for a number of years to reduce public spending on health and social care. One way of achieving this is to induce individuals to make their own provisions for care via private insurance schemes and stakeholder pensions, or to rely upon charities.

Charities are under great strain, as they have to deal with increasing numbers of individuals who need assistance. While they receive some help from central government and local authority grants, they must increasingly rely on their own funds and public generosity, which is also waning.

Of course, some fortunate individuals will always be able to pay for their own health and care requirements. In fact, having significant personal resources puts such individuals well out of reach of the NHS and Community Care Act. They do not need to be assessed for need or for wealth. These individuals are the only ones to have genuine free choice in health and social care services today.

Activity 7

Find out the maximum level of income that a person in your local area can have before they would contribute financially to residential care.

Private insurance for health and care is used elsewhere in the world, for example in the USA and the Republic of Ireland. Some common problems of this method of funding include increased spending on health care, as unnecessary investigations and treatments are provided, without resulting in improved health generally. In addition, insurance payments often fall far short of the true cost of treating serious illnesses, leaving many sick people in serious debt. It has been argued that the encouragement of private medicine and care in Britain has been at the expense of resourcing statutory services.

Activity 8

Find out what the cost of residential care is in one local authority and one private residential home. Discuss with your colleagues why you think there are differences in cost.

Access and entitlement to care

Entitlement to care is very carefully controlled by government, as to make it obligatory to provide care can have massive cost implications. The NHS and Community Care Act recognises this in that it is the right of an individual to have an individual care plan provided by the Social Services Department. There is no legal entitlement to any care identified in the plan. However, once a service has been provided it is illegal for Social Services Departments to withdraw it without a reassessment of the client's situation. The High Court has ruled that services cannot be taken away without reassessment. However, it also ruled that local authorities can take their level of resources into account when drawing up care packages and care plans. This ruling may put paid to the myth of needs-led assessment, as authorities can take into account whether they can afford the provision of a service when drawing up care plans with clients.

Beds blocked by funding crisis

by Linda Steele

Bed blocking and granny dumping. Catchy or insulting the jargon may be but it all amounts to the same thing – a shortage of resources and human misery. Hospitals have warned that beds are 'blocked' by elderly and disabled patients who cannot be discharged because community care services are not available. Patients needing long-term care are caught in the crossfire of the local government and community care funding crisis, and health-service underfunding and the closure of continuing-care NHS beds.

In some cases, this has meant 'granny dumping', with distraught families trying to insist on continuing NHS care because they can neither care for dependent elderly relatives at home nor afford private nursing homes. In other cases, patients have found themselves placed in private nursing homes, where they often have to pay. Elderly people, robbed of the belief that free health care is a cradle-to-grave right, have watched as their savings are eaten away. The crux has been a distinction between medical care, provided free by health authorities, and social care, means-tested and organised by local authorities. Sometimes, the distinction is so fine and the pressure on resources so great that health and local authorities can't agree who's responsible.

In a celebrated case, the Health Ombudsman ruled that the NHS had a duty to provide long-term care to a profoundly brain-damaged man whom a Leeds hospital had discharged to a private nursing home, leaving his wife to foot the bill.

The government has stepped in, not to increase the number of beds or fund care adequately but to end the right to free, long-term NHS care.

Source: Unison Magazine, April 1995

> ### Case study
>
> #### Access to hospital – waiting lists
>
> Many people do not believe the government's assertion that there is a reduction in hospital waiting lists. People have pinpointed methods that may be used to reduce the waiting lists artificially:
>
> * Hospitals may increase the length of time that patients wait before they see a consultant and their name is put on the waiting list in the first place.
> * Patients may be removed from the waiting list, followed by a letter asking them if they still want treatment. If they say yes they are put back on the waiting list as new patients.
> * Private hospitals can be paid to carry out the operation.
> * The procedure or operation may be removed from the list of those that are offered by the NHS.

Activity 9

The costs to the health services of treating a person with lung cancer are high. Is it possible to reduce the incidence of the disease by stopping people from smoking? Discuss with your class colleagues how this could be done.

Key Skills

You can use Activity 9 to provide evidence for Key Skills Communication C3.1.

Ways that people can access care

Having established something of the organisation, structure and staffing of the caring services, it is important to look at how people can make use of the services offered. There are basically three ways that a person can be referred to the care services:

* *Self-referral* – where people seek help themselves, which may involve support from family members.
* *Referral through professionals* – a doctor, social worker, nurse, teacher or other professional may assist the person to obtain care.
* *Compulsory referral* – where the person in need of care is taken into care by someone who is authorised (social worker, doctor, police officer, NSPCC officer) for that person's own (or others') protection.

Self-referral

This is often the first route for most people receiving health and social care. Within the health service self-referral may simply mean turning up at the GP's or dentist's surgery. The first point of contact can also be through a health visitor. Within social care, referral may be to a central office, a local office or direct to a care facility, such as a day care centre or a nursery.

In all cases, the initiative is with the person requiring care, or a friend or relative making the initial contact, e.g. a spouse of a person who is behaving oddly who seeks professional help, or a parent looking for nursery provision for a young child.

Activity 10

List as many services as you can in your locality that a person can refer themselves to.

Self-referral at the GP's surgery

Referral through a professional

Unless they are admitted to hospital as an accident or emergency case, the only way that people can voluntarily receive hospital treatment is by referral from another professional, normally a GP. Where a GP diagnoses or suspects ill-health that requires specialist treatment, the patient is referred to an outpatient clinic or admitted direct to a ward if the case is urgent.

In social care, an example of referral by professionals might be when a teacher in a school suspects child abuse and refers the case to the duty social worker. Under the Children Act 1989, all schools should have a named person who is responsible for making such a referral. Another example might be referral through the police if they have given a 'warning' to a child who has committed an offence and they feel the child should be referred to social services.

Case study

The story of John: a child in need of care

People often think that children are placed in care at birth for the purpose of adoption. There is always a flood of offers to adopt an abandoned baby. The reality of care under the Children Act is very different and many decisions have to be made to enable children to access care. John's story is typical of many cases and is based upon that of a real person, modified sufficiently to protect the confidentiality of the people involved. This scenario gives an indication of the people and agencies involved, and their roles in protecting and assisting young people.

John was the youngest of six children. His mother had been diagnosed as schizophrenic. Her first husband, father of four of the children, had died of a heart attack. At the time of John's birth his mother was living with her third husband. The neighbours had noticed that the children appeared to be well cared for, although they did not always go to school and at times appeared to be left in the care of the oldest child (a 12 year old). The school had also reported the sporadic attendance of the children to the Education Welfare Officer (EWO).

On visiting the home, the EWO noticed that the mother's drugs were left on the kitchen work-surface and that her level of anxiety and actions gave cause for concern. With the mother's permission, the EWO contacted the family GP, who arranged for her admission to a psychiatric hospital. John's father refused any help and insisted that he could cope with the children. However, after a week a neighbour contacted the NSPCC because he had heard one of the children crying for over an hour during the Saturday evening and when he called round had discovered that John's father was working overtime to earn enough money to support his children. The father had impressed on the oldest child that nobody should know that he was out or they would all be taken away to children's homes.

The NSPCC social worker called and worked hard to find ways in which the family could stay together and be provided with support. This included setting up regular after-school care for the children, along with counselling and guidance. It was during the after-school care that carers noticed disturbed behaviour from three of the younger children. Observing and listening to them convinced the carer that the children had been abused either physically or sexually by one or the other of their parents. This was reported to the social worker.

The evidence was significant enough for the social worker to call a case conference and issue an emergency protection order, as it was thought that all the children were in danger. A care order was later sought and granted by the court. After many weeks of work with the children in care, and with both parents, it was decided that in the best interests of the children they should be placed for adoption. This decision had come about as a result of the father's prosecution and conviction for assault, and the mother's requirement for long-term mental health care.

At this point the care of the children was transferred to the local authority social services. This was no reflection on the NSPCC, but shows the way in which the various organisations co-operate. Under the Children Act the needs of the children are paramount and one of those needs was thought to be for them to stay together. Another need was for them to be removed from institutional care and placed within a family environment.

It was not possible to find one family prepared to adopt all the children and so the decision was made to split them up. At the same time the arrangements for care had to be agreed with the court. The judge agreed the details and made a recommendation that the children should meet up on at least two occasions a year.

Eventually, all the children were adopted. John, being the youngest, was easiest to place and eventually ended up with his 12-year-old sister, who, after a long search for adoptive parents, was placed with John's new family.

@ *Discuss with class colleagues the different scenarios that can lead to people seeking care and identify the people who might assist them.*

Compulsory referral

Protection of children

The purpose of compulsory referral is usually to protect people unable to protect themselves. One of the most vulnerable groups in society is children, and so there has been much legislation relating to children in need of care. This has been brought into some sort of logical order with the Children Act 1989.

Compulsory referral – children

In summary, compulsory care and supervision can come about as a result of the following:

- *A care order*, which places the child in the care of the local authority to safeguard and promote the child's welfare. The authority shares parental responsibility and must work with the parents. The order lasts until discharged by the court, or the child reaches the age of 18 years or marries. Where the care is in dispute, courts are required to make or approve arrangements taking the child's needs as paramount. To safeguard the needs of the child the court appoints an independent social worker to act as guardian *ad litem* (GAL). The GAL prepares a report based on local authority records and interviews with carers, parents and others to assist the court in reaching a decision.
- *A supervision order*, where the child stays with the parents but is supervised by a social worker or probation officer. The parents retain parental responsibility. Orders last for 1 year and may be extended for up to 3 years.
- *An emergency protection order (EPO)* – when a child is likely to suffer significant harm a court may grant an EPO which lasts for a maximum of 8 days (extendible by a further 7). Care is passed to the local authority. The child, parent or carer can apply to the court for the order to be discharged after 72 hours. The police can also remove a child into protection for a maximum of 72 hours, but they must allow reasonable contact with parents/carers in the child's best interests.
- *A child assessment order*, which requires a child to attend for medical, psychiatric or other assessment. This remains in force for 7 days.
- *An education supervision order* is made where a child of compulsory school age is not being properly educated. Supervision is by the education authority and the order lasts for 1 year.

It must be emphasised that all of these orders are made as a result of placing evidence before a court and the order is made by the court.

Compulsory referral – elderly people

The National Assistance Act 1948 placed a duty on local authorities to provide residential accommodation for older people who were unable to look after themselves. It also gave them the power to remove people in need of care and attention to suitable premises on the recommendation of a named medical officer to prevent injury to the health of, or serious nuisance to, others. The local authority has to make an application under Section 47 of the Act, supported by a medical officer (community physician), for the compulsory removal from their home of those who are suffering from grave chronic disease or who, being aged, infirm or physically incapacitated, are living in insanitary conditions, are unable to devote proper care and attention to themselves and are not receiving this from other people.

These compulsory powers are used in approximately 200 cases each year. Much of the debate surrounding this section of the Act is among doctors and social workers, and focuses on the ethical desirability of compulsory removal of people from their own homes.

Compulsory referral – mentally ill

A compulsory referral may also be made under the Mental Health Act 1983. Section 2 of the Act lays down procedures by which a person unwilling to receive treatment for a mental disorder may be compulsorily admitted to a suitable hospital for assessment. Application can be made by either the patient's nearest relative or a social worker who has been authorised by a local authority to act as an approved social worker (ASW). The application must be supported by two doctors, one of whom has previous acquaintance with the patient, usually the patient's GP. The detention can last for up to 28 days.

An emergency admission for up to 72 hours can be made on an application supported by only one doctor. Within this 72-hour period a second medical opinion can be added and the detention can then be extended to 28 days.

There is provision within the Act for courts to hear objections from nearest relatives to compulsory admittance. There is also the option for courts to refer people convicted of a criminal offence to be admitted and detained in a specified hospital such as Broadmoor or Rampton special hospitals. Crown Courts can also impose restrictions on discharge from these hospitals.

Activity 11

a Describe in detail how clients gain access to services.
b Identify any barriers to access.
c Discuss how these barriers could be lessened or removed.

Key Skills

You can use Activity 11 to provide evidence for Key Skills Communication C3.2, C3.3.

Ethical dilemmas experienced by practitioners who use compulsory powers

When using compulsory powers, under either the Mental Health Act, the National Assistance Act or the Children Act, we must ask the question: For whom is the situation a problem? People's behaviour is often seen as problematic, socially disruptive or a nuisance to those around them. The behaviour of mentally ill or of elderly dependent people is seen as deviant and an embarrassment. Their behaviour may cause anxiety, fear and anger in others, e.g. when a confused elderly person does not eat properly or occasionally leaves the gas taps turned on. Relatives and neighbours may feel that they are unable to control the elderly or mentally ill person. The relatives may resort to legal controls not because the person is a danger to themselves or others but because the carer or relative or neighbour feels anxious. This anxiety may be transferred to social workers and doctors, who may then take action in situations where they might not do so if pressure from relatives was not so great.

/ **Activity 12** /

The following situation was reported in a national newspaper. A woman and her children were removed by a GP from his list because she would not agree to have her children vaccinated.

a Do you think that a GP should have the legal right to do this?
b Do you think that the GP was ethically right to do so?

Write down your answers and discuss them with your class colleagues.

Issues relating to access (information)

It is clearly the responsibility of health and social care organisations to promote access through effective marketing. This means publicising the services in a positive way and ensuring that information about the services reaches the individuals who are most likely to make use of them. It also means destigmatising services and generally making people feel good about using them.

However, many public sector care organisations have been notoriously poor at marketing or letting people know what services they provide. There are several reasons for this:

- Marketing is a dirty word in public sector services.
- Many public sector organisations do not employ marketing experts.
- There is often a conscious attempt to de-market services – i.e. to limit access to them because of financial constraints.

The last reason is an important one. In reality, many health and social care organisations dare not actively promote access to their services through fear of not being able to respond to the genuine levels of need in the community.

5.4 Funding of services

Health care funding

When the NHS was first formed one of the important aims was to improve the health of the nation. One of the tenets of the provision was that, while initial costs would be high, there would be a reduction in costs later as health improved and demand for health care decreased.

/ **Activity 13** /

a The table below details the cost of the National Health Service. Use these figures to plot a graph of NHS costs in actual and inflation-adjusted terms.
b Why have the costs in real terms increased? Consider issues such as life expectancy and advances in medical techniques, among others.

The cost of the National Health Service

Year	Total (£m)	Total at 1949 prices (£m)
1949	437	437
1950	477	477
1951	503	466
1952	526	499
1953	546	452
1954	564	459
1955	609	477
1957	664	489
1958	764	515
1959	826	549
1960	981	623
1961	–	–
1962	1025	628
1963	1092	655
1964	1190	695
1965	1306	728
1966	1433	769
1967	1556	816
1968	1702	861
1969	1791	875
1970	2040	929
1971	2325	950
1972	2682	997
1973	3054	1054
1974	3970	1171
1975	5298	1229
1976	6281	1271
1977	6971	1258
1978	7997	1288
1979	9283	1324
1980	11 914	1434
1981	13 720	1498
1982	14 483	1479
1983	16 381	1584
1984	17 241	1581
1985	18 412	1602
1986	19 690	1670
1987	21 488	1737
1988	23 627	1797

Source: OHE (1989) and C. Hamm, Health Policy in Britain, 3rd edn (Macmillan, 1992)

In 1992/93 the total gross expenditure of the NHS in the UK was £29.3 billion and was funded as follows:

- 80.8% from general taxation
- 13.9% from National Insurance contributions
- 3.9% from charges to patients
- 1.4% from capital sales.

The major charges to patients include:

- attending a person involved in a road traffic accident and their initial outpatient treatment
- accommodation and services for private patients
- non-emergency NHS treatment of overseas visitors
- drugs and appliances supplied on prescription by a doctor or dentist
- dental treatment.

Initially, health service funding was provided to hospitals directly from central government through the structures then in place. The way funds were allocated was not controlled directly by demand. While there were constraints on spending and demands for planning of provision, the provision was controlled by the individual units in consultation with district and regional authorities.

More recently the NHS and Community Care Act 1990 has divided the functions of providing funds for health care from the provision of care. The purchaser–provider relationship was introduced with the idea of freeing up the marketplace and introducing a level of competition – the aim, of course, being to reduce the costs of health care.

Old should be spared 'inhumane' treatment, says study

Call to curb surgery on terminally ill

Chris Mihill
Medical Correspondent

SOME old and sick patients are suffering needlessly because operations are carried out without a realistic hope of success, a report published yesterday says.

The report, produced by the royal medical colleges, says of such operations: "Surgery should be avoided for those whose death is inevitable and imminent. A more humane approach to the care of these patients should be considered."

It also blames a shortage of facilities, unsupervised surgery by junior doctors and a lack of research, for causing post-operative deaths.

The inquiry, which looked at 1,400 of the 18,000 adult deaths within 30 days of surgery from April 1991 to March 1992 in England, Wales, Northern Ireland and the Channel Islands, identifies four problems.
• Lack of an operating theatre reserved for emergencies;
• Inadequate intensive care facilities, leaving some operations for old and sick people little chance of success;
• Emergency operations at night on old and sick patients, by unsupervised doctors in training grades;
• Poor standards in the appointment of locum doctors.

Some 7,000 consultants were invited to take part in the investigation, but 24 per cent declined to do so, often because they could not find the case notes or other medical records.

Professor John Blandy, chairman of the inquiry, said: "There are roughly 3 million operations per annum in this country and about 18,000 deaths – a rate of 0.6 per cent – almost entirely restricted to the very old and the very sick."

The death rate has remained unchanged since a previous survey. "The vast majority of operations for the vast majority of patients are safe," Prof Blandy said. "However, this report is an effort by anaesthetists, gynaecologists and surgeons to see if they can't do better."

Prof Blandy said some of the large-scale desperate operations on very sick patients were carried out to reassure relatives that everything possible was being tried, but in some cases it was difficult to understand why they had been done.

He said patients, as well as health districts placing contracts, should ask questions about the surgical facilities available in hospitals.

The report says it "is no longer acceptable" for trainees to work alone without suitable supervision and direction by consultants.

Some patients are being given far too much fluid while they are unconscious and unable to pass urine. This can build up until it damages the heart and lungs, says the report.

Some examples of "hopeless" operations given in the report included that of a 74-year-old woman with a head injury who was operated on although she appeared lifeless. She later died from broncho-pneumonia.

A 68-year-old man with inoperable spread of cancer in the brain was recommended for surgery, and later received a second operation the same day to relieve fluid pressure in the brain. He died soon afterwards.

A senior registrar operating on an 80-year-old woman with a perforated duodenal ulcer also discovered she had womb problems. He carried out a hysterectomy, but the patient died from a heart attack. "There was no justification for this hysterectomy," the report said.

The report of the National Confidential Enquiry into Perioperative Deaths 1991/1992; 34–35 Lincoln's Inn Fields, London WC2A 3PN; £9.00

Source: *The Guardian*, 8 September 1993

The purchasers are able to purchase health care from any provider, whether NHS, private or voluntary. The providers lose the 'automatic' funding of current provision, and have to look at costs and quality. The concept of customer care becomes more important. All care has to be paid for and there must be a limit on the money available. All care agencies have to predict expenditure, and do so, rather as insurance agencies predict risk. However, there is never enough money available to provide all the services people would like. In social care this tends to mean that statutory services are provided and decisions are made to provide only some of the 'optional' services defined in enabling legislation. In health care it is often non-urgent treatment that is delayed. Advances in medical care mean that funding decisions become even more complex. Is it better to provide kidney transplants and save life or carry out plastic surgery on burns victims and improve quality of life?

Activity 14

Read the newspaper article above.

a What are your views on the issue?
b How might medical decisions be affected by funding issues?

Controlling access to care: shepherding the resources

There are many demands on resources in the NHS. One of the ways in which these demands can be managed is to consider the value added to a patient's quality of life. This can lead to a purely numerical system for determining the benefit of carrying out an operation. It is clear that it would not benefit the patient greatly if a kidney transplant were carried out on an 87-year-old man with terminal cancer and with an estimated life expectancy of a month. Lack of improved quality of life and the risk of going under the anaesthetic would indicate the unreasonableness of carrying out the operation. More difficult decisions need to be made where the risk of the operation means that life expectancy is not improved although quality of life may be.

There have been cases where access to care has been conditional on patients changing their lifestyles in some way. An orthopaedic surgeon may insist that a patient lose weight before carrying out a hip replacement. The logic for this is that the reduced weight will make the operation easier and will improve its long-term success. It is not an unreasonable request. Of more concern is the insistence that a person give up smoking before being treated for an unrelated illness. There was a case of a person who was refused access to an investigation for heart bypass surgery unless he gave up smoking. He subsequently died of a heart attack. In this case the argument was almost the same as the one put forward at the start of this case study: the operation had a reduced chance of success; continued smoking would recreate the problem, thus making the original cost a waste of money!

The difficulty with all of these decisions is that it is easy to theorise and make pronouncements about general situations but the needs of individual patients are real, not theoretical. In the end, to be efficient,

213

funding has to look at cost benefits. In terms of immunisation it is cheaper in the long run to provide rubella vaccine for all women before they have a chance of getting pregnant than it is to provide care for a damaged child for its lifetime. Similarly, the cost of providing domiciliary support for an Alzheimer's disease sufferer and carer is less than providing full-time residential care. It could be argued, however, that in the latter case the additional cost is the carer's loss of quality of life.

The population changes in the UK over the next half century mean that, as people live longer, the cost of care will increase while the workforce is decreasing. Legislation already recognises this problem: the NHS and Community Care Act 1990 requires local authorities to assess need but does not require them to meet all the assessed need. Greater demands are now being made on the relatives of people needing care. The cost of caring for these carers has yet to enter the equation.

Case study

Care in the community: Alice's tale – the long bereavement

Alice had been a professional with 15 people working under her. She had responsibility for the care of several hundred children. She and her husband moved to a large house in the country before they both retired, with the aim of pursuing their joint interest in gardening.

About two years after she retired, friends and family began to notice small changes. Alice was constantly talking about her old job as if she were still there. She still remembered the grandchildren's birthdays, but the presents didn't reflect the fact that they were growing up. She started to forget what she had said and so often repeated herself. Everybody put it down to the delayed reaction following her retirement from a job she had enjoyed and done well.

Her GP gave her a check-up and initiated treatment for high blood pressure. He continued for the next two years to issue repeat prescriptions and give infrequent check-ups. People close to Alice didn't notice much change other than she was starting to slow down and needed more time to think.

Four years after her retirement, Alice's forgetfulness started to show more clearly. She needed prompting to recognise her daughter, visiting her after a long absence. She called her son by her brother's name. Alice's husband started to become concerned when what he had not noticed as major changes were pointed out to him. The GP arranged for an appointment with a geriatrician.

The next six months showed a sharp decline in Alice's health. She became very forgetful and also very angry towards her husband. She became incontinent, especially at night, and so her husband's workload increased with all the extra washing. Eventually, a care plan was agreed, with Alice attending a day centre three days a week and going into residential care one week in four. Also domiciliary support would be provided to help wash and dress Alice on two days a week

Over the period of time before the next six-monthly review Alice deteriorated. It became more difficult to get her into the car and take her to the day centre. She became incontinent during the day, putting an even greater workload on her husband. Also, for financial reasons, it was decided to reduce the residential weeks to one in five. Alice's husband is awaiting a review of her case under the Care in the Community legislation.

Clearly he is coping and making limited use of the social services resources. The care plan originally agreed needs urgent review but, because he can cope and Alice's needs are being met, there is likely to be little change – possibly more domiciliary support and collection from home by ambulance as she will soon find it impossible to travel by car. It is unlikely that full-time residential care will be available because Alice's needs are being met by care in the community.

Care in the community is working for Alice. But for her husband it is not. He retired with plans for his garden – it is a wilderness. He looks forward to the respite care time to get basic housework done. He is unable to go out as Alice cannot travel far by car and, when he goes anywhere with her, it has to be somewhere that can cope with Alice's needs. Like many people in his situation, he will be alone for Christmas. His only conversation will be with relatives and friends over the telephone. He could be with family but refuses to allow his children to 'ruin' the young grandchildren's Christmas by taking them away from home.

Alice has Alzheimer's disease. She cannot talk, feed herself or in any way care for herself. The personality her husband married is no longer there, it has died and only the living body remains. He and his family know the meaning of the other name for the disease – 'the long bereavement'.

Q *What are Alice's needs? How are they being met?*

Q *What are her husband's needs? Which voluntary organisations might provide support for him?*

Q *Investigate provision in your area that might be made available, remembering that Alice and her husband live 7 miles from the nearest town.*

Alzheimer's disease: some facts

- Over 600 000 people in the UK suffer from Alzheimer's disease.
- Every day 42 more people develop the disease.
- It affects one in every 20 people over 65, and one in 5 over 80.
- It can affect people as young as 40.
- Alzheimer's disease is on the increase simply because advances in medicine mean that people are living longer.

Private health care

The Act of Parliament that formed the NHS has been described as a structure based on compromise. Many health professionals, in particular doctors, were unhappy at the thought of giving up their private practices. They were concerned, in part at least, that their freedom to charge for their services outside the NHS should be maintained. In fact, so strong was this feeling that, in order to bring doctors into the NHS, it was agreed that doctors would be able to work both within the NHS and in private practice.

Private health care can occur both within NHS-owned institutions, with the client paying for the services, or within totally separate 'private' health-care facilities. With the current move towards a mixed economy of care and the concept of purchases and providers, the distinction becomes blurred. Purchasers (e.g. district health authorities, **primary care groups**) are free to purchase care from any provider, not just those within the NHS. So NHS patients may receive treatment in 'private' establishments.

Is free health care for all possible?

The economic argument must be that total health care provision for all is impossible. It is clear that if all renal dialysis units are fully utilised then a new patient cannot be accommodated. To buy a new dialysis machine would be possible, but the money would have to come from somewhere.

Activity 15

Discuss with class colleagues whether it would be reasonable to have an extra dialysis machine for a single patient, especially if not buying the machine would pay for several hip replacement operations or more incubators for premature babies.

With any provision, the funding will always be insufficient. The costs of the NHS represented almost 12% of public expenditure in 1950 and almost 15% in 1988, and are still rising. Any increased government funding must come either from increased taxation or from reductions in other areas.

Another issue has to be the increased complexity and cost of health care. As knowledge and techniques improve so people can be treated for more and more things. Often, it is the emotive areas that point up these issues. In 1967, abortion was made legal up to the 28th week of pregnancy. This time limit was partially fixed by the then current knowledge that no child born prior to that date was able to survive. Developments in technology now mean that some children born at

24 weeks survive. The monetary cost is high and the potential for physical and mental impairment is high, but public expectation is that the provision must be made available. At the same time, such developments open moral and ethical debates.

Services free at the point of delivery

Social services	*Early years services*	*Health services*
Social work	Nursery class	Hospital care
Approved social work	Primary education	GP services
	Educational psychologist	Health visiting
	Educational social worker	Community nursing

Services not free at the point of delivery

Social services	*Early years services*	*Health services*
Residential care	Play group	Prescriptions
Day care	Nursery care	Glasses
Home care		Dentist
Meals-on-wheels		

Management issues

The NHS and Community Care Act 1990 attempted to use market forces to improve management of care provision. It also helped to rectify a problem that occurred when people in need of further care were discharged from hospital. In the past people were occasionally discharged into the community without their needs being met and without referral to the social services. Now the requirement for the DHAs, Trusts, primary care groups and local authorities to work together in assessing care need should reduce the risk of people 'dropping' through the system. In the next few years we will see how effective these measures have been.

Who receives care?

The principal outside influence on social welfare policy is the structure and size of the UK's population. Population structure refers to such variables as age, social class, gender, family and household status, marital status, employment or health status and religion. Estimates of current and future population structures form the basis for health and care policy planning. Population structures can therefore affect health and social care priorities.

Mortality trends would seem to indicate potential for people to live longer, particularly those over 65 years of age. However, people may live longer but do they gain in quality of life? If people are expected to live longer, but also as they grow old to become dependent, what effect does this have on the health and social care services?

Activity 16

What effect upon health and social care services will people living longer have? List the services that you think will be affected most and explain why.

Changes in family structure also affect funding. Marriage is now less popular than it has been for some centuries – this unpopularity is linked to a fall in fertility. However, the relationship between marriage and childbearing is becoming weaker and weaker. Marriage is been replaced by cohabitation, with no foreseeable decline or increase in the birth rate. The rise in single parents might indicate that childbearing is becoming a matter for women alone. All these changes have implications for household and family structures.

Activity 17

Access data in your school or college library and find out the percentage of single-parent families in your locality. Are there any differences in the percentages in different wards in your local authority? Why should these differences occur?

Independent of changes in the family, the population of the UK will age considerably in the decades to come. The timing of this ageing is linked with the 'baby boom' of the 1950s and the decline in the birth rate after 1970. In the UK the most rapid rise in the number of those over pensionable age is expected between 2000 and 2030, with a rise in the number of those over 80 years of age coming some years later.

Access to health and social care is not simply about the procedures of achieving treatment or care. There is the very important issue of who receives care and whether access is equal to all groups in society. It was hoped that the introduction of the welfare state would remove inequalities of access to care. One of the tenets was access to all, free at the point of delivery. If access to care is equal for all who need it, then there should be no inequalities and the health of the general population should improve.

The Black Report of 1980, which looked at inequalities in health, highlighted issues of differing mortality and morbidity levels related to social class. It emphasised the significance of broad social, economic and environmental influences on health. It argued that attention needed to be paid to factors such as housing, income support and nutrition if class differences in health were to be reduced.

These issues were at the heart of the development of the welfare state and the legislation that went before it. The three prongs of health care, social care and welfare benefits were intended to reduce the differences between social classes in terms of access to health and social wellbeing. The evidence is that in many ways the divide is just as great today as it was in 1946.

The effects of demographic changes upon funding

Demography is the study of population. It consists of two primary aspects: structures and processes.

- *Structures* examine how the population is made up, e.g. how many individuals over 70 or how many single-parent families live in a particular area.
- *Processes* examine the rate of change of variables such as births, deaths and migration.

There is a regular flow of statistical information from census returns, surveys and registration of births, deaths and marriages. The demographic scientist identifies trends and makes projections. These trends and projections are major factors in resourcing health and social care. The trend toward an increasingly large dependent elderly population is one of the factors the government uses in promoting private care, pensions and insurance schemes. They claim that the taxpayer cannot and will not support the needs of older people.

Activity 18

Using nationally produced statistics work out the proportions of people in the following categories in the UK:

a those under 16
b those over 16 and under 60
c those over 60.

Do this for the most recent data available to you and also for data 10, 20 and 40 years old. How is the population changing?

The three categories shown in Activity 18 represent potential wage earners (16–60) and others who may take more in terms of services than they contribute to the cost. The results of the Activity will indicate some of the trends in the population in terms of:

- birth rate
- length of life.

Other statistics would show the increased incidence of 'costly' diseases such as cancers and heart disease. In earlier times treatment was limited. Now it is available but often at a high cost.

If you consider the costs to the caring services of increased life expectancy, improved treatment of disease and dysfunction, and decreased birth rate, it becomes clear that potential costs will increase while the number of taxpayers will fall, along with the number of workers available to provide care. This demographic time bomb is already seriously affecting the structure of the welfare state in the UK.

Central government control and funding and access to individual care

The demographic information is worrying. If you expect to need to use the caring services in the future then you expect the government to be able to provide. There are two extremes in terms of this provision. The first would be to make each individual responsible for paying for care. This would require an increased use of private insurance systems. The second extreme would be for the government to increase taxation to pay for the caring services. In both cases the costs would be met by the population. In the first case the costs would be met by the individuals (through insurance); in the second the costs for older people and children would largely be met by taxpayers. As the population ages a greater burden would fall on a smaller number of taxpayers.

The government is trying to resolve the dilemma. Much of the most recent legislation has been to ensure that entitlement can be paid for through the statutory provision but that non-statutory services are, at least in part, paid for by the client. There has also been some encouragement through taxation for individuals to take out insurance related to potential care needs.

It is important to recognise that, while the solutions may vary according to the political party in power, the demographic time bomb will not be affected by party politics. The future problem will not go away whichever political party is in power.

Government control also arises as a result of political dogma and ideology. As almost all funding for the services comes from government (local and national), there is an opportunity to use funds to support different aspects of the services. A party that believes in traditional family values might focus funding to encourage mothers to stay at home and rely on a partner to provide the family income. This would disadvantage single-parent families. A party that believes strongly in equality of opportunity might fund services, such as child day care, that would allow mothers in particular to retain paid employment.

The role of the independent sector in influencing access to care provision

The term 'independent sector' refers to all non-statutory organisations that contribute to social care. The majority are not set up by government. Many are charities and many are private businesses.

Many independent agencies act as a focus for fundraising to provide for people with specific needs. The funds are then used to purchase the equipment or care required. Others, such as Anchor, provide specific residential or sheltered accommodation for older people.

The traditional image of the independent sector is of well-meaning amateurs. This image is not true of the sector today. While some charities work with unpaid volunteers, almost all of the larger ones and many others are staffed by salaried staff. The term 'independent' refers to the status of the organisation, not to the status of the workers.

Case study

The NSPCC

One example of an independent voluntary sector organisation is the National Society for the Prevention of Cruelty to Children (NSPCC). This organisation, formed in 1884, is in the interesting position of having statutory powers. It has the authority to take legal action on behalf of a child and has access to records such as the register of children at risk. To carry out this work it employs qualified social workers and works closely with the statutory social services and the police. Thus, a child may be referred to the NSPCC, which investigates the case and works with the family. If there is a need for the child to be taken into care, then the case may be taken to court by the NSPCC or passed over to the local authority social services. The emphasis of the organisation is on working with families and seeking to prevent their break-up.

How can clients be encouraged to take control to improve access?

The case of Mrs Johnson on page 239 illustrates how this can be done. There are many other ways in which clients can be empowered by giving them information and advice so that they can make appropriate informed decisions. Clients should be encouraged to take responsibility for their own lives, which involves choosing the services they want and taking decisions about their lifestyle. This assumes that they will be able to take risks to maintain their freedom and independence. Services should be delivered in a manner that respects the dignity and value of the client. Services that are offered should be appropriate to the client's situation, culture and lifestyle.

Information

Clients need information and knowledge of the services provided. The government encourages agencies to publish details of services available. In order to make informed choices clients must have adequate information about services and also about complaint procedures. This information should be accessible to all and produced in appropriate languages and formats. The National Health Service and Community Care Act 1990 requires social services departments to provide 'information accessible to all potential service users and carers, including those with any communication difficulty or difference in language or culture, setting out the types of community care services available, the criteria for provision and services, the assessment procedures to agree needs and ways of addressing them and standards by which the care management system will be measured'. This is done by publishing a Community Care Plan annually and also by setting up consultation procedures with clients and carers. Booklets and leaflets are also used to provide information.

The involvement of clients in the improvement of services

Many social services and health authorities have set up consultative groups as one way in which clients can influence services. Communication is at the centre of what most health authorities and health care trusts seek to do. These agencies do this by explaining the role of authorities and trusts to the local community, and by listening to local voices and involving local people in the consideration of care and health service standards and priorities. This is done by involving user groups, special interest groups, local advisory groups, Community Health Councils and voluntary groups.

A number of authorities have developed new initiatives to encourage users of services to become involved in the planning and management of services. The Margin to Mainstream project, funded by the Rowntree Foundation, enables clients and carers to become involved in the organisation, management and delivery of services. This initiative gives people who use and provide services to come together to distribute funds, meet each other and organise workshops. The project supports a direct payment scheme which allows for community care finance to be paid to users who can, in turn, purchase and manage whatever services they wish. Other schemes under this project facilitate users' input into training schemes and develop ways in which clients can influence public policy.

Sheffield Social Services Department has developed an Older People's Reference Group, which meets every two months to consider day services, home care and residential care facilities. This group also plays a direct role in the preparation of strategic plans and is developing a Direct Payment to Users Scheme for older people to enable them to purchase the services that best meet their individual needs (Sheffield's Community Care Plan 1994/95).

The Patient's Charter

The first nine national standards:

1 *Respect for privacy, dignity and religious and cultural beliefs*: practical arrangements should include appropriate meals and private rooms for confidential discussions with relatives.
2 *Arrangements to ensure everyone, including people with special needs, can use the service*: an example is the provision of access for people with wheelchairs.
3 *Information to relatives and friends*: there must be arrangements to inform relatives and friends of progress, subject to the patient's wishes.
4 *Waiting time for an ambulance service*: for an emergency ambulance this must be no longer than 14 minutes in an urban area and 19 minutes in a rural area.
5 *Waiting time for initial assessment in an accident and emergency department*: the standard requires immediate assessment of the need for treatment.

6 *Waiting time in outpatient clinics*: each patient should be given a specific appointment time and be seen within 30 minutes of that time.
7 *Cancellation of operations*: this should not happen on the day of arrival in hospital. If an operation is cancelled twice, it should be carried out within 1 month of the second cancellation.
8 *A named qualified nurse, midwife or health visitor responsible for each patient*: the standard says that this should be the case.
9 *Discharge of patients from hospital*: before being discharged a care plan should be made to meet any continuing heath or social care needs. Arrangements should be made with agencies to undertake this care before the patient is discharged.

From 1 April 1992, these first nine standards were increased by the requirement for local standards relating to:

• waiting time for first outpatient appointments
• waiting times for treatment after assessment in accident and emergency departments
• waiting times for transport home where a doctor identifies a medical need for the transport

- signposting of hospitals internally, for visitors
- ensuring all staff in contact with the public wear name badges.

These extra standards can also be increased by locally agreed standards.

5.5 How health, social care and early years services are organised today

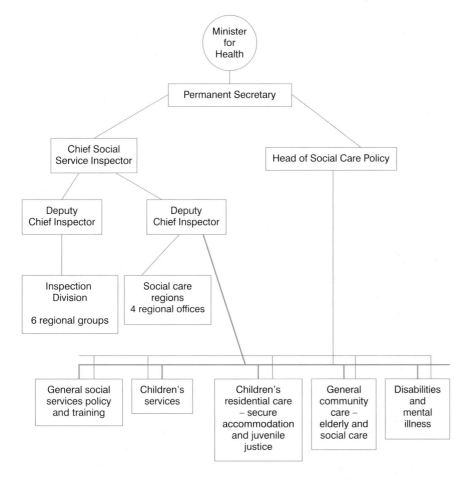

Structure of the Social Care Group of the Department of Health 2000

The government has set out to modernise the health, social care and early years services because they see it as a priority to improve the health and wellbeing of the population. Reducing health inequalities is also a government priority.

The overall aims of the Department of Health's key objectives are:

- the reduction of avoidable illness, disease and injury in the population
- the treatment of ill people quickly, effectively and on the basis of need alone
- the support of dependent people so as to allow them to live as full and normal lives as possible
- the maximisation of the social development of children within stable family settings.

The government hopes to meet these objectives by:

- tackling the root causes of ill health
- breaking down barriers between services
- ensuring uniform high standards
- maximising value for money
- making services more responsive and convenient.

The government has set national priorities, which are as follows:

- **Social Services priorities**
  - *Children's welfare* (to promote and safeguard the welfare of socially excluded children, and particularly of children looked after by local authorities)
  - *Interagency working* (to improve the extent and quality of co-operation between different public agencies with responsibilities to support looked after children, children in need and other children at risk)
  - *Regulation* (to ensure through regulatory powers and duties that adults and children in regulated services are protected from harm and from poor care standards).
- **NHS priorities**
  - *Waiting lists/times* (to meet the public's expectations for faster and more convenient access to modern and dependable services by reducing NHS waiting lists and times)
  - *Primary care* (to develop primary and community services in order to address inequality, improve the quality and convenience of services and increase efficiency)
  - *Coronary heart disease* (to reduce the death rate from heart disease and provide high-quality, cost-effective and responsive services for the presentation and treatment of coronary heart disease)
  - *Cancer* (to improve the quality and effectiveness of, and speed of access to, cancer services).
- **Joint health and social services department priorities**
  - *Cutting health inequalities* (to improve the health of the worst off in society at a faster rate than the rest of the population)
  - *Mental health* (to improve the mental health of the population and improve treatment and care of those with mental health problems through the provision of a comprehensive range of high-quality, effective and responsive services)
  - *Promoting independence* (to ensure the provision of services that help adults achieve and sustain the maximum independence in their lives, including, for those of working age, their capacity to take up, remain in or return to employment).

Source: *Modernising Health and Social Services Action* (Department of Health, 1998)

The government hopes to achieve these objectives by targeting funds and encouraging the development of Health Improvement Plans (HimP), which will involve local authorities, NHS Trusts, primary care groups, voluntary organisations and local communities. The main organisations (NHS, primary care groups and social services departments) will be expected to reflect these plans (HimP) in their objectives. These objectives are also reflected in the organisation of the present NHS and social services departments.

Services based on need

In 1997, the government set out to change the structure of the NHS so as to provide an up-to-date, quicker and more responsive service. This commitment was stated in a White Paper, *The New NHS – Modern, Dependable* – to provide a service based on people's need and not on their ability to pay. This new service is based on:

- making it easier and faster for people to get advice and information about health, illness and the NHS so that people can better care for themselves and their families
- the provision of a new service – '**NHS Direct**', a 24-hour telephone advice line staffed by nurses and in some cases with the support of GPs (who advise patients) – which is available across the whole country from 2000
- swift advice and treatment in the community in local surgeries and health centres with GPs working alongside other health care staff to provide a wide range of services
- prompt access to specialist services in hospitals linked to local surgeries and health centres.

NHS Direct

This service is well used. One centre in West London received a total of 3098 calls in one week. The callers received advice as follows:

Nurse advice/self-care	38.6%
Referral to primary care centre	15.1%
Home visit by GP	9.5%
Referral to GP next day	8.0%
Referral to non-clinical service	7.4%
Referral to Accident and Emergency Department	7.0%
Referral to GP surgery	5.8%
Told to seek GP advice	2.2%
Referral to other providers	2.1%
Ambulance	1.7%
Community services	0.8%
No action	0.7%
Information	0.3%
Other	0.2%

The National Health Service – the Health Act 1999

The Act provides for new arrangements aimed at improving the quality of the care provided to the community. The Act's main purpose is to make changes to the way in which the National Health Service is run in England, Wales, Northern Ireland and Scotland. The Health Act 1999 abolished GP fundholding in England, Wales and Northern Ireland. It amended the National Health Service Act 1977 to make provision for the setting up of new statutory bodies in England and Wales to be known as Primary Care Groups (PCGs).

The government believed that the service that operated under the National Health and Community Care Act 1990 fragmented decision-making and caused unfairness to some patients (some GPs did not become fundholders, for example). To replace this system, the Health Act 1999 moved away from outright competition to a more collaborative approach delivering a national service against national standards and working more closely with local authorities so that patients' needs could be at the centre of the process. All these ideas were incorporated into the Act.

Primary care groups

Over a period of time health authorities will relinquish their direct commissioning roles to primary care groups (PCGs). Health authorities working with local authorities, NHS Trusts and primary care groups will take the lead in drawing up 3-year Health Improvement Programmes, which will provide the framework within which all NHS bodies will operate.

Primary care groups became a reality on 1 April 1999. A total of 481 groups were set up in England on that date. Health authorities decided the boundaries; the NHS Executive confirmed their size and format. A number of these groups will only support the health authority, in an advisory capacity, in commissioning care for its population; others (called Level 2 groups) will take responsibility for managing the health-care budget in their area (the health authority will allocate a budget to the PCG), acting as part of the health authority. The Primary Health Care Group board can transfer money between hospital and community services to use the money where it believes it is needed most.

Primary care groups are run by boards, the members comprising GP and other professionals such as nurses and hospital doctors. The role of the PCG board, which is at present led by GPs, is to ensure that other stakeholders, such as nurses, patients and other health professionals, also have an opportunity to have their say about health-care planning and service delivery in their area. PCGs also employ staff to develop and implement policy. The population they serve varies from 206 000 people in York to 54 467 people in Wakefield (south).

It is proposed that some of these PCGs will become trusts in their own right (primary care trusts – PCTs).

Primary care group – England

The PCG Board is accountable to the Health Authority and will consist of:

- GPs (between four and seven) – a GP is usually the chairperson
- nurses (community and practice nurses) (up to two)
- a member of the health authority
- a lay member from the community
- a representative from the social services department.

The role of the PCG:

- improve the health of and address health inequalities in the community
- develop primary care and community health services in its area
- improve the quality of care provided through supporting GPs and their health providers in the delivery and integration of services
- advise on or take on commissioning of hospital services for patients so as to meet appropriately patients' needs.

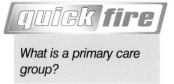

What is a primary care group?

Monitoring of primary care groups

The government has set up a new Commission for Health Improvement (CHI) whose job is to inspect health authorities and primary care groups. It is a standards watchdog that will visit hospitals and primary care groups, promoting good standards and rooting out the bad.

GP fundholding

The White Papers *The New NHS* and *Putting Patients First* set out the Labour government's proposals to replace the NHS internal market. To enable this to happen, GP fundholding ceased to exist in England, Wales and Scotland in March 1999. All GPs are now covered by a primary care group.

Primary health groups

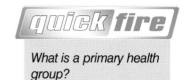

What is a primary health group?

Primary health groups are made up of GPs and community nurses, who work with NHS Trusts to plan the new services to deliver prompt, accessible, seamless care delivered to a high standard. These groups work to set quality standards agreed between health authorities and primary care groups.

NHS Trusts

NHS Trusts will provide patient care in hospital and in the community under long-term agreements with primary care groups.

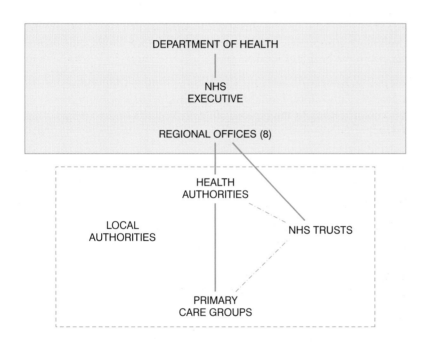

The NHS 2000

Health authorities

Health authorities have a number of key tasks:

- to assess the health needs of the local population
- to develop a plan for meeting those needs
- to decide on the range of services necessary to meet needs
- to allocate resources to primary care groups
- to make primary care groups do their job.

Health Action Zones (HAZ)

There is growing concern about the widening inequalities in health in Britain. To give priority to areas of greatest need, the government has set up **Health Action Zones** to help reduce these inequalities.

Inequalities in health – Life expectancy

Area	Years
Men	
East Dorset	77.7
Cambridge	77.5
Fareham	77.2
Liverpool	71.1
Tower Hamlets (London)	70.8
Manchester	70.1
Women	
East Dorset	83.7
Epsom & Ewell	82.5
Cambridge	82.0
Knowsley	77.2
Liverpool	77.2
Manchester	76.9

Health Action Zones will bring together local health organisations with local authorities (housing, education, social services departments, etc.), community groups, voluntary groups and local business to deliver measurable and sustainable improvement in the health of local people.

In Health Action Zones GPs have the flexibility to fund joint health and social services projects (Innovation Fund Schemes). This means that more money could be put into poor housing or unemployment, which in the long term would reduce the workloads of GPs.

Examples of HAZ Innovation Fund Schemes

- *Mersey – 'Building Bridges in Minority Ethnic Communities'*. Full-time mentoring to support young people with high drug misuse, behavioural problems and poor education performance.
- *Luton – 'Tackling Health Inequalities Through Action on Unemployment'*. Joint bid with the employment services to improve the health of the worst off by focusing on unemployment.

Key Skills

You can use Activity 19 to provide evidence for Key Skills Communication C3.1a, C3.1b.

What organisations will make up a Health Action Zone?

Activity 19

Accurately describe the function of the NHS and explain its purpose and function to a group of your colleagues.

Hospital and specialist services

Some 280 major hospitals in England provide services to a range of people. Hospitals are traditionally seen as institutions where people who are too ill to be cared for at home go for treatment on an inpatient or outpatient basis. In hospitals the medical personnel are organised into teams of doctors whose role is to diagnose, prescribe and monitor the success or otherwise of treatment. People are normally referred to a hospital specialist by their GP. Many are initially seen by the specialist as outpatients following this referral, or they may attend hospital for inpatient treatment.

The hospital medical teams are supported by personnel from other disciplines, such as radiologists, occupational therapists and physiotherapists, who have specialist knowledge and skills that allow them to provide services to assist the doctor in diagnosis and treatment. This is known as a multidisciplinary team.

NHS Staff (thousands), 1997	
Nursing, midwifery and health visiting	508
Medical and dental staff	57
Administration	167
Support staff	82

Specialist staff, such as occupational therapists, provide assistance to help the hospital doctor diagnose and decide treatment

Local health group boards – Wales

Local health group boards are the equivalent of primary care groups in England. Unlike in England, GPs are not in a majority on these groups. The groups will be coterminous with (have the same boundaries or borders as) the 22 Local Health Authorities.

These boards are health authority subcommittees and will in the first instance have an advisory role. The Welsh Assembly will make the final decisions as to the role of these groups.

What does the term 'multidisciplinary team' mean?

Local Health Group Boards – Wales
Executive Committee
• Chairperson (usually a GP)
• Other GPs
• Representative of health authority
• Representative of local authority
• A 'responsible officer'.

Board

- Maximum of four GPs
- Pharmacist
- Dental practitioner
- Optometrist
- Two representatives from nursing, midwifery or health visiting
- Second health authority representative
- Second local authority representative
- Representative of local voluntary organisation
- Lay representative.

Reforms in Northern Ireland

New reforms set out in the paper *Fit for the Future: A New Approach* are proposed for Northern Ireland. Health reforms in Northern Ireland will be delayed until the Northern Ireland Assembly takes shape. GP fundholding will be abolished in 2000 if and when the new structures are to be introduced.

Health and social care partnerships consist of primary care co-operatives (PCCs), serving 50 000 to 100 000 people. These groups will assess health and social care needs in their area, and oversee health and wellbeing improvement programmes.

PCCs will hold budgets for commissioning health and social services, for drugs and staff and premises. It is expected that at least 3 years' development will be necessary before they become fully functioning.

Northern Ireland

Health and social care partnerships

- Made of primary care co-operatives
- Will assess health and social needs in area
- Oversee health improvement programs.

Primary care co-operatives

- Hold budgets for commissioning health and social services.

The role of district health authorities in meeting the needs of their population

The District Health Authority is responsible for planning and assessing the health needs of the population living in its area; almost all have produced strategic plans and consultative documents. They are a major influence in the internal market of the NHS. The DHA is accountable to the Regional Health Authority (RHA). The RHA monitors the performance of the DHA, which works closely with other agencies such as primary care groups in drawing up its purchasing plans. These plans must include a statement of priorities, statements about how improvements in service are to be achieved and monitored, and the range of services to be funded. DHAs also have overall responsibility for services not provided by self-governing Trusts. In these cases, they agree contracts with providers for a particular standard and level of service. The National Health Service Management Executive

(NHSME) was set up to manage self-governing Trusts, which are accountable directly to the Secretary of State for Health. The NHSME has regional offices to deal directly with the self-governing trusts. This structure is shown in the figure on page 227.

Activity 20

Assess the impact of government funding upon the NHS and Social Services.

Key Skills

You can use Activity 20 to provide evidence for Key Skills Communication C3.2.

Under the GP fundholding schemes (now abolished), GPs received a budget that covered the cost of running their practices. This fund also allowed them to purchase drugs, non-emergency hospital services and also some community health services. Those GPs who were fundholders were in effect purchasing authorities, which could contract with other health providers to give a service to patients on their list.

The primary health care team (PHCT)

The PHCT involves a wide range of professionals – nurses, health visitors, midwives, social workers and the general practitioner. The White Paper *Promoting Better Health* (1987) removed the restriction on the type and number of staff that GPs could employ at their surgeries. *Promoting Better Health* encouraged a GP-led service and as a result GPs were able to employ practice nurses.

The health visitor

The National Health Service Act 1946 established the preventative and social aspects of the health visitor's work. The role of the health visitor is that of a 'health educator' and social adviser who acts 'as a common point of reference and a source of standard information, a general advisor on health teaching, a common factor in family welfare'. The majority of the health visitor's work is with families and young children, advising and mobilising resources. Health visitors focus on healthy people rather than those who are ill; their work is concerned with the prevention of illness rather than treatment. Health visitors visit clients on their own initiative, without needing a specific request for help. They also work as part of a multidisciplinary team involving the GP, district nurse and care staff.

The district nurse

The district nurse is an important member of the community care team and is responsible for assessing, implementing and evaluating the nursing needs of patients living in their own homes. Because of their relationship with patients and their carers they also have an important role to play in health education.

The community midwife

The first thing to remember about midwives is that they are not just nurses, they are independent practitioners responsible for the care of the mother through pregnancy and for some time after birth. The community midwife provides a service to all women during pregnancy and for up to 28 days after the birth. The midwife works closely with the GP and health visitor in providing a service to the mother. Education is a vital part of the role of the midwife, who may provide information on breast feeding and general care of both the mother and her child.

The general practitioner

New working arrangements introduced for GPs in 1990 place emphasis on the provision of information to patients and the extension of health promotion activities, including advice on lifestyle and general health education. Health promotion activities now include detection of risk factors for disease, advice and counselling on the maintenance of good health, chronic disease management and tertiary prevention.

Almost all GP practices include antenatal, postnatal and family planning clinics. In many practices other services are offered: screening clinics for the preschool child; hypertension and coronary risk clinics; and well woman clinics.

The practice nurse

The practice nurse holds clinics for people with chronic conditions at the GP's surgery. The practice nurse can also be involved in well woman and well man clinics as part of the health promotion role. They also conduct routine health checks, checking blood pressure and urine specimens, and offering general health advice on such issues as weight, smoking, alcoholism, asthma and diabetes.

The chiropodist

The chiropodist treats patients' feet; their patients have a number of footcare problems. Chiropodists treat the existing problems of their patients and also provide preventive services through health education and health promotion projects. They give talks on foot care and also advise on appropriate footwear to prevent foot problems.

The dietitian

The dietitian's primary role is to draw up food plans for those who are ill and anyone who needs a special diet for any reason. Dietitians work in hospitals, the community and industry. One important role of the dietitian consists of encouraging individuals, groups or communities to eat a healthy, balanced diet. Devising new ways to influence eating habits is also part of their remit. Dieticians often work with groups in the community, such as groups of elderly people or mothers and toddlers.

The Social Services Department

The Social Services Committee, established by the Local Authority and Social Services Act 1970, has responsibilities in four areas:

- *Childcare* – under the various Children Acts and Adoption Acts, including the Children Act 1989 (see below).
- *Provision and regulation of residential accommodation* for older people and people with disabilities – under the National Assistance Act 1948 and the Registered Homes Act 1984.
- *Provision of welfare services* for older people, people with disabilities and those who are chronically ill, and statutory powers under the various Mental Health Acts.
- *Power to delegate* some responsibilities to other organisations and to provide necessary assistance.

The ways in which local authorities manage their roles and responsibilities through social services committees varies across the UK. An example of the organisational structure for one local authority social services department is given in the figure on page 238.

Local authority personal services expenditure by client group, 1997 (£ million)

Elderly	Children	Learning disability	Adults	Mental health
4575	2142	1208	748	468

Case study

Nursing care

Mr Jackson, who is 90 years of age, has become very infirm and is in need of nursing home care. His local authority purchases a place for him in a local nursing home. His local authority is responsible for paying for general nursing care needs and the cost of incontinence services.

Mr Jackson's district health authority is responsible for purchasing physiotherapy, chiropody and the provision of specialist nursing services that he needs.

The professionals involved in delivery of social care and early years services

Activity 21

a   Make a list of all of the key personnel involved in delivering care, both health and social care. Identify whether they are providers or purchasers of care.
b   Where might each be based?

In your health-care list, you should easily have identified: care manager, doctors, nurses, physiotherapists, occupational therapists, speech therapists, radiographers, dentists, dental hygienists, opticians, pharmacists and ambulance personnel. You may have thought of health-care assistants, nursing auxiliaries, porters and the many people who work in catering, cleaning and administration. The list could go on. In your social care list you should have included: social workers, residential and day care staff, home helps (domiciliary support workers), probation officers and nursery nurses. Again, this ignores many of the administrative roles but shows something of the range. The relationships between health-care and social-care operations are shown in the figure on page 234. We will take each area separately and look at the personnel involved, their roles and how people access the services.

Local authority social services staff, 1997 (thousands)

Field Work Staff (social work etc.)	115
Residential Care Staff	65
Day Care Staff	31
Central Office Staff	16

The care manager

The care manager is the person who co-ordinates the social-care assessment of clients' needs in the community. The care manager is not usually involved directly in providing any service for which the client has been assessed. The care manager can be from any profession, but is usually employed by the local social services department.

The role of the care manager is:

- to assemble and co-ordinate services to meet the assessed needs of individuals in conjunction with service users and within agreed criteria and budgetary limits
- to co-ordinate comprehensive assessments of individual needs in conjunction with staff of the social services department and other organisations, and with the applicants for services
- to devise, agree and record individual care plans with clearly identified priorities within county policy and available resources, and in conjunction with service users and, where appropriate, their carers
- to make recommendations to the care management co-ordinator regarding expenditure on individual care plans
- to amend the care plan and negotiate changes to provision of care required within the allocated budget
- to negotiate with service providers – this will include costing and prioritising services to be provided, and preparing and agreeing with the service user specifications of the service required
- to monitor and evaluate the provision of care in line with the care plan
- to review care needs in conjunction with the service user at intervals agreed in the care plan and to review the provision of services
- to monitor needs and make recommendations as appropriate for the development of services.

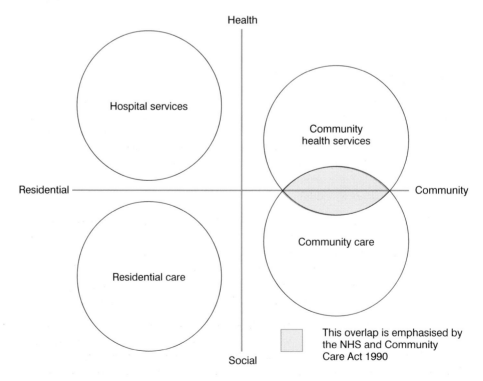

The relationship between health care and social care

Monitoring the services

We have already discussed the government's objectives for modernising the health and social services. To monitor the SSD's performance the government is setting up a new approach. It intends to provide a new and enhanced role for the Regional Social Services Inspectors. Their job will be to review and inspect new performance assessment indicators, which will be put forward by the Department of Health.

The roles of other sectors (voluntary and private) in planning and providing care

So far we have only considered the roles of the statutory sector (NHS and statutory social services). Both the voluntary and private sectors play a vital role in the delivery of care. Whereas in the past a statutory provider of care could reasonably expect to receive funding to provide care within an area, there is now a requirement to view the voluntary and private sectors as potential providers of care. This has brought in an element of competition, which has made the statutory sector look at issues around quality. The voluntary and independent sector has also been active in the provision of health and social care services on a contractual basis. It does not really matter to a patient if the care is provided by the statutory, voluntary or private sector, so long as the care is appropriate and meets the patient's needs. In the days of little competition it was not unusual to hear of people waiting for hours to see specialists or being given little support by carers. Now the service providers have developed quality standards, stating clearly the level of service a client can expect. There is clearly a level of accountability to the client for the service quality.

Activity 22

Write a report on the ways in which a local voluntary organisation monitors change in government policy and how it alters it services as a consequence.

Key Skills

You can use Activity 22 to provide evidence for Key Skills Communication C3.3.

Multiagency schemes

Health authorities also have powers to make payments to local authorities and other agencies to purchase services such as personal services and housing. They are used to support people already in the community or to support their transition from hospital to community. 'Multiagency' refers to any arrangement where joint funds are used to pay of the care of groups or individual clients.

Multiagency examples

Sheffield Health Authority and Sheffield Social Services Department have established a multiagency strategic planning group whose role is to prepare multiagency strategies for drug and alcohol services and recommend an annual investment plan for the services. Other multiagency services are provided for people with HIV/ AIDS, covering counselling and advice, social care, health care and housing services; and HIV prevention and health education. A variety of agencies are involved.

Other multiagency plans involve the independent or voluntary sector. For example, the Family Welfare Association (FWA) in Wandsworth developed a 3-year programme to provide services for families and individuals with long-term mental health problems. The services provided include day care and social work assessment and counselling. A number of social work counselling sessions take place in GP practices.

Some of the personnel involved in delivering health and social care

You can use Activity 23 to provide evidence for Key Skills Communication C3.2.

| Activity 23 |

Describe how social services departments co-ordinate or interact with at least one other service.

Assessing the needs of the local population

One of the main challenges facing health authorities and social care providers is to assess and map the needs and demands of the local population. Many authorities argue that it is futile to map needs when they have not got the resources to meet them. Although the NHS and Community Care Act 1990 placed emphasis on a needs-based service, recent court cases have began to erode the concept of a needs-led service by allowing authorities to provide only services within their resources. All local authorities and health authorities have to publish an annual community care plan whose purpose is to report progress with implementing the government's community care reforms. The other aim of the plan is to describe the plans for the provision and development of community care services for the locality.

How provider services are changing to meet the demands of purchasing and providing

The NHS and Community Care Act 1990 urged local authorities to consider changes in their structure to separate the provision of services from the purchasing arm of the agency. The purchaser–provider split was seen as essential to identify the true costs of provision and to ensure that there was no favouritism in the market for contracts. Another reason for this split was to weaken the influence of those who provided the services and so hopefully move the power to the users rather than the providers. Many social services moved to an organisation that recognised this split (see the figure on page 238). This structure allows social services departments to purchase services from a range of agencies, statutory, voluntary and independent, in the community. This system's intention is to improve the quality of services, involve the user (client and family) in the planning process, increase choice and obtain better value for money. In 1991, the Department of Health expected that these changes in the way local authorities managed services would provide the following benefits:

* more client choice
* needs-led planning
* needs-led budgeting
* individual assessment and care packages that were needs-led
* improved value for money
* improved services
* development of a mixed economy of care
* development of service specification and standards
* development in monitoring of quality of service.

Contracts

Social services departments have used contracts to buy services for clients for many years. Children placed in private or voluntary children's homes were placed there under a contract of some kind. The voluntary organisation or private agency agreed to provide a service (look after the children, feed them, house them and in some cases offer therapy) and in return the local authority would pay a fee. Standards were usually inspected by either the authority's social workers or government inspectors.

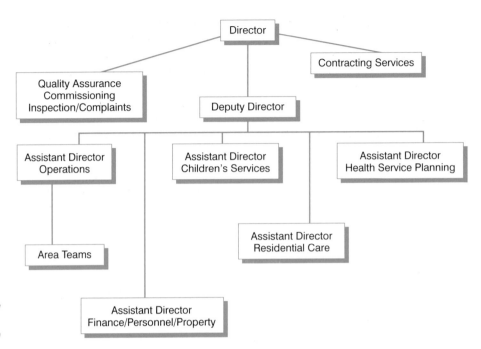

A typical structure of a
local authority Social
Services Department in
England in 2000

Any contract agreed by either a health authority or a social services department must comply with certain specifications. These specifications set out what the agencies want for the client or group for which the contract is intended. The specification sets minimum standards relating to quality of inputs and outcomes. For example, the contract may specify the qualifications of staff, who the users must be, a complaints procedure, care practices, equal opportunities, and involvement of clients and users. These specifications form the basis of a legally binding contract. Authorities usually print all the specifications in one publication and in many cases advertise for agencies to apply to provide the service. This procedure is called tendering. It has been used for residential care, domiciliary care and meals-on-wheels services, among others. Open competitive tendering allows everybody to make a bid to run the service. The Women's Royal Voluntary Service (WRVS) has recently won the tender to provide the meals-on-wheels service in Derbyshire.

Types of contract – individual clients

- *Spot contracts for individual clients* – in this situation providers remain independent agents and may accept or reject a contract in any given situation.
- *Block contracts* are those where the provider is given a contract for a group of clients. Health authorities are encouraged to use block contracts, which give the provider a fixed payment for services given.

Standards of care are enforced by inspection units of local authorities and health authorities. These units increase the pressure for explicit standards that can be inspected and measured.

Client involvement

Associated with the accountability and quality issues has been the need to involve client choice in the delivery of care. The Children Act 1989 made it clear that the needs and wishes of a child had to be listened to and used in making decisions about care needs. The NHS and Community Care Act 1990 also identified the importance of client choice.

The effects have been for individuals to be given much more information about the options available for care. They have become much more involved in planning care. The care organisations also monitor the quality of their services by using questionnaires to elicit client views. One of the effects of all of this is to empower clients to make decisions about care rather than have care thrust upon them. Since 1987 patients in the health service have been able to gain access to their medical records if they are held on computer and from 1991 if they are held on manual systems. The introduction of the Patient's Charter in 1992 was an attempt to make the public sector more responsive to the consumer.

The emphasis on the customer comes over very strongly in the various charters (see the Patient's Charter) produced nationally and by individual trusts. These set out the expected level of care and attention that a person should receive. They also highlight the systems for complaining if the provision does not meet the minimum standards. It is a requirement that the units monitor compliance with the charter standards. Results of this monitoring have to be published, in part at least to enable purchasers of the care to determine where the 'best' treatment is available.

In some respects these processes are compatible with the ideals of the original National Health Service, with more care being available and so provision for all, free at the point of delivery, coming closer. The reality is that in a broad sense it works, but there are areas where facilities have been threatened with closure on economic grounds, with an increased risk to potential patients.

Case study

Mrs Johnson is 90 years old. She is an independent lady but has suffered a stroke at home. She was found by a neighbour, who called an ambulance, and she was admitted to hospital. After a few days in hospital the care team held a conference to co-ordinate Mrs Johnson's care and treatment. The conference was attended by the doctor who was responsible far her medical treatment, the nursing staff responsible for her nursing care, the dietitian who looked after her diet (Mrs Johnson is a diabetic), the physiotherapist who was helping her retain the use of her limbs and the speech therapist who would help her learn to speak correctly again. The social worker was also present to liaise with community services when Mrs Johnson was well enough to go home or into residential care.

After some weeks Mrs Johnson was ready for discharge and a further case conference was held with staff from the hospital and the care manager from the local authority. A number of local authorities have agreed a protocol for hospital discharge; this requires hospitals to provide:

- written information to all patients regarding assessment and discharge arrangements
- referral of all patients requiring a full needs assessment to the hospital social work service, completion of assessments within an agreed time scale
- development of a care plan on completion of the patient's hospital treatment
- identification of appropriate placements for patients within an agreed period of completion of the treatment plan.

Mrs Johnson felt very strongly that she wanted to return to her own home, although the doctor and physiotherapist did not agree. However, it was agreed that Mrs Johnson's wishes should be adhered to and arrangements were made for her return home. The care manager called together all the people who would have some input into helping Mrs Johnson function as independently as possible in her own home. The hospital and local social worker, health visitor, occupational therapist, home help, meals-on-wheels. district nurse, GP and Mrs Johnson herself all met up. The hospital social worker provided the link between the hospital and community services and was a person with whom Mrs Johnson could relate as they had built up a relationship in hospital. A care plan was agreed with Mrs Johnson:

*   she would receive meals-on-wheels 7 days a week until she could cook her own meals again
*   the health visitor would advise her on general health problems
*   the district nursing service would provide a bathing service three times a week
*   the home help would cook Mrs Johnson breakfast and evening meals and help her get out of bed each morning
*   the occupational therapist would help her to learn basic living skills
*   the social worker would co-ordinate all these different services.

Mrs Johnson's health and social wellbeing improved for about 6 months. However, during the winter months, she became depressed and expressed a wish to the social worker to go into a residential home. A meeting of all the care workers who were providing services for Mrs Johnson was called, with Mrs Johnson present. After some discussion, it was agreed that she should enter a residential establishment.

The social worker made arrangements for Mrs Johnson to visit a number of establishments. After she had decided on one, a member of staff and a key worker came to visit her in her home and discuss with her a date for admission. On admission to the home she was met by the key worker and introduced to the other staff and residents. She was encouraged to keep her own GP, although she was given the option to register with a GP who came into the home regularly.

Key Skills

You can use Activity 24 to provide evidence for Key Skills Communication C3.2, C3.3.

Activity 24

Describe and present a through and clear account of how one aspect of the Social Services Department has developed as government policy has changed and new legislation has been introduced.

Moving into purchaser-only roles

Historically, all statutory agencies have been the providers of health and care services. The moves over the last few years have been towards purchaser-only roles. Internal departments within statutory agencies will have to compete with the independent sector in order to continue to exist. For this reason, many internal departments are developing arm's-length relationships with their organisations.

Example

Most hospitals have pathology laboratories. Pathology laboratories are where tissue samples are examined for disease and where post-mortem examinations are often carried out. The total market for pathology services is comprised of those services presently within NHS hospitals and a newly flourishing private sector. It is highly unlikely that all these pathology services can remain viable in a competitive market. Many are likely to close.

Increasingly, one might find a small hospital in the Midlands sending pathology specimens to a laboratory in Scotland, or the other way around. Pathology consultants may not have the personal relationships with local colleagues that they presently enjoy. Pathology services will go out to the lowest tender, which may not be the hospital's own department. Many pathology consultants have been sent for training in management and marketing, in order to prepare then for the competitive market.

Increasingly, local authority social services residential homes are unable to compete with the 'lean and mean' private sector. Their wage bills are higher and the management is sometimes relatively complacent. Many authorities do not have the money necessary to bring their own homes up to the standards of the private sector, although they are required to do so. Consequently, some local authority homes are closing. Others have formed independent Trusts. It is evident that social services departments are moving towards a purchasing and inspection role only. They cannot afford to stay in the provider market; for example, over 80% of residential care provision is now provided by organisations other than local authorities.

This rapidly changing commercial environment into which care services are moving has not had all negative consequences. Concepts such as customer care and marketing have increasingly higher profiles. Marketing in particular is helping to shape services more to meet consumer needs.

Wishful thinking

On his return to Earth after his famous moon walk in 1969, American astronaut Neil Armstrong was asked what occupied his thoughts most while in space. He replied that he had been hoping that the contract to produce the millions of electronic components used in the mission had not gone to the lowest tender.

Activity 25

This activity is designed to support your investigation of a single care organisation. It allows you to examine the strategies for care adopted and the organisational constraints on care delivery. You will be expected to investigate how and when different strategies are used and link them to organisational constraints.

a Identify a care organisation within your community, and obtain and read any documentation that identifies the mission, charter standards, aims and objectives of the organisation. Use this to try to identify any care strategies adopted and also to help you to plan the next task.

b Arrange an interview with an appropriate staff member in the care organisation to discuss their strategies for care in different situations. Investigate how they determine what strategies are appropriate and what constraints affect these (e.g. budget, decision-making processes, organisational and management structures).

c From your interview, the documentation and if possible direct observation identify one constraint that affects the care strategies. Describe how it affects the delivery of the service and the service users. Identify how a removal of the constraint might affect service delivery from both the staff's and the service users' point of view.

Key Skills

You can use Activity 25 to provide evidence for Key Skills Communication C3.2, C3.3, Application of Number N3.1, N3.2, N3.3 and Information Technology IT3.1.

Volunteers in the independent sector

Volunteers also have a clear role to play in social care. There are a large number of people willing to take on work without pay to provide a variety of forms of care. This may be with the statutory or voluntary services. In many areas this may be co-ordinated by the local Council for Voluntary Services. The functions of this organisation are as follows:

- *Co-ordination* – It tries to bring together the various local voluntary organisations, in part at least, to reduce the duplication of provision. It also acts as a pressure group for the constituent organisations.
- *Review* – It constantly monitors local provision and seeks areas of unmet need. As part of this, it helps to form new organisations and seek funding for new projects.
- *Organisation* – It co-ordinates and interviews volunteers. In doing this, it attempts to match people wishing to volunteer with a role that they are suited for. There is also a follow-up to monitor the success of the matching from the volunteer's and the agency's point of view. The agencies involved can be from the voluntary and statutory sectors.

Case study

WRVS: professional but voluntary and independent

The term 'voluntary' in the title of the Women's Royal Voluntary Service defines a non-statutory organisation but does not imply a lack of professionalism. Many of the workers are unpaid volunteers but the range of their work is phenomenal, as the advertisement indicates.

The table below shows the range and commitment of just one of the many voluntary organisations. The support of the statutory services can be measured in manpower, in the donations of money and in materials, but this does not reflect the true value of the organisation in its unquantifiable support for individuals and families by the simple fact that it is there.

WRVS facts and figures for 1999

In communities

- 43 toy libraries
- 95 contact centres
- 236 Magistrates' Court tea bars
- 323 trolley services in residential homes
- 1100 social clubs (Darby & Joan)
- 1630 books on wheels rounds for 18 602 clients

In prisons

- 5 visitors' centres
- 6 play areas and créches
- 94 tea bars

In emergencies

- 12 374 volunteer on call 365 days of the year
- 1021 volunteers assisted at 130 emergencies including Glastonbury Festival where they served hot drinks and gave out sleeping bags
- 2663 volunteers assisted at 236 community events including Cowes Week, Isle of Wight, where they ran information desks
- 1278 volunteers took part in 148 exercises feeding 56 RAF and rescue personnel at Pal-Y-Nant, Betws Garmon during mountain rescue practice

With food

- 12 million meals on wheels delivered to more than 100 000 recipients and served around one million meals at lunch clubs. WRVS is the largest single provider of meals on wheels.

In hospitals

- 581 shops and cafés
- projects in 444 hospitals
- 283 trolley services to the wards
- 274 hospital trusts partnerships
- 133 reception and guiding services
- 39 flower arranging services
- 29 libraries and book trolleys

The table is not exhaustive. Did you know that the WRVS delivered 15 million meals-on-wheels to more than 120 000 housebound/elderly people in 1992?

Volunteering

New Kids on the Block

by Victoria Butterworth, regional PR officer

A group of Merseyside teenagers were so impressed with WRVS that they have set up their own emergency services team.

Pupils from Archbishop Beck High School, Aintree, became involved with WRVS through projects at Walton and Fazakerley Hospitals where they help out with the WRVS cafe. But as the students learned more about the work of WRVS and their emergency services role, they decided that they wanted to set up their own 'disaster response' team!

Andrea Davis, who teaches at Archbishop Beck High School, said: "We are always looking for work experience for students studying towards a GNVQ in Health & Social Care. We contacted WRVS locally and found that their projects fit in perfectly with the syllabus to provide the practical experience they need.

"The pupils did a WRVS food hygiene course before they started work in the hospital, but then decided they would also like to set up an emergency services team."

"Once again the students were given training and then had to work through mock situations. They are delighted at their vital new role and are looking forward to putting it into practice at an emergency exercise."

Aintree's newest team, all aged 17 (clockwise from left) Lela Kimela, Clare Murphy and Lisa Pinnington.

Activity 26

Contact your local WRVS and identify just what they do in your area. Personal experience is that they are always ready to accept volunteers and the work can be enjoyable – you don't even have to be a woman! The number to call for more information is 01235 442951.

Private enterprise in the independent sector

Increasingly, many health and care services are being provided by private companies. Privately owned independent services are having a significant impact in areas such as residential and nursing care services, nurseries, private medicine, home care services and hospital support services.

The government has encouraged competition among independent organisations for work previously done wholly within the public sector. Competition is fierce. Within many care markets and geographical areas, there is an oversupply of private services, driving prices down. This is, of course, the aim of the exercise – to reduce costs.

Key Skills

You can use Activity 27 to provide evidence for Key Skills Communication C3.2, C3.3, Application of Number N3.1, N3.2, N3.3 and Information Technology IT3.1.

Activity 27

This activity is designed to allow you to examine a particular social care or health or early organisation and how well it satisfies the needs of local people. It also provides you with an opportunity to investigate the interlocking roles of workers from the agencies or agency you have decided to investigate.

a Select a service or agency to investigate. Read relevant documentation on the role and objectives of the agency. Reference all sources in the text of your report (see **d**).

▶▶

b Decide how you are going to collect the relevant data on such areas as:
  i   what legislation influences the provision of the service
  ii   how the service is funded
  iii   how the agency prioritises its services
  iv   key personnel
  v   the referral process
  vi   how users gain access to the service
  vii   what services are provided
  viii how well the service is used
  ix   advantages and disadvantages of the service for users.

c Decide on a system for recording information you will receive from individuals you are intending to interview. Draw up an interview schedule (or several) to ensure you make the most appropriate use of your time and that of the people you interview.

d Write a report in covering all the areas mentioned in **b**. Use appropriate charts, diagrams or graphs to illustrate and highlight the points you make. Give your conclusion on how effective and efficient the organisation is, supporting your conclusions with facts and figures. Give realistic recommendations on how the service might improve its efficiency and effectiveness.

5.6 *Informal carers*

Informal care is the care undertaken by relatives, neighbours and friends. This informal care-giving takes place within a relationship, and brings both stresses and satisfactions to the carer. The main aim of a carer is to ensure that the person they care for is all right and getting the most appropriate support. If adequate support is available, for the statutory services such care may be far more effective than care in an institution. Some argue that the **informal carer** is used as a dumping ground for long-term patients whom it would be expensive to care for in hospital or residential care, to save public money.

There has been a movement over the past 20 years towards self-help and greater involvement of care in the community; much of it supplied by informal carers. Governments encouraged informal care by families and friends. For example, the government in 1981 stressed that the care of the elderly and other vulnerable groups was a community responsibility and that care in the community must increasingly mean 'care by the community' (*Growing Older*, HMSO 1981). For many this meant a heavy responsibility. This policy was based on the view that, wherever possible, people should be cared for in their own homes. This is a view shared by many informal carers themselves and the people they support. The role of statutory services is now seen as being to support informal carers so that they can continue to look after their relatives or friends in their own homes. The present government sees the role of the carer as being an essential aspect of community care (*Modernising Health and Social Services*, DOH 1998). The government sees its strategy for carers as been underpinned by three key approaches: information for carers, support for carers and care for carers.

The schedule-structured interview

The most structured form of personal interview is the schedule-structured or highly **structured interview**, in which the questions, their wording and their sequence are fixed and are identical for every respondent. The respondents in this situation do not have the opportunity to enlarge on any of their answers. This type of interview is based on three crucial assumptions:

- that the respondents have a sufficiently common vocabulary, so that the interviewer and respondent have the same understanding of the words used in the question
- that all the questions are phrased in a form that is equally understood by all the respondents
- that the sequence of the questions is the same for all the respondents.

The semi-structured interview

In the semi-structured interview (conducted by means of set questions but which allows for some flexibility either in the question or in the range of responses) the respondent will have opportunities to answer outside the structure of the interview schedule. With little or no direction from the interviewer, respondents are encouraged to relate their experiences, to describe whatever events seem significant to them, and to reveal their opinions and attitudes as they see fit. The interviewer has therefore a great deal of freedom to probe various areas and to raise specific queries during the course of the interview.

Example: 'Do you think that people who kill policemen should be hanged?'

In a semi-structured interview, both those people who answer 'yes' and those who answer 'no' may be asked why they gave that answer. In a structured interview they cannot explain this.

Interviews may, however, consist of structured and non-structured elements.

The advantages and disadvantages of personal interviews

Advantages

- The interviewer may get all the sample to respond to the questions
- The interviewer can ask the respondents to explain their answers
- The interviewer can see if the respondents understood the questions

Disadvantages

- They are time-consuming and may cost a lot if you have to pay the interviewer
- It is difficult to interpret the data
- Interviewers have to be trained
- Personal interviews may intrude unnecessarily into people's lives

Activity 8

Key Skills

You can use Activity 8 to provide evidence for Key Skills Communication C3.2, 3.3, Application of Number N3.1, N3.2, N3.3, Information Technology IT3.1.

a Choose a subject for the interview, one that people usually have strong feelings about – the local football team, cricket, traffic, the government. Read as widely on the subject as you can before you interview or start designing any questions.

b Think of a few neutral questions, say six, that will put the person you are interviewing at ease and lead them into your chosen subject. Write down notes of what they say in a notebook.

c Decide who you will need as respondents. For example if your chosen subject is football you might consider interviewing:
  i rank and file respondents – people in the street
  ii football team followers.

d Depending on whom you are interviewing, talk to respondents about their feelings on the subject matter. Get their answers as nearly verbatim as possible. This means in their own words, not in a summary by you.

e Read over each interview before embarking on the next. Watch for points that you will want to follow up in this and subsequent interviews.

f By the time you have finished your interviews, you should have some interesting information concerning the topic you have chosen to investigate. Read your interviews and make notes concerning points you wish to make and the questions you wish to use in your report.

g Write a report including the following:
  i a brief statement of the topic of study and what aspect of that topic you intend to investigate
  ii a brief list of questions you asked in the order in which they developed, from the introductory ones to those that were more focused
  iii an explanation of why and how you selected participants, your sampling technique – explain why at least two other sampling techniques were not thought to be more suitable
  iv a discussion of your findings and the supporting evidence, taken from interviews, to back them up
  v a discussion of the pertinent areas or hypotheses for further study
  vi a discussion of the problems you encountered in carrying out the interviews and any suggestions you have for surmounting them in the future
  vii a list of sources of information and a bibliography.

Sampling methods

Selecting a sample

At first glance, it sounds a very simple exercise to select a sample. We sample things every day; for example, people sample wine or food in a supermarket. In practice, good sampling is a far from easy matter. For example, to be fully comprehensive and accurate a survey should be completed by everyone to whom it applies. If you wish to find out about users of a cinema feel about it, in an ideal situation you should ask every user. This would, however, take too long and would be expensive. You must therefore question a sample of the users.

How large should the sample be?

Size of sample

The size of the sample will depend on what you want to do with the results. If you want to generalise, then you must interview as large a sample as possible. If you only interview six mothers who use a day nursery on a Friday, you cannot state that their views represent those of the users on the other days of the week. If you want to generalise about users of the day nursery, you must interview all users or a sample of those who use it on every day throughout the week.

Activity 9

a If you wanted to find out how people in your locality felt about their local councillors and it was only possible to interview people in the high street one morning at 11 a.m., which groups of people might be missed out on any day?

b How would you go about getting a representative sample?

The size of the population you study is important but to believe you have a good sample is not just a matter of how large the sample is, it also depends on how well you have chosen the sample. The principles underlying all sample design are:

- to avoid bias in the selection procedure
- to achieve the maximum precision for the resources available.

The goal of science is to find uniformities or 'patterns' in nature. Obviously, scientists cannot examine all instances of the data they are studying. For example, the botanist cannot look at all plants, nor the social scientist all juvenile car theft. A poor sample can be disastrous – it can provide misleading information and result in errors. Even if researchers cannot observe all of the population, for example all people with an experience of hospital admission, they will wish to be able to generalise to all similar cases from the data they collect. The problem is: how can the researcher be sure that the sample studied will be representative or similar to the rest of the people (population) who were admitted to hospital at some time?

Activity 10

How can a researcher be sure that the sample studied will be representative of or similar to the rest of the people (population)?

A population may be a group of students, people over 65 years of age, residents of a home, shoppers or home owners. The specific nature of a population depends on the purpose of the investigation or research. The first step is to define the population to be sampled. This task is not as easy as it sounds. No sample of a population is perfectly representative; the smaller the sample, the more unrepresentative it will be. If you wished to interview students in your college or school about their attitude to a particular issue, could you interview every student?

Activity 11

A researcher comparing the activity of children in two separate playgroups may have difficulty in duplicating the research with the same groups. List as many reasons as you can why this might be so. Can the researcher extrapolate these findings to other groups?

You can use Activity 11 to provide evidence for Key Skills Communication C3.1a.

Would you choose five from every class or form? If you decided to do this, how would you select them? Would they be representative of the rest of the students? Similarly, if you wished to interview people who used a meals-on-wheels service, would those who received meals on Monday be representative of people who received them at weekends?

If you are going to generalise from your results to the general population then you must choose your sample according to the rules of statistical theory. It may be wrong to select, say, volunteers, friends or people who happen to be at hand.

Finally, the idea of sampling is not new and it is economical. It is obviously cheaper to collect information from 100 students than from 1000. Sampling also saves labour and time.

If you apply the rules of statistical theory, can you generalise from your results to the general population?

Random sampling

Random does not mean 'haphazard'; it means the very opposite. It implies a very careful preselection plan. A random method of selection is one that gives each of the units (people) in the population to be studied a calculable probability of being selected. Each member of the population to be studied has an equal chance of being selected for the sample.

How might we draw a **random sample**? First, as already mentioned, you need to define the population that you wish your sample to represent.

Example of a random sample

If you wish to study students at your particular school/college, you first need to define what you mean by a student.

- Who is included in the population?
- Do you want to include full-time and part-time students?
- Do you wish to include night/evening students?
- Do you wish to include students over 65 years of age?

When you have clarified the target population, you need to locate or complete a list of all of its members, say every full-time student under 65 years of age (known as a sampling frame). If you do not have such a list then random sampling cannot be used and other methods will be more suitable. Many lists are suspect and do not list all the population. A telephone directory is not an adequate listing of people in a town because it will not include people who cannot afford a telephone or those who wish their telephone number to be unlisted. Are all people over 18 years of age on the electoral roll?

Assuming that you have a list (sampling frame) of all the members of the population you wish to study, how do you select your sample? There are a number of methods of probability sampling.

Simple random sampling

Simple random sampling is the basic probability sampling design. It gives each of the known sampling units of a population (N) an equal chance of being selected. To ensure that this happens one of the following methods may be used.

The lottery method

Each member of the population is represented by a disk or a piece of paper with his or her name or a number corresponding to the position of the name on the list. The pieces of paper or disks are placed in a box, mixed well and a sample of the desired size is drawn. Every member of the population has an equal chance of being selected.

Table of random digits

The random number tables were devised to meet the two criteria of random selection:

* each number has the same chance of being selected
* each number is independent of the others.

The procedure is simple. Each member of the population is listed and numbered. A number is selected from a table of random digits. Each number that appears in the table of random digits corresponds to the numbering of a sample unit in the list. That sampling unit is selected for the sample. The process is continued until the desired sample size is reached. Random numbers can also be generated by computer.

Example

You have a population of 100 students and you want a 10% sample. You list all the students serially and give each one a number between 1 and 100. Randomly decide where to start in the table of random numbers. Select one column and one row at random. For example, suppose you choose the 13th vertical column and the 9th horizontal row. The point on the table is numbered 17. Thus the first number is 17. You therefore identify that person and the number on the list of your sample. You next read down the column and find the next number, which is 13; that person is also included on your sample list. You continue down the column until you have selected 10 numbers (17, 13, 69, 55, 88, 80, 72, 75, 92, 18). The 10 chosen people will be a random sample of the population you wish to study.

1	36	45	88	31	28	73	59	43	46	32	00	32	67	15	32	49	54	55	76	17
2	90	51	40	66	18	46	95	54	65	89	16	80	95	33	15	88	18	60	56	46
3	98	41	90	22	48	37	80	31	91	39	33	80	40	82	38	26	20	39	71	82
4	55	25	71	27	14	68	84	04	99	24	82	30	73	43	92	68	18	99	47	54
5	02	99	10	75	77	21	88	55	79	97	70	32	59	87	75	35	18	34	62	53
6	79	85	55	66	63	84	08	63	04	00	18	34	53	94	58	01	55	05	90	99
7	33	53	95	28	06	81	34	95	13	93	37	16	95	06	15	91	89	99	37	16
8	74	75	13	13	22	16	37	76	15	57	42	38	96	23	90	24	58	26	71	46
9	06	66	30	43	00	66	32	60	36	60	46	05	(17)	31	66	80	91	01	62	35
10	92	83	31	60	87	30	76	83	17	85	31	48	13	23	17	32	68	14	84	96
11	61	21	31	49	98	29	77	70	72	11	35	23	69	47	14	27	14	74	52	35
12	27	82	01	01	74	41	38	77	53	68	53	26	55	16	35	66	31	87	82	09
13	61	05	50	10	94	85	86	32	10	72	95	67	88	21	72	09	48	73	03	97
14	11	57	85	67	94	91	49	48	35	49	39	41	80	17	54	45	23	66	83	60
15	15	16	08	90	92	86	13	32	26	01	20	02	72	45	94	74	97	19	99	46
16	22	09	29	66	15	44	76	74	94	92	48	13	75	85	81	28	95	41	36	30
17	69	13	53	55	35	87	43	23	83	32	79	40	92	20	83	76	82	61	24	20
18	08	29	79	37	00	33	35	34	86	55	10	91	18	86	43	50	67	79	33	58
19	39	29	99	85	55	63	32	66	71	98	85	20	31	83	63	91	77	21	99	62
20	65	11	14	04	88	86	28	92	04	03	42	99	87	08	20	55	30	53	82	24
21	66	22	81	58	30	80	21	10	15	53	26	90	33	77	51	19	17	49	27	14
22	37	21	77	13	69	31	20	22	67	13	46	29	75	32	69	79	37	23	32	43
23	51	43	09	72	68	38	05	77	14	62	89	07	37	89	25	30	92	09	06	92
24	31	59	37	83	92	55	15	31	21	24	03	93	35	97	84	61	96	85	45	51
25	79	05	43	69	52	93	00	77	44	82	91	65	11	71	25	37	89	13	63	87

Part of a table of 1000 random digits

Systematic samples

Using the simple random sampling method, each member of the population under study is given a number, and then a subgroup is taken for study. For example, if we wished to study a subgroup of your school or college, every student would be given a number, and then a subgroup, say a particular class or students of a particular age or hair colour, would be taken for study.

Systematic sampling

Systematic sampling consists of selecting every 10th, 20th or 30th (*k*th) person (sampling unit) of the population after the first person (sampling unit) is selected at random from the first *k* sampling units. So, if you wished to select a sample of 100 students from a population of 1000 at a college, you take every 10th student ($k = N/n$, where *k* is the interval of selection, *N* is the total population and *n* is the sample (so 1000/100 = 10)). The first selection must be chosen by the random process.

Suppose the fourth person was selected, the sample would then consist of students numbered 4, 14, 24, 34, 44, 54 and so on.

Stratified sampling

This method can only be used when there is detailed knowledge of the population under study. It is usually used when there are variations in the sample, e.g. different age groups, people with differing disabilities. Stratified sampling is used primarily to ensure that different groups of a population are adequately represented in the sample. For example, if you knew that the student population was made up of 20% female students and 80% male students, a simple random sample might not give you a representative sample of these groups. You may find that all females had been selected. The survey would then tell you little about the male population.

Give one situation in which you would use stratified sampling.

The answer to this problem is to draw from each group a random sample proportionate to the size of the group; you will then be sure of having both male and females in your sample.

Non-probability sampling

If a list of a population is not available, this type of sampling may be used. In non-probability sampling, there is no way of specifying the probability that each unit has been included in the sample; there is no assurance that every unit has some chance of being included. The major advantages of this type of sampling are convenience and economy.

Convenience sampling

A convenience sample is obtained when the researcher selects whatever sampling units are conveniently available. Thus you may select only students in your class or the first 100 people you meet in the street who are willing to be interviewed.

Purposive sampling

Sometimes this method is referred to as judgement sampling. The researchers attempt to obtain a sample that appears to them to be representative of the population they wish to research. The chance that a particular person will be selected depends on the subjective judgement of the researcher.

Quota sampling

The aim of this method is to try and select a sample that is as closely as possible a replica of the population to be researched. For example, if it is known that the group to be researched has equal numbers of males and females, the researcher selects an equal number of both. If it is known that the group or population has only 20 males then the researcher would select an appropriate percentage.

You can use Activity 12 to provide evidence for Key Skills Communication C3.2 and Application of Number N3.2. N3.3.

Activity 12

A large college is to open a new creche. The Principal is to hold a wine and cheese party after the official opening and wishes to invite representatives of each of the sectors in the college in proportion to the numbers working in each sector. There is only space for 50 people at the party. How many will be chosen from each of the following sectors?

Sector	No. working in the sector
Health and Social Care Department	50
Engineering Department	78
Business and Finance Department	60
Building supervisor's staff	20
Catering staff	26
Admin./clerical	100

Sources of information

Primary sources are usually the first publication of a work, article or paper. Primary sources contain the original primary data collected in carrying out research, such as measurements from laboratory experiments, data from field observation, archive data, information gathered by questionnaires and interviews. Always try if possible to read the primary sources.

Secondary sources are generally in the form of indexes and classifications of primary sources, such as text books, subject abstracts and monographs. This type of data varies from highly quantitative statistics to more qualitative documents such as autobiographies, log books or diaries. These sources will be subject to the problem that they were collected for purposes other than the researcher's present work and will also suffer from the biases and inaccuracies of the author.

Major sources of secondary data are technical publications, books and journals, official publications, trade association data and computer databases.

Secondary data has considerable attractions for research students, particularly those in the social sciences and especially if they are engaged in short research projects. Secondary sources are more quickly available than primary sources and they exist in considerable quantities. However, before you use secondary sources you must evaluate how reliable the information contained in it is. You should ask the following:

- Who collected the data? If, for example, a survey was studying the effects of cigarette smoking, how reliable would it be if it was carried out by cigarette manufacturers? Similarly, how would you treat a report on the side-effects of a drug if the drug company who manufactured the drug published the report?
- For what purpose was the data collected? How was it collected? Was the sample size large enough for the results to apply to your research?

> **Remember**
>
> If possible, always go to the primary source of data.

Case study

In 1995, the Home Secretary announced a national fall of 5.5% in recorded crime – the largest reported fall in 40 years. In Greater Manchester, crime was reported as having fallen by 12% in 1994. However, in South Yorkshire the crime rate had risen by 5%. Were people in South Yorkshire more likely to be the victims of crime?

Researchers have looked at these crime figures to try and explain the differences. They found that crimes had been reclassified, which in turn affected the figures. Some police forces no longer recorded such crimes as malicious telephone calls, vandalism, deception, minor criminal damage and assault. This lack of recording could have accounted for the fall in reported crime in some areas.

In South Yorkshire the Chief Constable, concerned about reports that some of his officers were not reporting crime, found that there was an above-average number of reports of damage to houses where the damage was valued at £20 or more. Those houses where the damage was valued at less than £20 were not reported in the crime statistics. The Chief Constable stopped this practice and this could have accounted for the rise in crime in South Yorkshire.

Activity 13

Choose an area of study such as residential care, day care or outpatient departments. Using the resources in your school or college library, make a list of primary and secondary sources of information or data for your chosen subject.

Key Skills

You can use Activity 13 to provide evidence for Key Skills Communication C3.2.

Tertiary sources include sources that facilitate the location of primary and secondary sources; it includes, for example, handbooks, bibliographies and encyclopaedias.

6.3 Methods of analysis, validation and how to present research results

Defining a research problem

A research project is a major undertaking and planning is necessary if you are not to waste time and effort. The first thing you will need to consider is the purpose of your research. Are you going to:

- review existing knowledge
- describe something new, or
- explain some situation or event?

A good definition of a research problem aims to develop a realistic plan of action, with clear objectives that take account of both resources and constraints, and with a high probability of being achieved.

One way to achieve this is to look at a broad subject area that you are interested in. For example, if you are interested in unemployment there are a number of major areas that you could look at.

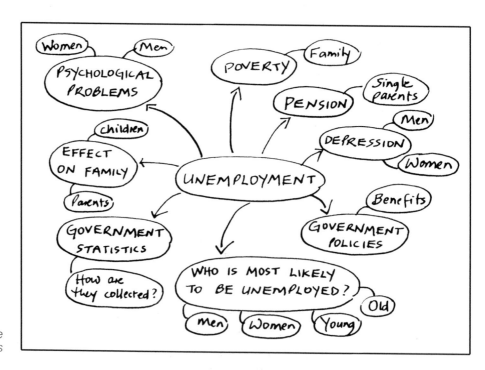

Some possible research questions

One way to link up ideas based upon a single concept, such as unemployment, is to produce a diagram such as the one above, writing down all the ideas that you can think of relating to unemployment and how they interact with each other. When you have drawn up a map of ideas you will be able to see that there are many aspects to unemployment. For example, you could look at the psychological aspects of unemployment, in particular what psychological effects it might have on men compared to women. When you have finally agreed on an area of interest to study, the next step is to develop a hypothesis.

Hypotheses

Not all research projects need a hypothesis, but you must have a clear idea in your mind of what you are planning to do. You may want to analyse a general problem (see below). However, let us assume that you want to carry out a piece of research that needs a hypothesis. A hypothesis is a proposition that can be tested, or the naming of the phenomenon that is to be tested. Any idea or theory that makes provisional predications is called a hypothesis. For example:

- all social care students are female
- all engineering students are male
- sports enthusiasts are less likely to smoke than people who take no part in sports.

The view of the issue that the researcher holds has an impact on the formulation of the hypothesis. You may believe that all social care students are female, but if you are to set out to prove it you must have an open mind and keep an objective approach to the research design. You set out to support or contradict the hypothesis.

The difference between research questions and hypotheses

A few examples will help clarify the distinction between research questions and hypotheses, and how hypotheses are constructed and expressed. Research questions are general questions. Here are some examples:

- What causes inflation?
- Who uses a playgroup?
- What types of student pass examinations?
- What causes football violence?
- Who becomes a leader in a group?
- What causes child abuse?
- What is the gender make-up of engineering students?

The researcher can then generate a hypothesis based on a general question.

Examples

1. From the general question 'Who becomes a leader in a group?', a hypothesis about how leaders develop in a group could be expressed as follows:

'As inter-group conflict increases, those people who are more aggressive and who are able to articulate are given power by the group.'

The researcher will then devise a strategy to observe behaviour in one or more groups to support or contradict the hypotheses.

2. When considering the general question 'What causes child abuse?', the researcher may feel that those who have suffered abuse as children are likely to abuse their own children. The hypothesis could be formulated as follows:

'Individuals who have experienced violent and abusive households are more likely to grow up to become child abusers than individuals who experience little or no violence in their childhood.'

Hypotheses can be derived from theories, observation, intuition or a combination of these. Ideas and background to any potential idea can be obtained by consulting bibliographies, indexes, abstracts, professional journals and statistical sources.

It does not matter if your research findings do not support your hypothesis – the researcher sets out to test a hypothesis, not to prove it.

- Research problems are intellectual stimuli calling for an answer.
- Hypotheses are tentative answers to research problems.
- Hypotheses should be clear, value-free and amenable to testing.

Key Skills

You can use Activity 14 to provide evidence for Key Skills Communication C3.1b.

Activity 14

Generate a hypothesis based on the following general question: 'Does having five GCSEs at grade E or higher indicate whether students can obtain a GNVQ at Advanced level?'

Planning

Once you have agreed on an area to study your next step is to look at what you need to do to complete your research, in effect a research action plan. How much time have you got to complete the work? Your tutor will have given you some idea of this – can you complete what you want to do in the time given? How much reading will you have to do? Are the books, journals and papers readily available or will the school or college librarian have to get them from another source? How long could this take? How will you get reliable, relevant, up-to-date knowledge?

Activity 15

How can you tell that your sources of knowledge/data are of good quality and valid?

If you have decided that your research needs interviews, how many people do you need to interview? How do you select your sample? Where are they? Have you time to interview as many as you would like? If not, what are you going to do about it? If you are going to use questionnaires, how long will it take you to design them?

How are you going to analyse your results? How long will it take you to write up your report? How accessible is your college computer resource – do you need to book a computer in advance?

When drawing up your research action plan you will need to answer all of these questions.

Designing questionnaires and interviews

Gathering and collecting data

When the researcher has formulated a hypothesis the next thing is to decide how to gather or collect data. We have seen that the most widely used methods are:

* the questionnaire
* the personal interview
* observation.

The foundation of all questionnaires is, of course, the question. Instead of observing what people do, would you get more relevant information if you asked people what they were doing or asked them their views on what they are doing? A questionnaire is simply a list of questions that provides a relatively fast, effective and cheap method of obtaining information.

The personal interview is a face-to-face, interpersonal situation in which the interviewer's questions are designed to obtain answers that are relevant to the research hypothesis. The interview can be tightly structured, with the interviewer asking questions from a prepared questionnaire, or it can be open, with scope to ask further questions in order to probe the respondent's feelings more deeply (see below).

Sometimes the researcher may make use of a self-administered questionnaire (see page 284).

A good questionnaire requires a lot of thought and planning

You must ask yourself:

* What questions am I going to ask?
* Who am I going to ask?
* How am I going to record the answers?
* What am I going to do with the results?

There are two main types of interview:

* the structured interview
* the unstructured interview.

Structured interviews

As discussed earlier in this unit, the structured form of interview is one in which the questions, the wording and their sequence are fixed and identical for each respondent. Any variations that appear in the responses can be attributed to the actual differences between the respondents and not to variation in the interview.

Structured interviews provide an objective exercise and the tendencies toward bias are less than with observation or unstructured interviews. A major advantage is that the information can be easily coded and analysed.

It is important to give a lot of thought to the design of the questionnaire, as structured interviews are only as good as the questions asked. It is also important to frame the questions in a language that the respondents will understand:

* avoid woolly generalisations
* avoid bias that might encourage the respondents to give the answer that you want them to give.

Example of a questionnaire for a structured interview

                                                      Code

Question 1
How often do you watch soaps on television?

Never	1
Every week	2
Two or three times a month	3
Once a month or less	4

Question 2
How much money do you spend on cigarettes each month?

Less than £50	1
£51–80	2
£81 or more	3

Question 3
Do you go to the cinema?   Yes/No
If your answer is No, is it because:

You don't like what's showing?	4
You prefer to watch it on video?	5
You are worried about the cigarette smoke?	6
Other reason (please state):	7

What is the advantage of the structured questionnaire?

Problems with structured interview questions

There are many problems with framing questions for structured questionnaires. Some questions may be unclear, or use words that the respondent may not understand. Leading questions are ones that encourage the respondent to give a particular answer.

Activity 16

Is either of the following a leading question, and if so in what way?

a Do you think that women should not work until their children are old enough?
b Don't you agree that there is too much violence on television?

A subtler example of the use of leading questions

Interviewer	What brand of soap do you use?
Respondent	Pearly Pink.
Interviewer	Why do you like Pearly Pink soap?
Respondent	Ah . . . um . . . I've never really thought about it.
Interviewer	Well, try to give me an answer. (*Pause*) Is it because of its smell?
Respondent	Yes, it's got a nice smell.

The interviewer writes down that the respondent likes the soap because of its smell. But perhaps the respondent is simply not prepared to admit that he or she likes the soap because it is the cheapest brand on the market or is helping to get rid of his or her facial spots.

Questions that presume take it for granted that the respondent has at some time done something specified in the question:

- When did you last go to a pop concert?
- How many cups of coffee have you had?

Double questions are questions with more than one part:

- Do you think that the college should spend less money on books and more on sports facilities?
- Do you think that there is too much violence at football matches and that this is responsible for the lowering of standards in society?

Activity 17

Compare the following two questions. Which question expects the answer 'Yes' and which the answer 'No'?

a Do you think people should be free to provide the best medical care possible for themselves and their families, free of interference from the state?

b Should the wealthy be able to buy a place at the head of the queue for medical treatment, pushing aside those with greater need?

Discuss your conclusions with your colleagues.

You can use Activity 17 to provide evidence for Key Skills Communication C3.1a.

Unstructured interviews

The least structured form of interviewing is the unstructured, or non-directive, interview, in which respondents are given no direction from the interviewer. They are encouraged to relate their experience and to reveal their opinions and attitudes as they see fit. This framework allows respondents to express their opinions as well as answer the questions. The respondents can let you know their real feelings about the subject of the question and, therefore, tend to answer more freely and fully.

Activity 18

Your task is to discover as many specific kinds of conflicts and tensions between children and parents as possible. Carry out the following unstructured interview with a teenager of your acquaintance. The five areas of possible conflict we want to explore are listed in question **c**. Questions **a** and **b** are to allow you to build up a rapport with the respondent.

a What sorts of problems do teenagers have in getting along with their parents?
b What sorts of disagreement do you have with your parents?
c Have you ever had any disagreement with either parent over:
   i staying out late
   ii friends of the opposite sex
   iii dating
   iv smoking
   v drinking?

Write a short report based on your findings and present your findings to your colleagues.

You can use Activity 18 to provide evidence for Key Skills Communication C3.1b.

Give one advantage of the unstructured interview.

The principles of interviewing

The aim in interviewing is to get the desired information. This can be done by following a few simple guidelines:

- The person you are interviewing needs to feel that the interview will be pleasant and satisfying.
- Interviewers should present themselves as being understanding and easy to talk to.
- The people being interviewed need to feel that the study is worthwhile.
- The interviewer also needs to overcome the respondent's suspicions.
- The interviewer should explain in a friendly manner the purpose of the study and the confidential nature of the interview. How can you put people at ease?
- Tell the respondent who you are and who you represent, and explain to them what you are doing in a way that will make them interested in your research.
- Tell the respondent how and why they were chosen to be interviewed. Any instructions should be brief.
- Create a relationship of confidence between yourself and the person you are interviewing.

Activity 19

a When interviewing, do you think that there are situations when the respondent might feel inhibited?

b Discuss with your class colleagues the effect on the outcome of an interview that the following scenarios might have:
- **i** a white interviewer and a black respondent
- **ii** a male interviewer and a female respondent.

Types of question

There are basically two types of question:

- factual questions
- opinion or attitude questions.

Factual questions

Factual questions elicit objective information. The most common type of factual question obtains information such as sex, age, marital status, education or income of respondents.

Example

At what age did you get married?

- 16 years   ☐
- 17 years   ☐
- 18 years   ☐
- 19 years   ☐
- 20 years   ☐
- 21 years   ☐
- Over 21 years   ☐

Please tick the appropriate box.

Other factual questions could elicit information about a respondent's social environment, e.g. 'How many people are living in your household?', or their leisure activities, e.g. 'How often do you go to the pub?'.

Opinion or attitude questions

Opinion or attitude questions are more difficult to construct. Before we examine how to develop an opinion or attitude question, we must first examine the difference between an 'attitude' and an 'opinion'. An attitude is the sum total of a person's prejudices, ideas, fears and convictions about any specific topic. Opinions are the verbal expression of attitudes.

Activity 20

Which of the following are opinions and which are attitudes?

a John says he likes Leeds Football Club.
b Mary refuses to allow her son to marry an Irish girl.
c Jim is convinced that anyone over 65 years of age should not work.
d Peter says that a woman's place is in the home looking after children.
e Jim refuses to allow his wife to continue working after the birth of their first child.

To obtain data about factual matters or attitudes, you can ask two types of question:

- closed questions
- open questions.

Closed questions

In closed questions respondents are given a set of answers from which they are asked to choose one that closely represents their views.

Closed questions are easy to ask, quick to answer and their analysis is straightforward. Answers can be more elaborate than open questions (see the second example below).

Examples of closed questions

Example 1: Driving a train is a man's job.

Strongly agree ☐
Agree ☐
Disagree ☐
Strongly disagree ☐

Example 2: Do you feel that you are really part of your class group?

Really a part of my class ☐
Included in most ways ☐
Included in some ways, but not in others ☐
Don't feel that I really belong ☐
Don't fit in with any class ☐

Please tick the appropriate box.

Open questions

Open questions are not followed by any kind of specified choice – the respondents' answers are recorded in full. For example, the question 'What do you personally feel are the most important problems the government should try to tackle?' is an open question. The virtue of this type of question is that respondents can express their thoughts freely, spontaneously and in their own way.

What type of question should you use?

In which situations should you use the different type of questions? The following points should be considered:

- *The objectives of the questionnaire* – Closed questions are suitable when you want to find out if the respondent agrees or disagrees with a point of view. If you want to find out how the respondent arrived at this view, an open question is more appropriate.
- *How much does the respondent know about the topic in question?* – Open questions give you the opportunity to find out how much the respondents know about the topic. Obviously, it is futile to ask any questions that are beyond the experience of the respondent.
- *Communication* – How easily can the contents of the answer be communicated by the respondent?
- *Motivation* – How motivated is the respondent to answer the questions?

Forms of response

Rating
One of the most common formats for questions in social science surveys is the rating scale. Here, respondents are asked to make a judgement in terms of strength of feeling.

Example
Old people should not be allowed to live on their own if they are very dependent.
Strongly agree ☐
Agree ☐
Disagree ☐
Strongly disagree ☐
Don't know ☐
Please tick the appropriate box.

These responses reflect the intensity of the respondent's judgement.

Ranking
Ranking is used in questionnaires whenever the researcher wants to gather data regarding the degree of importance that people give to a set of attitudes or objects. For instance, in a survey on the quality of life of students, respondents could be asked to rank in order various dimensions they considered important to student life.

Example

I would like you to tell me what you have found important in student life. Would you please look at this card and tell me which of these is most important to you as a goal in your life, which comes next in importance, which is third and so on?

Meeting other students

    1st rank
    2nd rank
    3rd rank
    4th rank

Academic life

    1st rank
    2nd rank
    3rd rank
    4th rank

Sport activities

    1st rank
    2nd rank
    3rd rank
    4th rank

Student's union

    1st rank
    2nd rank
    3rd rank
    4th rank

Ranking is a useful device for providing some sense of relative order among judgements. It is particularly important in the social sciences where a 'numerical value' cannot be applied. The rank order method is an extremely easy method to use. One of the most basic assumptions is that attitudes towards various statements may be expressed along a continuum from least to most favourable.

Semantic differential measuring method

The **semantic differential** measuring method is one of the most adaptable yet, ironically, underutilised scaling methods in the social sciences. This scale, with minor variations, is adaptable to any attitude measurement. The semantic differential measures a subject's responses to stimulus – words, concepts or phrases – in terms of bipolar (opposite to each other) adjective ratings. An example is shown in the figure below.

With a list of such bipolar adjective scales, it is possible to measure the effect experienced by any person towards any statement.

```
                        A social worker is
  good       ---------------------------------------   bad
  powerful   ---------------------------------------   powerless
  honest     ---------------------------------------   dishonest
               3     2     1     0     1     2     3
```

A bipolar adjective rating scale

| Activity 21 |

Design a bipolar adjective scale to measure people's attitudes to the role of the police.

The self-administered questionnaire

The self-administered questionnaire, as a method, is cheaper than others and avoids the problems, such as bias, associated with the use of interviewers. It may be handed out to people or sent through the post to be completed in the respondent's own time.

The self-administered questionnaire has some positive advantages. People are more likely to express less socially acceptable attitudes and feelings when answering a questionnaire alone than when confronted by an interviewer. The greater the anonymity the more honest the response. Aside from the greater honesty that they may produce, self-administered questionnaires also have the advantage of giving a respondent more time to think.

This type of survey gives no opportunity for the questioner to probe beyond the answer given. The questions should be simple and straightforward, and be capable of being understood with the help of minimal printed instructions.

Give one advantage of the self-administered questionnaire.

How to encourage people to complete and return questionnaires

With all surveys there is the problem of people who may refuse to fill in your questionnaire or simply forget to do so. This makes your results less accurate. If your response rate is low, what can you do to improve it? There are various methods that you can use to improve the response rate, including:

- *follow-up* – write or telephone the people who have not responded
- *length of questionnaire* – the shorter the better, as longer questionnaires tend not to be answered
- *who gave out the questionnaire* – if the respondents know you or the school/college, then they are likely to reply; however, where questions are of a confidential nature this may not be the case – in these instances you must stress confidentiality in your introductory letter
- *introductory letter* – an appeal to the respondents to emphasise that they would be helping the interests of everyone seems to produce the best results
- *method of return* – a stamped addressed envelope produces the best results.
- *format of the questionnaire* – a title that will arouse interest helps, as does an attractive and clear layout with plenty of room for handwritten answers.

Analysis and interpretation of data

Validity

Validity is defined as the degree to which researchers have measured what they set out to measure. Validity also provides a direct check on how well the questions fulfil their function, the determination of which usually requires independent, external criteria of whatever the questionnaire is designed to measure.

Validity determines whether researchers are really measuring what they say is being measured. For example, a questionnaire asking home support workers what they do for clients may not produce valid data indicating what they actually do in the clients' homes; the results may not be valid. The only way to find out what a home support worker actually does in a client's home is to observe him or her doing it. This data *would* be valid. Do the questions asked in a survey actually measure the concepts the researcher intended them to measure? For instance, from the wording of a question, the researcher assumes that the respondent who agrees that 'all policemen are hostile' is indicating a distrust of the police. Undoubtedly, one of the most important questions that needs to be raised regarding any questionnaire is the validity of the questions, i.e. do they actually measure what they purport to measure?

Example

A measuring tape may measure in feet or metres, not in pounds or grams. You do not measure height by standing on a weighing scale.

Tests for validity

One of the common tests for validity is face validity. For example, if the concept the researcher wishes to measure is 'How satisfied is a person with his or her car?', the question 'Do you like your car?' has face validity because it is relevant to the concept in question and it is unambiguous. The answer that you will get from such a question will usually make sense. Face validity can be checked by discussing the questions in a questionnaire with respondents, who can give their opinions as to their validity (do they make sense?). For example, if you are constructing a questionnaire on the work of teachers, then asking members of that profession about the relevance of your questions would go some way to providing face validity.

The question you should therefore ask yourself is, 'Will the questionnaire look valid to the subjects who respond to it and to the personnel who make use of it?'.

Reliability

Reliability should be distinguished from validity. It refers to consistency – to the ability to obtain the same results again and again under similar circumstances. Will the same methods used by other researchers produce the same results? Reliability measures consistency between independent measurements of the same phenomenon.

Many argue that in the social sciences 'true' answers do not exist. Or true answers may exist, but they may change over time. However, some sort of criterion is available that can be applied to the realm of 'factual questions' such as 'Is bathing residents part of your job?' or 'Do you think that shaving residents is part of your job or of someone else's?'. Such questions would produce a true answer, if the researcher could find time to observe the member of staff at work. If another researcher asked the same staff the same questions the answers ought to be the same, i.e. show high reliability. If questions are poorly phrased and obscure, the respondent may answer differently to the same question on different occasions. The answers may reflect the respondent's current mood.

It is rare for researchers to obtain perfect reliability between independent measurements in the social sciences. Your questions may not be interpreted in the same way by the respondents the second time around.

Analysing qualitative data

It is very unlikely, because of time constraints or financial constraints, that you will be asked to carry out a study that will require you to analyse qualitative data. However, you should be aware of some of the basic techniques for doing so. Most qualitative data consists of descriptions of what took place, what was observed, expressed in words. Remember what was said earlier about qualitative research, often called fieldwork or participant observation. This method of collecting data does not usually involve asking standardised questions of large, representative samples of people. Qualitative research is about exploration and low evidential value. However, this type of research can provide valuable information. Once observations are made and data gathered, the researcher needs to evaluate and interpret the results of the study. The data might be a verbal description of everything observed, a video tape or audio tape.

Qualitative research permits discretion on the part of the researcher. The researcher is bound by the rules set for the collection of data but not by strict rules of sampling for example (see below). So, when reporting the results of their research, researchers can exercise considerable discretion as to what they report, since qualitative data will come from diverse series of incidents written up as notes, rather than explicitly measured **variables**. It is difficult for researchers to describe in detail the research procedures that led to their conclusions or to present a summary of the evidence supporting a particular conclusion. However, qualitative researchers can write up their experiences to give the reader some insight into the development of their analyses.

An excellent example of qualitative research was a study by Goodlove, Richard and Rodwell. This research involved an observation study of elderly people in different care environments. Researchers observed, in pairs, for periods of 6 hours at a time, the activities of staff and residents in care settings. They observed such activities as eating and drinking, formal exercise, occupational therapy, personal care and recreational activities. They used different methods to report and analyse their results. The table below, for example, shows the percentage of the population who did any 'rehabilitative activities' in the differing settings.

Percentage engaging in rehabilitative activities

Day centres	76.9%
Local authority homes	13.3%
Day hospitals	80.0%
Hospital wards	7.6%

Source: Goodlove et al., 1984

This method of presenting data allows the reader to see at a glance the analysis of data in a clear readable format. These data show quite clearly the different policies on rehabilitation in the different settings.

This way of presenting data is useful in summarising the differences between the activities carried out in the differing environments. However, data presented in this way does not give any indication of what was observed in respect of individuals and what they were doing or experiencing. To bring the data more alive the researcher used the method of describing what was observed. The following is an example from the research we discussed above.

On the day of observation, Mrs H sat in the lounge all morning, apart from a 5-minute visit to her bedroom. She read a little and talked to other residents a little but mostly sat and stared or dozed, sometimes picking at the fabric of her dress. Her only contact with staff was when a care assistant spent 30 seconds combing her hair (talking to her for at least 10 seconds) – Mrs H walked unaided and ate lunch unaided. She talked occasionally during lunch. After lunch she returned to the lounge and spent the afternoon almost exactly as she had spent the morning.

Source: Goodlove et al., 1984

Illustrations such as this one, unfortunately, are not by themselves strong evidence – is this example typical? What happened in the other settings? Many examples were given in this report. However, no matter how many examples are illustrated, they can often form the basis of differing interpretations and cannot stand as very strong evidence in support of the researcher's analysis.

The research report then went on to discuss the relevance of the observed data and its usefulness for social policy and planning.

Analysing quantitative data

Statistics is a science that deals with the collection and analysis of numerical data. It can be divided into two main areas called descriptive and inferential statistics. Descriptive statistics covers methods of summarising properties of data such as frequency, central tendency and variability. Inferential statistics involves methods of generalising from properties of samples to properties of populations. For example, if after carrying out a survey of the work of staff in a children's home you find that staff give no choice of menu to children, could you infer that this would be the case in every children's home? You might be able to extrapolate (infer that it would happen in other establishments) that it would happen if your sample had been selected in a proper manner. You could not extrapolate if you had studied only one establishment or one type of establishment.

The average shapes of frequency distribution

One of the main reasons that we use statistics is to describe sets of numbers in a brief and understandable way. It is difficult to deal with information when it is presented in the form of large groups of numbers. It takes time to read through them and is difficult to see the wood for the trees. A way must therefore be found to present data in a manner that can be understood. One way to do this is to find out what the average is.

Mean (or arithmetic mean)

If we collect a large number of results we could split up the total range of values into a large number of small intervals and calculate the proportion of results falling into the intervals. If we mark in this proportion, at the midpoint of each small interval, and then join up the points, we get a **frequency distribution**. For any given distribution researchers want some measure of the centre of the distribution. The most widely used is the **mean**. The mean is the measure to which we usually refer when in everyday life we use the word 'average'. The mean can be defined as the value each item in the distribution would have if all the values were shared out equally among all the items. It is a measure of central tendency. For a sample, the mean is simply calculated by adding together all the values and dividing the result by the total number of values. The mean for a distribution is the sum of the scores divided by the number of scores. It is by far the most useful of all measures of central tendency and has the advantage of taking into account all the values in a distribution. The formula for calculating the mean is:

$$X = \frac{Ex}{n}$$

Activity 22

Calculate the mean for the sample scores 3, 6, 8, 9, 10.

$$X = \frac{Ex}{n} = \frac{3 + 6 + 8 + 9 + 10}{5} = \frac{36}{5} = 7.2$$

Example: Age of residents in High Cross Residential Home

Resident	Age
Jack	65
Mary	66
Eamonn	68
Joan	80
Mary	75
Joanne	76
Peter	70
Jose	86
Ken	90
Alice	88
Mark	94
Clia	98
Patrick	106
$n = 13$	Total ages 1062

From the data in the table above, the mean age for this sample is 81.69 years. This was calculated as follows:

List the numbers (ages) in the vertical column.

Add the numbers (ages) together = 1062 years.

Count the number of items (residents) making up the list, to get n.

As the list comprises 13 residents, therefore $n = 13$.

Divide the total (1062 years) by the value of n (13), so 1062/13 = 81.69.

Therefore, the mean, or average, age of residents is 81.69 years.

$$X = \frac{Ex}{n} = \frac{1062}{13} = 81.69$$

This method is not as easy to use as the other two averages, the **median** and **mode**, and it takes time to calculate. Also it is not suitable to use with all sets of data. The mean may not be of the same value as any of the individual sets of data. For example, none of the residents in the example was 81.69 years of age. If numbers in your data vary widely then the mean can mislead. In our example, the youngest resident was 65 and the oldest was 106. Other measures can be used to give a more meaningful picture.

Activity 23

a   Calculate the mean of the following: 36, 21, 6, 18, 78, 90, 6, 67, 66.
b   Is the following set of data suitable for the mean formula: 30, 30, 30, 30, 30, 30, 56, 78, 30, 30, 30?

The median

The **median** is that value in a distribution such that exactly one-half of the scores are less than or equal to it, and exactly one-half are greater than or equal to it. The purpose of the median is to determine the exact midpoint of a distribution. The median measure of the central or middle point of the distribution is the value of the central result when the values are arranged in order of magnitude. If you want to obtain a figure that represents the central point then the median is a useful measure to use.

If we have an odd number of results, then the median is simply the value of the middle result. If we have an even number, as in the example below, then there is no single middle result and we take the average of the two middle results.

Example: Age of residents (in order of magnitude) in High View Residential Home	
Resident	**Age**
Peter	70
Mary	75
Jack	78
Joan	80
Jose	86
Alice	88
Ken	90
Mark	94
Total (8)	661

The two middle results are 80 years and 86 years: (80 + 86)/2 = 83 years.

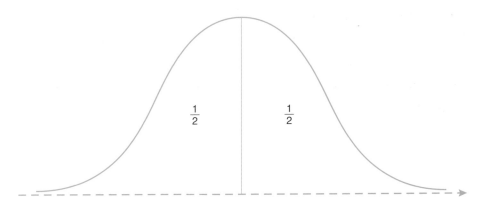

Frequency distribution showing the median

The median is sometimes a useful estimate of the middle of a distribution when the distribution is not symmetrical, i.e. when there is a long tail on one side and not on the other. An example of this would be salaries where most people have fairly moderate salaries but a small number have very large ones. Most people would have salaries below the mean. This kind of distribution, which is not symmetrical, is called skewed. In this case, the median salary would be a sensible estimate of the middle of the frequency distribution of salaries. Half the individuals would have salaries below this and half above.

This method is less useful when we have many numbers but on the other hand it is not affected by extreme values. Would it be appropriate to use the median if you had the following set of figures: 24, 26, 31, 36, 37, 37, 38, 109, 140?

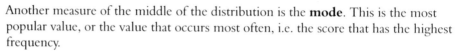

> ## Activity 24
>
> Calculate the median for the following values:
>
> **a** 22, 33, 45, 46, 48, 89, 99
> **b** 4, 6, 9, 23, 44, 44, 48, 78, 90
> **c** 5, 5, 5, 5, 9, 9, 9. 9, 9
> **d** 14, 15, 15, 16, 16, 16, 16, 18, 18, 18, 18.

Mode

Another measure of the middle of the distribution is the **mode**. This is the most popular value, or the value that occurs most often, i.e. the score that has the highest frequency.

In the following set of figures the number 11 occurs most often, so it is the mode: 2, 3, 6, 7, 11, 11, 11, 11, 13, 15, 17.

In what situation would you use the median?

The mode is a useful measure of the middle of a distribution when the variable the researcher is interested in is discrete, i.e. confined to certain restricted values. For example, the mode would be useful as a measure of the number of children in a family in the UK. If the most frequent number of children in a family is, say, 2, then the modal value would be 2. One of the reasons that you might want to use the mode is when you want to indicate a 'normal' value or figure.

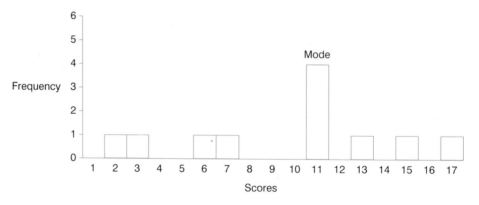

Frequency distribution showing the position of the mode for the above data

Choosing a measure of central tendency

- Use the mean when the scores in a distribution are more or less symmetrically grouped about the centre.
- Use the median when extreme scores may distort the mean.
- Use the mode when all that is required is an approximate value of central tendency.

In what situation would you use the mode?

Using statistics to help simplify and describe data is only the first step in analysing the results of a research study. The rest of the analysis is concerned not so much with the specific subjects that the researcher has tested (the sample) as with what those subjects can tell the researcher about a larger group (the population).

Frequency distribution

The data that we have been looking at so far have all been in 'sets' or 'groups'. In this section we shall be looking at the distribution of the 'sets' or 'groups' of numbers or values. Finding a single figure that indicates the location of a distribution is not easy. The distribution may be spread out over a wide range of values and to choose one to represent its location is like trying to find a single person who can represent one student in a college or one patient in a hospital. When data are purely quantitative, the simplest way is to count the number of cases in each category.

For instance, in an analysis of the census of students in a large college, one of the variables of interest is the number of males and females in each faculty. To summarise the data, we count the number of students in each faculty by sex. The results are shown below:

Number of students by faculty and sex

Faculty	Engineering	Social care	Science	Art
Male	300	20	400	250
Female	20	200	100	200
Total	320	220	500	450

The count of individuals having a particular quality is called the frequency of that quality. The frequency for male students in the science faculty is 400. The proportion of individuals having that quality is the relative frequency or proportional frequency. The relative frequency of male students in the science faculty (of all students) is $400/1490 = 0.27$ or 27%. The set of frequencies is called the frequency distribution of the variables. Below is another example of a frequency distribution.

Number of students by marks in examination

Marks	Number of students (frequency)
20–29	2
30–39	3
40–49	8
50–59	12
60–69	13
70–79	7
80–89	4
90–99	0
Total	50

An arrangement such as this is called a grouped frequency distribution. It shows the overall pattern clearly – in this case, a bunching of observed values in the middle. This way of presenting information does not tell you what actual marks the individual students obtained.

Measures of dispersion

The median, mode and mean are single numbers that indicate the central tendency or location of that number on a scale. Each is incomplete as a descriptive measure because it does not tell us anything about the scatter or dispersion of the values or set of numbers from which it is derived. In some cases these values will be clustered closely, as in the first table on page 291, while in other cases they will be scattered as in the second table. The importance of dispersion can be seen from a simple example. Say that we tested a sample of four lightbulbs of type A, and found that the bulb life was (in turn) 20, 23, 25 and 26 months, assuming that each bulb was used for 2 hours daily. The mean life of the A bulb is 23.5 months. Next, we tested four bulbs of make B and found that they lasted 4, 10, 25 and 55 months. The mean life for these bulbs is also 23.5. In such cases we need a way of specifying that the life of make B bulbs is more variable than make A. If you were planning activities for adults attending a day centre and you were told that the mean age of those expected to attend was 25 years, it would be helpful to know the range of ages. Are those expected all within the range 20 to 30 years? If so, you could plan activities for this age group, but if some 60 year olds are expected, some other activities might be more suitable. One way to specify the variability of data is to simply state the range.

The range

The range is the difference between the smallest and largest observation. The range is the simplest measure of variability and tells us about the interval between the highest and lowest scores in a distribution. It is calculated by subtracting the lowest score from the highest score. In the case of the B lightbulbs, with a mean life of 23.5 months, the range is $55 - 4 = 51$ months. This wide range is because of the rather low and very high values at the extremes. This problem, however, can be overcome by working out the range between the lower and upper quartiles.

If we have a set of measurements or values arranged in order of size, the lower quartile is that value that has a quarter of the observations below it and three-quarters of the observations above it. The upper quartile has three-quarters of the observations below it and one-quarter above it. If the quartiles fall between observations, they are given a value that is the mean of the numbers on either side of them. Below is an example of quartile positions based on the set of numbers for the A lightbulbs:

20/23, 25/26

The lower quartile falls between 20 and 23, so has a value of 21.5; the upper quartile has a value of 25.5. The interquartile range is therefore $25.5 - 21.5 = 4$, compared to the full range of 6. However, when we look at the set of data for the B lightbulbs the interquartile range is 33 (compared to the full range of 51 months). This shows that the interquartile value is less affected by extreme values than the range. The interquartile range gives a more reasonable indication of the dispersion in these two examples than does the full range.

Because the range takes account only of the two most extreme scores it is limited in its usefulness, since it takes no account of how the scores are distributed. The problem of extreme scores can be overcome by using the interquartile range, which uses the central half of the scores to calculate the range.

Standard deviation

The best measure of dispersion around the mean is the standard deviation (see the figure on page 293). Like the mean, the standard deviation takes all the observed values into account. If there were no dispersion at all in a distribution, all the observed values would be the same. No value would differ from the mean. However, in real life the observed values always deviate from the mean; some a lot, some a little. The larger the dispersion, the bigger the deviations and the larger the standard deviation. The standard deviation is calculated as follows:

- All the deviations (differences) from the mean of the set of numbers are squared.

- The mean of the squares is then calculated.
- The square root of this mean is the standard deviation.

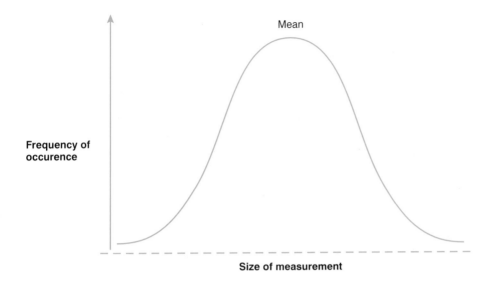

Pictorial representation of standard deviation

Example

Let us look at what the standard deviation is for the following set of values:
111, 114, 117, 118, 120 (mean = 116).

Value	111	114	117	118	120
Deviation from mean (116)	−5	−2	+1	2	+4

Note that if you take an average (mean) of the deviations it will be zero – the negative deviations will always cancel out the positive ones. To overcome this difficulty, each deviation is squared; this gets rid of the minus signs.

Deviation from mean (116)	−5	−2	+1	+2	+4
Squared deviation	25	4	1	4	16

The mean of the squared deviations is called the variance:

$$\text{Variance} = \frac{25 + 4 + 1 + 4 + 16}{5} = \frac{50}{5} = 10$$

To obtain the standard deviation we take the square root of the variance and the result is then the standard deviation.

$$\text{Standard deviation of distribution} = \sqrt{\frac{25 + 4 + 1 + 4 + 19}{5}} = \sqrt{10} = 3.16$$

The standard deviation is therefore 3.16.

If the standard deviation is large, then there is much dispersion around the mean. If the standard deviation is small, then the degree of dispersion is much less. The standard deviation does not in itself tell us much; on its own it is of limited value. It comes into its own when you have a number of sets of data and you wish to compare standard deviations.

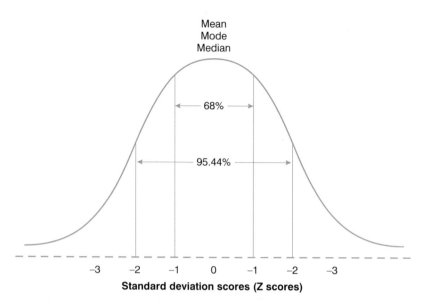

The normal distribution

A normal distribution has about 68% of all scores lying within one standard deviation on either side of the mean and approximately 95% within two standard deviations of the mean. You can use these percentages to give you some idea of the proportion of the values you could expect to find within certain limits.

The normal distribution is a bell-shaped curve, as illustrated in the figure above. The three measures of central tendency – the mean, mode and median – all lie on the same point on the curve. The term 'normal distribution' does not mean that it is the typical or most often observed distribution. 'Normal' is used in the sense that the bell-shaped curve is a 'norm' or idealised version of a distribution against which you can compare the distribution of your data.

When you have a normal distribution you have 50% of the observations on each side of the centre. The standard deviation is a way of showing how much your data vary from the mean.

Relationships between variables

One helpful technique when examining the association between two variables is to examine their joint distribution on a scattergram (see the figures on page 295). A scattergram is a plot on which the position of each observation is designated at the point corresponding to its joint value on the dependent and independent variable. The independent variable is plotted on the horizontal axis and the dependent variable on the vertical axis. If the points that you plot bunch together like a thin tube, as in the first figure, the association between the variables is strong, but if they bulge out at all sides like a balloon, as in the second figure, the association is weak.

Example

You might want to investigate if there is a relationship between how many books a student reads and the student's age. Age is the independent variable and so is plotted on the horizontal axis. In the first figure on page 295 there is a positive correlation between the two variables.

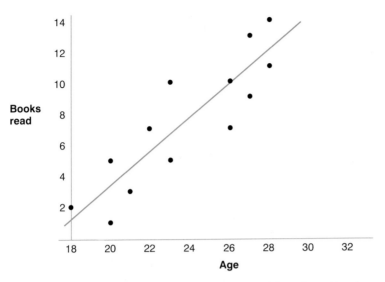

A scattergram showing a positive correlation between age and number of books read

Negative correlation is shown in the figure below. You might normally expect to find that the larger the discount on the disks the more (volume) that you might sell. However, the data in the figure show that there is little relationship between the discount given and the numbers sold.

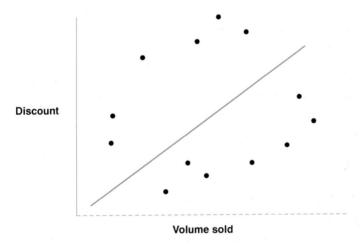

A scattergram showing lack of correlation between size of discount offered on blank floppy disks and number sold

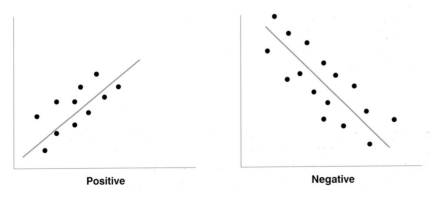

Positive   **Negative**

Scattergrams showing positive and negative relationships

Presentation of data

Information or data can be presented in the form of:

- diagrams
- graphs
- pie charts
- tables.

Each of the four different methods helps you to present information in an understandable and logical way.

Diagrams

Diagrams are a way of presenting a lot of information in picture form. A good diagram will help you cut down on the amount of writing you would otherwise have to do to describe the information presented in it.

Graphs

A bar chart or graph shows the relationship between two variables; one is usually quantitative and the other qualitative. Information can be presented in a variety of graphical forms. Graphs can be used to show changes in a particular variable over a given period of time. The graph can be used to reinforce points made in writing.

Bar graphs

Examples of bar graphs are shown below.

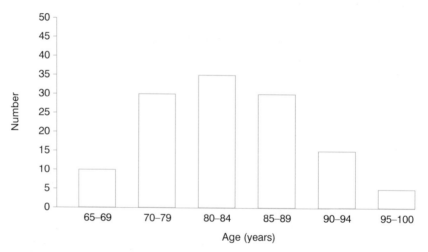

Bar graph to show the number of elderly people admitted to day care in Uptown Local Authority, by age, 2000

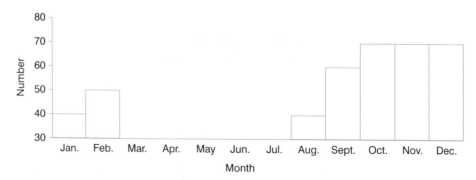

Bar graph to show the number of elderly people in residential care in Uptown Local Authority, by month, 2000

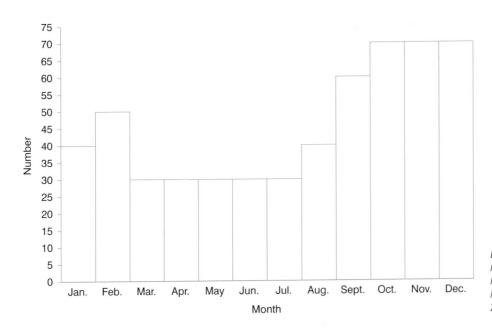

Bar graph to show the number of elderly people in residential care in Uptown local authority, by month, 2000

Key Skills

You can use Activity 25 to provide evidence for Key Skills Application of Number N3.2, N3.3.

Activity 25

a Construct a bar graph from the data in the following table:

Children on the at risk register at 31 March 2000, by age

Age	Number
14	200
5–8	67
9–12	100
13–15	75
16+	8

b Look at the two figures (one at the foot of page 296, and one on this page) about elderly people in Uptown. Although they give the same information, do they look different? Do they seem to be conveying the same message? Discuss the reason why they look as if they are giving different messages based upon the same data.

c From the data in the table below, construct a bar graph.

Referrals for meals-on-wheels support to Downside Social Services Department, 2000

Month	Number	Month	Number
January	100	July	55
February	81	August	50
March	84	September	60
April	81	October	70
May	73	November	75
June	60	December	85

Line graphs

A line graph is another useful way to illustrate increasing or decreasing values. Two examples are given below.

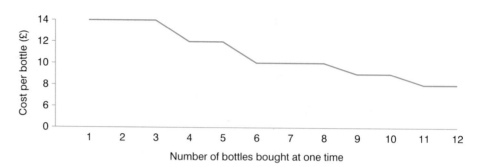

Line graph to show the advantages of buying wine in bulk

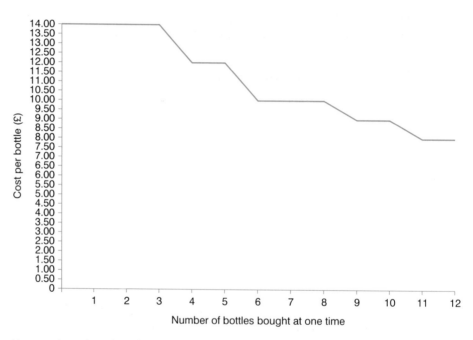

Line graph to show the advantages of buying wine in bulk

Activity 26

a Look at the two figures above and consider the following questions:

  i   What is the cost of one bottle?
  ii   What is the cost of five bottles?
  iii What is the cost of seven bottles?
  iv   What is the cost of ten bottles?

b Compare the two line graphs. Why does it look as if a bottle of wine is more expensive in the second figure?

How do you arrive at a percentage?

Look at the table on page 297 which shows the number of meals-on-wheels referrals. We can work out the percentage of referrals for the month of April as follows:

Divide the number of referrals for April by the total number of referrals for the year:

Total referrals for the year = 874
Number of referrals in April = 81
81/874 = 0.093.
Then multiply by 100 to obtain the percentage:
$0.093 \times 100 = 9.3$.

The percentage of referrals for the month of April is 9.3%.

Activity 27

Look at the information in the table below. Copy the graph axes and draw either a bar chart or a line graph using the data in the table.

You can use Activity 27 to provide evidence for Key Skills Application of Number N3.2, N3.3.

Child care assistants by age

Age	Number	Percentage
Under 20	19	1.5
20–29	163	9.0
30–39	433	24 0
40–49	643	36.0
50–59	418	23.5
60+	101	6.0
Total	1777	100.0

Pie charts

A pie chart is a visual presentation that breaks down a total figure into different components. Look at the pie chart below, which illustrates the percentages of patients attending as outpatients at a hospital. The percentage figures were derived from the following table:

Number of patients attending the outpatients department at St Jack's Hospital

Type of patient	Number of patients
Adults	400
Children	200
Elderly 60–79 years	100
Elderly 80+	100
Total	800

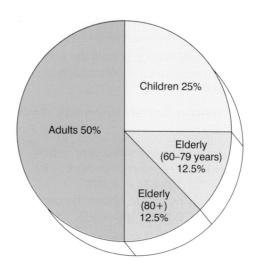

Pie chart to show the percentage of patients attending the outpatients department at St Jack's Hospital

Activity 28

Construct a pie chart to illustrate the data in the following table:

Qualifications held by Uptown Social Services staff

Qualifications	Number	Percentage of staff
Cert. Social Service (CSS)	86	9.9
Diploma in Social Work	180	20.7
HND Care	20	2.3
GNVQ	26	2.6
Other	23	3.0
None	532	61.5
Total	867	100.0

Tables

Tables enable you to show much more data than, for instance, a bar graph. The table below shows the response rate to a postal questionnaire that was sent to a sample of home helps (Group A) and a sample of auxiliary nurses (Group B) in a national survey.

Response rates to a postal questionnaire

	Group A No.	%	Group B No.	%
Questionnaires distributed	1302	100.0	1961	100.0
Questionnaires returned	1170		1482	
Uncompleted questionnaires	133		144	
Total analysed	1037	79.6	1338	68.2

From the data we can see that, although Group B were sent more questionnaires (1961), the percentage response (68.2%) was lower than in Group A (79.6%).

Activity 29

You have recently taken up a post as junior research officer in a social services department. Your first task is to conduct a survey of residents in Summerfield home for the elderly to find out some information about the residents.

The home has 50 residents and you have selected 25 from which to obtain data.

a Describe three sampling techniques that you could use to obtain a representative sample of the population in the home.

b The home has 40 female and 10 male residents. How would you ensure that you included male and female representatives in your sample? How would you minimise possible sources of error?

c The ages of the population you have selected are: 72, 74, 76, 72, 76, 76, 77, 76, 78, 72, 80, 77, 98, 72, 73, 74, 76, 79, 100, 87, 92, 72, 80, 82.

  i What is the number sampled as a percentage of the total population of the home?

  ii Express the number of 72 year olds selected as a percentage of the total population sampled.

  iii Express the number of 76 year olds in the sample as a percentage of the total population.

  iv Draw up a frequency distribution table from the above data showing the frequency of distribution of residents in the home.

  v Calculate the range of the sample.

  vi Calculate the mean age of the sample.

  vii Calculate and explain the mode of the sample population.

  viii Calculate the mean average distribution of the sample population.

  ix Calculate the standard deviation of the sample population.

Key Skills

You can use Activity 29 to provide evidence for Key Skills Application of Number N3.2, N3.3.

How to write up your research

Production of the final report

There is no one way to organise a research report. Your tutors will also have their own ideas about how your final write-up should look. The following headings are provided as guidelines.

1. Title

The title should indicate the nature of what you have been researching. For example 'A report on attitudes of further education students on smoking' or 'A survey of the workload of care assistants in four residential establishments for the elderly in Downtown Local Authority'.

2. Summary

It may appear strange that a summary of what you have done appears at the beginning of the report and not at the end. A summary (abstract) is written so that other readers can quickly see if the research is of interest to them before they read the main body of the report. The summary should be about 100–150 words long, explaining what you did, your methods and results.

3. Introduction

In the introduction you should give the reader a general description of the research problem that you have looked at, why you undertook the work and what your hypothesis is. You can also give a clear picture of the aims of your research.

4. Review of the literature

You should give a review of the literature that you have read directly relating to your research. This gives the reader an overview of the field that you are studying.

5. Methodology

Under this heading you should describe your methodology, how you chose and sampled your population, how you developed your questionnaire, etc. You should provide enough information so that anyone reading your report could repeat your research if they wished.

6. Results

This section gives you the opportunity to present your results. To do this you can use tables, graphs or any other medium to present your data. Do not put your working calculations or computer printouts in this section; keep all this type of data for the appendix, if appropriate.

7. Analysis and discussion

This is where you discuss to what extent your results support or do not support your original hypothesis. This can be done by discussing your results and providing the evidence from these results to support (or otherwise) your hypothesis. You can also discuss your methodology and any problems that you have encountered, and what you could do to overcome them if you had the chance to carry out the research again.

8. Conclusions

Present any conclusions you have drawn from your results and any recommendations that you might wish to make based on these results.

9. List of references

You must give detailed references for all the sources that you have used in your report.

There are a number of ways that you can do this. For example, if you have used quotes from Edwards & Talbot p. 35 (1994) in your text then the reference might appear as: Edwards, A. and Talbot, R. (1994) *The Hard Pressed Researcher*. Longman, Harlow, p. 35.

If you quote from a journal then the reference might read: Garnham, N. and Williams, R. (1980) Pierre Bourdieu and the sociology of culture. *Media, Culture and Society*, **2**(3), 116–126.

6.4 Ethics of research in health and social care

Social research with human subjects is rarely physically intrusive (unlike medicine or research on animals) and the risks to the subjects are not as great as in some biomedical research. Nevertheless, issues of deception, invasion of privacy, informed consent and subject's rights apply. The issue of **ethics** can be a major problem for researchers. Research is a nosy activity and it can be difficult sometimes to know where to draw the line. The research process involves a series of decisions that must be made by the researcher before observing even a single subject or asking one question. The researcher in planning the research has the obligation to weigh carefully the potential benefits or contributions of the proposed research against the costs to the participants – costs such as affronts to the participants' dignity, anxiety, embarrassment, loss of trust in social relationships and lowered self-esteem. A commitment to research at whatever level raises a number of ethical issues. These must be taken seriously as an integral part of a health or social care professional's responsibility.

Moral relationship

Health and social care staff, when they carry out research, enter into a moral relationship with the people they study. This relationship can become problematic when the research is looking at areas that are sensitive. The general public and users of social care or health services have a right to expect adherence to a recognised code of conduct from the researcher who wishes to undertake research. Social care researchers, when they undertake to carry out a research project, enter into a personal relationship with the people that they are studying. The more sensitive the topic to be studied the more problematic the relationship becomes. If there are potential consequences for the participants, then the relation of researcher to participant needs careful thought. If the issue to be researched is a sensitive one (e.g. looking at staff rolls, which could be used by management to promote or redeploy staff or even make them redundant), the range of methods that can be used is restricted. Research on sensitive issues is frequently open to misrepresentation by those who see opportunities in such misrepresentation and by those who see opportunities to exploit the findings. Before you embark on any research project in health and social care, you should ask yourself the following questions:

- What are the aims and purpose of my research?
- Am I presenting any unnecessary risks or inconveniences to clients, staff or anyone else? (No person should be hurt or put at risk by the completion of the research or publication of the report.)
- Does my work respect confidentiality and anonymity? How will I be able to keep confidential the identity of participants?
- Am I competent to undertake the project (have I the experience or qualifications)?
- How much support do I need?
- For what do I intend to use the research findings?

All those involved in the research process – staff, clients and carers – are entitled to information on these points. It is part of the research code of ethics to explain the research to all the people involved in it.

The *Nuremberg Code,* developed after the Second World War, emphasises the need for those who carry out research with people to be appropriately qualified, to use only voluntary participants and to relieve them of pain if it becomes excessive. Other groups have drawn up codes of confidentiality, including the British Medical Association, the British Association of Counselling, the British Association of Social Workers and nurses' organisations.

Participants' right to take part or not to take part

One of the most important safeguards in any code of ethics is that the subject must always have the right to refuse or to discontinue participation at any time, even after having agreed to take part. It should always be the subject or participant who decides to take part in the research. Researchers should not gather data until they have received the unequivocal consent of the participants. This means informed consent (discussed below): the researcher must provide prospective participants with enough information about the research to enable them to make informed decisions about whether or not they wish to take part in it.

Informed consent

There is now widespread acceptance of the doctrine that research involving human beings should only be performed with the informed consent of the participants. Informed consent is essential whenever participants are exposed to substantial risks such as taking part in experimental or new medical research. Researchers should not proceed to gather data until they have received the subjects' unequivocal consent. However, it may be relatively easy to obtain written or verbal consent, but informed consent is a more problematic issue. Informed consent means the researcher must provide participants with all relevant information concerning the nature and value of the research and its likely dissemination. Participants should know that their involvement is voluntary at all times and they should receive beforehand an explanation of the benefits, risks, rights and dangers involved as a consequence of their taking part in the research.

Why do we believe that informed consent is important? The idea derives from cultural values, the care value base and also legal considerations. Participants should be free to decide their own behaviour because of the high degree of importance we give to self-determination. For someone to be fully informed, consider supplying them with the following:

- a fair explanation of the procedures to be followed (in simple language – no jargon, technical language or use of statistics that the participant may not understand, etc.)
- a description of the risks involved
- a description of the benefits
- the opportunity at any time to question the procedures or their involvement
- clear instructions that the participant can withdraw at any time.

Confidentiality

In the data collection stage of the research, participants should be given clear, accurate information about the meaning and limits of confidentiality. Keeping confidential the identity of individuals may prove difficult at times: people may be identified by the description of the job they do or their disabilities. For example, the manager of a residential unit may be identified if that person's role is discussed because an establishment tends to have only one such manager. Likewise, a user may be identified by his or her disability if, for example, there is only one client who uses a wheelchair. Remember, other people have to live with the consequences of what you write and your conclusions.

Case Study

Confidentiality

Even in some cases the use of information that has been made anonymous can be a breach of trust and also illegal. The High Court has ruled (July 1999) that Department of Health guidelines to GPs stating that patients' consent was not needed if anonymised data was accessed by researchers were incorrect. The High Court ruled that the patient's consent was necessary even if it was not possible to identify the patient from the data accessed.

This ruling also indicates that implied consent was not adequate. Leaflets or notices in a GP's surgery stating that information about patients' treatment etc. might be given to other organisations (no patient could be identified from this information) was not adequate, even if patients did not object. GPs using this implied consent method risk being sued by patients. Each patient must give informed consent for any information to be given to a third party.

/ **Activity 30** /

Louise has been given permission by the manager of a residential care establishment to carry out research involving the use of a questionnaire to be given to elderly residents. There are 2 male and 20 female residents. The manager has not spoken to the residents or obtained their permission.

a What issues should Louise address before she begins her work? For example, what information should she give the residents to enable them to make an informed decision as to whether to take part or not?
b What issues of confidentiality should be addressed?

Key terms

After reading this unit you should be able to understand the following words and phrases. If you do not, go back through the unit and find out, or look them up in the Glossary.

Ethics
Extralinguistic behaviour
Frequency distribution
Hypothesis
Mean
Measures of dispersion
Median
Mode
Primary sources
Qualitative research techniques

Quantitative research techniques
Random sample
Response rate
Secondary sources
Semantic differential
Spatial behaviour
Structured interview
Validity
Variable

Review questions

1 Give an example of the main advantages of using observation as a data collection technique.
2 What are the main disadvantages of the observation method of collecting data?
3 Explain what is meant by the term 'random sample'
4 Explain what is meant by the term 'measure of probability'?
5 Suggest two examples of a frequency count.
6 What is meant by the term 'semantic differential?
7 In what situation would an in-depth interview be the most appropriate way to collect information?

8 Give an example of a situation in which you would use one of the following:
   a frequency count
   b mean
   c median
   d mode.
9 Give two examples of probes and prompts to support open questions.

Assignment

Produce a report of a research project you have carried out relevant to health, social care or early years settings.

To gain a merit or distinction you are asked to analyse and/or evaluate certain situations or tasks. Analysing means breaking the task down into detailed parts and discussing the pros and cons of the situation. To evaluate you must present facts to support your opinions or findings and you must also determine the value of your findings and appraise them.

Tasks

1 Give a rationale for the research project that you have chosen.

2 Identify, accurately describe and apply an appropriate research methodology to the research project that you have chosen.

3 Carry out a review of the relevant literature, and clearly and appropriately summarise what is already known in the area of your research.

4 Identify and explore the ethical issues that are relevant to your project.

5 Use appropriate methods to present your findings.

6 Select and apply an appropriate research methodology independently and explain clearly why you chose the method.

7 Review the validity of your research sources and identify possible sources of error or bias in your work that might have an influence on your conclusions.

8 Analyse the effect of ethical considerations on your research.

9 Present your research and findings accurately, clearly and coherently.

10 Take a comprehensive approach to the design of your project and in carrying out the methodology.

11 Draw realistic and valid conclusions from your findings and say how your work might be improved.

12 Make realistic recommendations for further research.

13 Justify your choice of research methodology and explain alternative research methods that might appropriately be used in relation to this type of project.

Get the grade

To get an **E** grade you must complete tasks 1–5

To get a **C** grade you must complete tasks 1–9

To get an **A** grade you must complete tasks 1–13

Key Skills

Key Skills	**Opportunity**
	You can use this Assignment to provide evidence for the following Key Skills
Communication C3.2	When reviewing relevant literature and research.
Application of Number N3.1	When analysing data and statistics to illustrate findings.
Information Technology IT 3.1, 3.3	If you use a computer to analyse data and statistics to illustrate findings.

choice, individual
  maintenance of 27
  promoting 8–11
  threats to 11–13
  see also rights
chromosome abnormalities 157
Chronically Sick and Disabled
  Persons Act 1970 14
Citizens Advice Bureaux 36
Citizen's Charter 16
class, social
  and attitudes 149
  discrimination 20
  and health 166, 168
  and socialisation 151
clients
  carer relationships 62–6
  communication and 44–5, 45
  confidentiality and 12–13,
    67, 73–4
  involvement 34, 220–2,
    238–9
  and research 303–4
  rights *see* rights
closed questions 48, 281
cognitive development theory
  180–2
cognitive skills 20, 127
Commission for Health
  Improvement (CHI) 226
Commission for Racial Equality
  (CRE) 14, 35
communication 42, 45
  assertive behaviour 56–8
  barriers to effective 45–6
    emotional factors 62–6
    physical 58
    physical environment
      58–62
    social factors 66–7
  and challenging behaviour
    27
  confidentiality 67, 73–4
  effective 46–7
  in groups 67–71
  in health and social care
    42–5, 221
  language development
    124–6, 127, 138
  neuro-linguistic programming
    53–4
  non-verbal 54–6, 58, 257–8
  promotion of equality and
    rights 3–4, 10
  skills 42, 47–8
    active listening 49–52
    giving information 52
    prompting 49
    questioning 48
    rapport 52–3

  self-disclosure 49
  skill evaluation 71–2
'community', use of the term 4
community midwives 231
complaints 34, 74
compulsory referrals
  children 208
  elderly people 208–9
  ethical dilemmas 209
  mentally ill 209
confidentiality 12–13, 67, 73–4
  and research 304–5
consensus management 190
consultants 188, 189
consultative groups 221
consumer benefit concept 42
continuous theories 175
contracts 237–8
controlled involvement 63
convenience sampling 272
cortisol 93
cost of services *see* funding
Council of Europe 36
Council for Voluntary Services 242
CRE (Commission for Racial
  Equality) 14, 35
Criminal Justice Act 1992 15
culture
  cultural diversity 4
  discrimination 20
  and socialisation 151

data
  observation recording 258–9,
    259, 260
  physiological measurements
    formulae 111–13
    recording 110–11
    secondary sources
      113–17
    taking 100–10
  presentation 296–301
  primary, secondary and
    tertiary 272–3
  qualitative research analysis
    285–7
  quantitative research analysis
    287–95
  reliability 285
  validity 284–5
  see also information
Data Protection Act 1984 12, 13, 73
defence mechanisms 148–9
demography
  research and 254
  and social welfare policy
    217–19
denial 146, 148
depolarisation 113
depression 166

descriptive research *see* surveys
development 122
  influencing factors
    health risks 159–65,
      171–3
    ill-health 165–8
    inherited gene disorders
      155–8
    nature-nurture debate 155
    role status 159
    socioeconomic 168–71
  life stages 122
    infancy 124–7, 136
    childhood 127–8, 136–7
    puberty and adolescence
      128–9, 137
    early and middle
      adulthood 129–30, 137
    later adulthood 130–5, 137
  of skills
    attitudes and values
      153–4
    emotional 141–9
    personality 139–41, 155
    self-concept 138–9
    social 149–53
  theories 174
    cognitive development
      180–2
    on differences between
      sexes 182
    Maslow's hierarchy of
      needs 184–5
    nature-nurture debate
      155, 174–5
    psychoanalytic theory
      177–80
    social interactionism
      182–4
    social learning theory
      175–6
DHAs (district health authorities)
  191, 192, 193, 194, 230–1
diabetes mellitus 94
diagrams 296
diastolic blood pressure 104, 105
diet 169–70
dieticians 232
digestive system 83–5, *84, 85*
disabilities, people with 15, 35, 165
  and discrimination 20
Disability Rights Commission 35
Disabled Persons Act 1981 & 1986
  15
discontinuous theories 174, 180
discrimination 17–19, 21–2
  common types of 19–21
  contexts in which may occur
    24–5
  legislation against 14–15

non-discriminatory practice 28–9
the vicious circle 22–3, *23*
disengagement theory of ageing 131–2
dispersion, measures of 291–4
displacement (defence mechanism) 149
dissociative reference groups 152–3
district health authorities (DHAs) 191, 192, 193, 194, 230–1
district nurses 231
diversity 4
dizygotic twins 155
double questions 279
Down's syndrome 157, 165
drugs 166
    alcohol 166, 173
    smoking 171–3
ducts 91
duodenum 94

ECGs (electrocardiograms) 113–15, *114*, *115*
Education (Handicapped Children) Act 1980 15
education supervision orders 208
ego, development of 178
egocentrism 127, 181
elderly people 137, 218
    compulsory referrals 208–9
    and discrimination 19
    theories of ageing 130–5
electrocardiograms (ECGs) 113–15, *114*, *115*
electrolytes 99
emergency protection orders (EPOs) 208
emotional development
    bereavement and loss 145–7
    change and transition 147–9
    in childhood 127
    in infancy 127
    stress 141–5
emotions, and communication 51–2, 62–6
empowerment 5, 25–6, 26–7, 46, 122
endocrine system 87, 91–6, *92*, 97
environment
    and communication 58–62
    and health 166
    nature-nurture debate 155, 174–5
Environmentalists 174
enzymes 84, 94, 96
epidemiology 254
epigenetics 174, 178
EPOs (emergency protection orders) 208

equality 3
    charters 16
    discrimination 17–23, 24–5
    ethical issues 26–7, 29–31, 31–3
    legislation 14–15
    maintenance of rights and choice 27
    monitoring quality 16–17
    non-discriminatory practice 28–9
    power and empowerment 25–6, 26–7
    principles underpinning 7–8
    promoting 3–5, 24
    staff training and development 26
    support and guidance sources 33–7
Equal Opportunities Commission 35
Equal Pay Act 1975 14
Erikson, Eric 129, 140, 178–80, 183
erythrocytes 117
ethical issues 5–6, 29–30
    handling 26–7, 31–2
    organisational responsibilities 32–3
    in research 302–4
    stakeholder concept 30–1
ethnic minorities 4, 17
ethnomethodology 184
European Convention on Human Rights 36, 73
European Directive on Data Protection 1995 12, 73
event sampling 258–9, *259*
exocrine glands 91, 94
experimental research 261–2
expiration 81
external respiration 80–1
extralinguistic behaviour 258
eye movements 53, *53*

face validity 285
facial expressions 55
factual questions 280–1
families
    and development 126, 127, 153
    and socialisation 150–1
    as social support group 249–50
    structure and social welfare policy 218
family health service authorities (FHAs) 192, 193, 194
family practitioner committees (FPCs) 191, 192
'feel good factor' 167–8

feelings
    and communication 51–2, 63
    see also emotions
females *see* women
FHAs (family health service authorities) 192, 193, 194
fieldwork *see* qualitative research
fluid balance, body's 99
formulae 111–13
FPCs (family practitioner committees) 191, 192
frequency distribution 287, 291, *291*
    arithmetic mean 287–8
    measures of dispersion 291–4
    median 289, *289*
    mode 290, *290*
    relationships between variables 294–5, *295*
Freud, Sigmund 129, 143, 177
funding 193, *198*, 203, 204
    central government and 219–20
    demographic issues and 216–19
    health care 210–14
    independent sector and 216, 220
    is free health care possible? 216–17
    and resource allocation 11

gaseous exchange 80–1
gastrointestinal tract 83, 84, *84*
gender 153–4
    and attitudes 149
    discrimination 20
    roles 127
general practitioners *see* GPs
genes
    inherited gene disorders 155–8
    nature-nuture debate 155, 174
gestures 56
glands
    digestive 84, 91
    endocrine 91–6, *92*
glucagon 94
glucocorticoids 98
glucose, blood 94, 98
glycogen 98, 141, 142
Goffman, Erving 183
gonadotrophins (sex hormones) 95, 128, 130
gonads 95
GPs 188, 190, 228, 231, 232
    fundholding 193, 194, *194*, 227, 231
    and primary care groups 226
    referral of patients 206

graphs 296–8, *296*, *297*, *298*
grief 146–7
groups 152
    membership 150–2
    reference 152–3
    working in 45, 67–71
growth 122–3, *123*, 124, *124*, 127
    see also development
growth hormone 92

habit 148
haemoglobin 81, *116*, 117
hallucinations 166
HAZs (Health Action Zones)
    227–8
health
    of children 170
    and diet 169–70
    housing and 168–9
    social class and 168
    see also health risks; ill-health
Health Act 1999 225
Health Action Zones (HAZs)
    227–8
health authorities 227, 235
    see also DHAs; FHAs; RHAs
Health Improvement Plans
    (HimPs) 224
health risks 159–60
    alcohol 173
    assessing 161, *162*
    children 160–1, 170
    smoking 171–3
    and statistics 162–4, *163*, *164*
health services
    1948–1974 188–9, *190*
    1974–82 190–1, *191*
    1982–1990 191–2, *192*
    1990–1999 192–5, *193*, *195*,
        196, 197
    present-day organisation
        223–32, *227*
    access to services 203–10
    assessing local needs 237
    costs 202
    funding 193, *198*, 203,
        210–22, *211*
    good practice responsibilities
        32–3
    multiagency schemes 235
    organisations involved in *199*
    Patient's Charter 16
    private 216, 235, 244
    purchaser-only role 240–1
    and social care services *234*
    staff 231–2, 233
Health Services Supervisory Board
    192
Health and Social Security Act 1984
    191

health status
    discrimination 20
    and social class 168
health visitors 231
heart 82, 83, *83*, 99, *114*
    monitoring 102, 109, 113–15
heredity
    inherited gene disorders
        155–8
    nature-nuture debate 155,
        174–5
HimPs (Health Improvement
    Plans) 224
HIV status discrimination 20
homeostasis 89, 96
    communication and control
        systems 97–9
    maintaining 96–7, *96*
homosexuals 14, 21
hormones 91, 92, 93, 94, 97
    adrenaline 89, 91, 94, 141,
        142, 166
    sex 95, 128, 130
hospitals 188, 192, 228–9
    waiting lists 205
housing 168–9
human development *see*
    development
hypothalamus 87, 96
hypotheses 255, 262, 275–6

identification
    defence mechanism 148
    socialisation process 150
identity development 128, 129, 153,
    177, 183
ill-health
    cancers 166
    physical disabilities 165
    psychiatric ill-health 165–6
    reduced 167–8
    socioeconomic and
        environmental factors
        166
    see also health; health risks
imaginary reference groups 152
immune system and stress 142
imposed membership groups 152
independence, client's 27
independent care sector 200, 202,
    220
    private services 216, 220,
        235, 244
    voluntary 220, 235, 242–4
independent variables 261
infancy 124–7, *136*
informal carers 245–6, *246*
    support for 246–7, 248–50
    women 159, 246, 248
    young 248

information
    for carers 247
    communicating 52
    confidentiality 12–13, 67,
        73–4
    exchange and communication
        44
    providing about rights 16
    publicising services 210, 221
    for research participants
        304
    research sources 272–3
    targeting 29
    see also data
informed consent (to research) 303,
    304
ingestion 84
inherited gene disorders 155–6
    chromosome abnormalities
        157
    control and cure 157–8
    single gene disorders 156–7
innate theory of language
    development 124–5
Innovation Fund Schemes 228
insincerity 65
inspiration (breathing) 81, 113
institutionalisation 9–10
institutional racism 25
insulin 94
insurance, private health and social
    care 203, 219
intellectual development 180–2
interaction *see* communication
interactionism, social/symbolic
    182–4
Interactionists 174, 183
interdependence, client/care service
    27
internal market *see* purchasers and
    providers
internal respiration 80
interpersonal skills 10, 27, 43
    see also communication
interpretivists 255
interviews 265–6, 277
    forms of response 282–3
    principles of interviewing
        280
    structure 266, 277–9
    types of questions 280–3
introjection (defence mechanism)
    148
Invalid Care Allowance 247
involvement, controlled 63

key life events 143, *143*, 145
kidneys 85–7, *86*

labelling theory and ageing 134–5

language 44
    barrier to communication 66
    determining attitudes 152
    development 124–6, 127, 138
    linguistic behaviour 258
    use promoting equality and
        rights 3–4
leading questions 278
learning
    cognitive development theory
        180–2
    observational 175, 176
legislation 6
    supporting equality and rights
        8, 14–15
Liberty (National Council for Civil
    Liberties) 36–7
life events, key 143, *143*, 145
life expectancy 163–4, *164, 228*
life histories 67
life stages 122
    infancy 124–7, 136
    childhood 127–8, 136–7
    puberty and adolescence
        128–9, 137
    early and middle adulthood
        129–30, 137
    later adulthood 130–5, 137
    see also development
life tables 163–4, *164*
line graphs 298, *298*
linguistic behaviour 258
listening skills 10, 49, 68
    paraphrasing 49–50
    reflective listening 51–2
liver 84–5
Local Government Act 1966 14
local health group boards 229
loss 145–6, 147
    coping with 146
    stages of grief 146–7
lungs 80, *80*, 81
    lung volume 107–8, 110,
        113, 117, *117*

males *see* men
management 217
    health services 190, 191–2
    structures and ethical issues
        32–3
Margin to Mainstream project 221
marital status discrimination 20
marketing 210, 241
Maslow, Abraham 184
mastication 84
mean 287–8
median 289, *289*
Medical Records Act 73
medulla oblongata 81, 99
melanin 92

membership groups 150–2
men
    and discrimination 20, 21
    male stereotypes 154
    role status 159
menopause 130
mental development 124, 127
mental disabilities 165
mental health 37
    discrimination 20
Mental Health Act 1983 15, 27, 209
mental illness 165–6
    compulsory referrals 209
meshing 52–3
middle-age 139–40, 140–1
    see also adulthood
mid-life crises 141
midwives, community 231
MIND 37
mirroring and matching
    communication skills 52–3
mixed economy of care 191–3
mode 290, *290*
modelling
    management and 33
    neuro-linguistic
        programming 53
molecules 83
monozygotic twins 155
mood, illness relating to 165–6
moral development 127, 180
moral relationships in research 303
motor nerves 88
motor skills 124, 127
multiagency schemes 235
myxodoema 93

National Association of Citizens
    Advice Bureaux 36
National Disability Council (NDC)
    35
National Health Service
    1948–1974 188–9, *189, 190*
    1974–1982 190–1, *191*
    1982–1990 191–2, *192*
    1990–1999 192–5, *193, 195,*
        196, 197
    2000 224–9, *227,* 230–2
    entitlement to services 200,
        202
    funding 193, *198,* 210–17,
        211, 218–20
    Patient's Charter 16, 222
    priorities 224
    staff *229*
    see also health services
National Health Service Act 1946
    188
National Health Service Act 1973
    190

National Health Service and
    Community Care Act 1990 15,
        34, 196–7, 203, 204, 221
National Health Service
    Management Executive
    (NHSME) 230–1
National Insurance Act 1911 188
Nativists 174
nature-nurture debate 155, 174–5
NDC (National Disability Council)
    35
needs 149
    assessing those of local
        population 237
    Maslow's hierarchy of 184
    need versus choice 11
nephrons 86
nerve cells 90–1, *90*
nervous system 87–91, *88, 97,*
    98
neuro-linguistic programming
    (NLP) 53–4
neurones 90–1, *90*
NHS *see* National Health Service
NHS Direct 225
NHSME (National Health Service
    Management Executive) 230–1
NHS Trusts 227
NLP (neuro-linguistic
    programming) 53–4
non-participant observation 256–7
non-probability sampling 272
non-verbal communication 44, 48,
    54–6, 58, 257–8
normal distribution 294, *294*
Northern Ireland health service
    190, 191, 230
notification procedures 33
NSPCC 220
Nuremberg Code 303
nurses
    district 231
    practice 232
nurture-nature debate 155, 174–5

observation
    of communication skills 71
    of non-verbal behaviour 56
observational learning 175, 176
observation research 256–7
    advantages and disadvantages
        260
    observable behaviour 257–8
    recording observations
        258–9, *259, 260*
oestrogen 95, 130
old age *see* ageing; elderly people
open questions 48, 282
opinion questions 281
oral phase of development 177, 178

outcomes 46, 52, 69
outreach services 29
ovaries *92*, 95
over-identification 64–5
oxygen 80, 81
oxytocin 92

pacing communication skills 53
pancreas *92*, 94
paraphrasing 49–50
parasympathetic nervous system 89, 98, 99
parathormone 93
parathyroid glands *92*, 93
parents and socialisation 150
participant observation 257
    see also qualitative research
participatory socialisation 150, 151
passive behaviour 57
patients *see* clients
Patient's Charter 16, 73, 222, 239
PCCs (primary care co-operatives) 230
PCGs (primary care groups) 225, 226
peak flow meters *108*, 109
peer groups 151
percentages 299
perception
    disorders of 166
    selective 147–8
peripheral nervous system 88–9
peristalsis 84
personality development 139–41
    cognitive development theory and 180–2
    nature-nurture debate 155
    psychoanalytic theory 177, 178
    social learning theory 176
personality theory of ageing 133
personal space 55
phallic phase of development 177, 178
PHCTs (primary health care teams) 189, 231–2
phenylketonuria 156, 158
physical contact 55
physical disabilities 165
physiological measurements 100
    body temperature 100–2
    cardiovascular system 102–5
    formulae 111–13
    potential sources of error 109–10
    recording of data 110–11
    respiratory system 107–8
    safe practice 108–9
    secondary source data 113–17

physiology 80
Piaget, Jean 127, 180
pie charts 299–300, *300*
pituitary gland 91–2, *92*, 99
play 127
political beliefs and discrimination 20
pons 99
population
    sampling 268–9
    and social welfare policy 217–19
positivists 255
postures, body 56
poverty and ill-health 166
power 25–6, 65
practice nurses 232
prejudices 4, 5
primary care co-operatives (PCCs) 230
primary care groups (PCGs) 225, 226
primary data 272
primary health care teams (PHCTs) 189, 231–2
primary health groups 227
private health and social care insurance 203, 219
private sector 216, 220, 235, 244
private space 55, 258
process recording 71
progesterone 95
projection (defence mechanism) 148
prolactin 92
prompting 49
providers and purchasers 192–3, *193*, 194, *194*, 197, 202, 212–13, 216, 237–8
psychiatric ill-health 165–6
psychoanalytic theory 177–80
psychological perspective on development 174
puberty 128–9, 137
publicity 210, 221
pulse rate 102, 109
punishment 175
purchaser-only role of statutory agencies 240–1
purchasers and providers 192–3, *193*, 194, *194*, 197, 202, 212–13, 216, 237–8
purposive sampling 272
pyrexia 100

qualitative research 255–6
    advantages and disadvantages 260–1
    analysing data 285–7
    observable behaviour 257–8

observation research 256–7
    recording observations 258–9, *259*, *260*
quality 16, 45, 235
    monitoring 16–17
quantitative research 261
    analysing data 287–95
    experimental research 261–2
    presentation of data 296–300
    sampling methods 267–72
    surveys 263–4
        forms of response 282–3
        interviews 265–6, 277, 277–80
        questionnaires 264–5, 277, 284
        types of question 278–9, 280–2
quartiles 292
questioning skills 48, 49
questionnaires 264–5, 277
    forms of response 282–3
    self-administered 284
    types of questions 280–2
questions 277
    closed 48, 281
    factual 280–1
    forms of response 282–3
    interview 278–9
    open 48, 282
    opinion or attitude 281
    type to use 282
quota sampling 272

race
    and attitudes 149, 151
    and discrimination 21
Race Relations Act 1976 14–15
racism 21, 24–5
    challenging 4
radial pulse 102, *102*
random sampling 269–70, *271*
range of data 292
ranking (questionnaires) 282–3
rapport 52–3, 54
rating scale (questionnaires) 282
reaction formation (defence mechanism) 148
reactive model of development 175
receptors 97
recessive disorders 156
reference groups 152–3
referrals 205
    compulsory 208–9
    self-referral 205
    through a professional 206–7
reflective listening 51–2
reflective practice 71, 72
reflex actions 89–90
    children 180

Regional Health Authorities
    (RHAs) 192, 193, 194, 230
regression (defence mechanism)
    148
reinforcement 175–6
relationships 27, 62–3
    communication and 44
    controlled involvement 63
    problems 64–6
    in research 303
    supervision of 63–4
    uniforms and 60
    see also communication
reliability of data 285
religion
    and attitudes 149, 151
    and discrimination 21
reminiscence 67
renal system 85–7, 86
repolarisation 113
reports, research 301–2
repression (defence mechanism)
    148
repressive socialisation 150, 151
research 254
    data presentation 296–301
    data reliability 285
    data validity 284–5
    defining a research problem
        274
    ethics 302–4
    final reports 301–2
    hypotheses 275–6
    planning 276
    purpose 254–5, 274
    qualitative 255–61
    qualitative data analysis
        285–7
    quantative 261–73
    quantitative data analysis
        287–95
    questionnaire and interview
        design 264, 266, 276–84
    researcher's perspective 255
    sources of information 272–3
residential care 202, 208, 241
resources
    allocation 11
    managing 213
    see also funding
respect for the client 64
respiratory rate 99, 107, 110
respiratory system 80–1, 80, 81
    monitoring 107, 107, 108,
        110, 117
response, care worker's 63
reversal (defence mechanism) 148
RHAs (Regional Health
    Authorities) 192, 193, 194,
    230

rights 2
    charters 16
    discrimination 17–23, 24–5
    ethical issues 26–7, 29–31,
        31–3
    of expression 57
    information about 16
    legislation supporting 14–15
    maintenance of 27
    monitoring quality of services
        16–17
    non-discriminatory practice
        28–9
    power and empowerment
        25–6, 26–7
    promoting 3–5, 8–11, 24
    staff training and
        development 26
    support and guidance sources
        33–7
    threats to 11–13
risks see health risks
roles 134
    adolescence 129
    gender 127
    interactivist theory 183
    in old age 131, 132, 134
    role status 159
role theory and ageing 134

salivary gland 91
sampling
    random 269–70, 271
    selecting a sample 267
    size of sample 268–9
    systematic samples 271–2
sampling frames 270
scattergrams 294–5, 295
schemata 180
schizophrenia 166
secondary data 272–3
selective perception 147–8
self 134, 138, 183
self-administered questionnaires
    284
self-awareness 64
self-concept 126, 138–9, 183,
    184
self-disclosure 49
self-esteem 63, 140
self-help groups 34
self-reflection 71
semantic differential measuring
    283, 283
sensitivity 63
sensory ability and discrimination
    21
sensory contact 44
sensory nerves 88
serotonin 166

sex
    biological and social
        approaches 182
    distinct from gender 153–4
Sex Discrimination Act 1975 &
    1986 14
sex hormones 95, 128, 130
sexuality and discrimination
    21
Sexual Offences Act 1967 14
shock stage of grief 147
sickle cell anaemia 157
sinoatrial node 113, 114
smoking 171–3
social care services 202, 232
    access to services 203–10
    assessing local needs 237
    and children 200
    development from 1948
        195–6
    entitlement to 200–2, 204
    expenditure 233
    funding 198, 203, 213
    good practice responsibilites
        32–3
    and health care services 234
    monitoring 235
    multiagency schemes 235
    NHS and Community Care
        Act 1990 196–7
    organisation 223–4, 223
    organisations involved in
        199
    and purchasing/providing
        237–8, 240–1
    residential care 202
    responsibilities 198
    staff 233–4
social class
    and attitudes 149, 151
    discrimination 20
    and health 166, 168
social cognition 126
social development 128
social exclusion 5
social interactionism 182–4
socialisation 149–50
    membership groups and
        150–2
    reference groups and 152–3
social learning theory 175–6
social perspective on development
    174, 182
Social Services Departments (SSDs)
    196, 197, 232
    care plans 204
    and carers 247
    responsibilities 198, 200
    typical structure in 2000 238
    see also social care services

social skills development 149–50
    sources of socialisation
        150–3
social space 55, 258
society, concept of 184
socioeconomic factors 168
    and children's accident risk
        170
    and children's health 166, 170
    and diet 169–70
    housing 168–9
    and ill-health 166
sociograms 259, *260*
spatial behaviour 55, 258
sphygmomanometers 104, *104,*
    109–10
spinal cord 88, *88,* 90
spirometry 107, *107,* 110, 113, 117,
    117
SSDs *see* Social Services
    Departments
stability versus change 175
staff
    interpersonal skills 42, 43, 45
    NHS *229*
    representative of community
        29
    selection 32
    training and development 26,
        32
    uniforms 59–60
stakeholders 30–1, 44–5
standard deviation 292–4, *293, 294*
Starlight Foundation 167–8
statistics 162, 287
    frequency distribution
        287–95
    gathering 162–3
    life tables 163–4, *164*
    physiological measurements
        111–17
    population 218–19
statutory services 200, 202
stereotyping 5, 8, 18, 24
    by infirmity 165
    males and females 154
steroid hormones 93
stratified sampling 271–2

stress 141–3
    bereavement and loss 145–7
    and caring relationships 65–6
    job-related 144
    measuring 143, *143*
    reactions to 145
structured interviews 266, 277–9
subcultures and socialisation 151
subculture theory of ageing 133–4
sublimation (defence mechanism)
    149
supervision of care workers 63–4
supervision orders 208
surveys 263–4
    advantages and disadvantages
        264
    forms of response 282–3
    interviews 265–6, 277,
        277–80
    questionnaires 264–5, 277,
        284
    sampling methods 267–72
    types of questions 280–2
Swann Report (1985) 24
symbolic interactionism 182–4
sympathetic nervous system 89, 98,
    99
symphysis pubis 87
systematic sampling 271–2
systolic blood pressure 104, 105

tables of data 300–1, *300*
taxation 219
temperature, body 98
    monitoring 100–2, 109
tendering 238
tertiary data 273
testes *92,* 95
testosterone 95, 130
thermometers 101–2, *101,* 109
thyroid gland *92,* 93
thyroxin 93
tidal volume of the lungs 81, 107
touching 55
Trades Union Congress (TUC) 37
trade unions 37
trait theory 138
transition *see* change

tripartite structure of health services
    190, *190*
TUC (Trades Union Congress) 37
twins 155

'underclass' 5
understanding 63
uniforms, staff 59–60
unstructured interviews 279
urethra *86,* 87
urine 86–7, 92

validity of data 284–5
values 2, 4, 7, 151
    care 2, 9, 25, 46
    conflicting 29–31
    development of 153–4
    ethical issues and 5
    and interpersonal skills 43,
        46
    see also attitudes
valves, heart 83, *83*
variables 286, 294
    independent 261
    relationships between 294–5,
        295
veins 82
ventral body cavity 83
verbal communication 44, 48
vicious circle model of
    discrimination 22–3, *23*
viscera 100
vital capacity 107–8
voluntary sector 34, 220, 235,
    242–4

waiting lists, hospital 205
Wales, health service 190, 191,
    229–30
whistle-blowing 33
women
    carers 159, 246, 248
    and discrimination 14, 20,
        21
    female stereotypes 154
    role status 159
women's refuges 248
WRVS 242–4